WHAT'S IN A NAME?

A History

of the

Community of the Holy Name

© Copyright 2015 Community of the Holy Name

British Library Cataloguing in Publication Data.
A catalogue record for this book is available from the British Library

ISBN 978 0 86071 698 3

A Commissioned Publication of

MOORLEYS
Print & Publishing
tel: 0115 932 0643 web: www.moorleys.co.uk

Foreword

When the CHN sisters sent me the history of their community written four decades and more ago by one of their community, I was struck immediately by the story it revealed. This was not just community memories or a general overview, but was based on serious historical research. Sister Constance had found many interesting facts about the early years of the community and those who paved the way for it coming into being. It was clear this was a text worth publishing and when better to do so than for the 150th anniversary of the foundation?

It seemed appropriate to bring the story up to the present day and Sister Julie has done an excellent job in writing the final sections of the book. The main part needed some small editorial changes but in general remains as Sister Constance wrote it. It tells an inspiring story that will be of interest not only to those who know the sisters but for anyone intrigued by the significant role that Anglican sisters have fulfilled over the past century and a half.

The Community of the Holy Name, like many Anglican foundations of the nineteenth-century, grew from humble beginnings in difficult circumstances. Against the odds, it flourished and over the past one hundred and fifty years its sisters have ministered in a variety of contexts, both in Britain and overseas. There are provinces today in South Africa and Lesotho as well as the UK. Much of the sisters' work has been hidden, often on an individual level, the effect of their support to countless people through the years being hard to quantify. Yet this history witnesses to all they have accomplished and chronicles the different places their love and compassion have reached.

There is much gratitude for all they have achieved and still achieve. I hope many people will read and enjoy this story as much as I have.

Petà Dunstan

WHAT'S IN A NAME?

A History of the Community of the Holy Name

Contents

Part One

Part Two

Note to Part One

As the text was written at the time in history when language
and values were contemporary to the day,
we are aware that these would not be used today.

Part One

Introduction

This history was written in two parts: the first part covers the years 1865 – 1953 in detail, and the developments of the years 1953 – 1970 are sketched in outline. Part two, written over forty years later, fills in the details for that latter period, and seeks to bring the story of CHN up-to-date.

It is difficult to understand a person's life without knowing something of the setting against which it was lived. Every good biography contains an account of its hero's parents, probably of his/her grandparents and other close relations, and sometimes a complete family history covering several centuries will be necessary for the elucidation of his/her life and character. The story of a community's life resembles that of an individual; it too cannot be written 'in vacuo'.

Therefore a history of the Community of the Holy Name cannot begin with the first sisters. It is necessary to learn something of its founder, the Reverend G W Herbert, and of the Vauxhall slum parish in which it came to birth. Indeed, we must delve even deeper, for the Community had a 'spiritual grandfather' whose influence (though indirect) had a profound effect upon its early development. For Robert Aitken was, under God, the instrument of Father Herbert's (evangelical) conversion; his second wife Wilhelmina was the aunt of the Community's foundress, Fanny Macdowell Grant; and his disciple William Haslam was responsible for the 'complete conversion' of its first superior, Charlotte Maria Broadley. Thus his influence was an important element in the spiritual experience of the three people on whom the Community's early development depended, and it served to unite them in a common outlook. Yet even this fails to indicate the full extent of his influence. For the 'Aitkenites', as the followers of Robert Aitken were called, formed a loosely knit group or 'school' bound together by ties of friendship, a shared experience and a common aim. So it was that Father Herbert and the early sisters were in frequent contact with the other members of this group and were influenced by them.

The histories of the nineteenth century Church contain little about Robert Aitken and his followers, for he was an isolated figure who stood aloof from Church parties and Church politics. Since it is unlikely, therefore, that the reader has much knowledge of this remarkable man, this history of CHN must begin with a brief account of his life and influence.[1]

CHAPTER 1

Robert Aitken and his Followers

Robert Aitken's early life was conventional enough. He was born in Scotland in 1800, the son of a poor schoolmaster, and left his home early to seek his fortune in England. He received ordination in the English Church and in 1824 settled in the Isle of Man as curate of St George's Church. His ecclesiastical duties were light, and he devoted most of his energies to the improvement of his property, for he had set himself up as a gentleman farmer.

Yet all the time his conscience was uneasy; again and again the thought recurred to him, almost as if a voice were saying to him, 'You fool! Were you sent into the world with no higher purpose than the draining of a bog?' A dramatic conversion followed. One day as he was working on a study of the Atonement he heard a voice saying. 'You are making a Gospel for God, instead of believing God's Gospel.' This was followed by another, even more distinct, 'All thy righteousness is as filthy rags.' He took these words as a divine warning and a period of intense mental anguish followed. His wife feared for his reason. After nights of sleeplessness he fell on his bed exhausted, crying, 'Now Lord, let me see thy salvation.' He woke with the joy of assurance flooding his soul.

His whole life was changed. He could hardly contain his joy. The great news of free salvation had to be shared with others, and so he began to preach all over the island. His fellow priests were scared of such enthusiasm and only two of them would allow him to use their churches, but the Methodists welcomed him and offered him their pulpits. The service he took in a disused chapel at Peel showed the form his ministry was to take.

After he had given the blessing, a Cornish Methodist from Mousehole came up to him and said, 'There are penitents in the chapel, sir.' Bewildered, he said that they had better go home and pray, but the little Methodist knew better. The scene which followed seemed to him to be one of wildest confusion as men prayed aloud and called desperately on God for mercy, but he had to remain until the souls awakened by his preaching had found their own assurance of salvation.

For the next eight years he preached from Methodist pulpits. Revival services were held all over the Isle of Man; then he crossed to the mainland and preached throughout England and the greater part of Scotland. His ministry was outwardly successful - during six weeks in Sheffield alone, three thousand people gave in their names as 'saved' - yet he was dissatisfied. Many of his converts were content with their conversion and saw no need to press on to holiness of life. He was also uneasy about his connection with the Methodist Church, which was then passing through the crisis of the Warren controversy.

He ceased preaching for the Methodists and set up his own society. Two proprietary chapels were established in London and one in Liverpool, and there were at least six others in the north and midlands. The new society was Methodist in its teaching and organisation, for he had no quarrel with these as such; it was the lack of zeal shown by the existing Churches in pursuing the work of conversion which impelled him to set up his own organisation. Therefore the first object of his 'Christian Society' was the conversion of souls, and its second the cultivation of holiness by its members. Conversion and holiness were to be focal points of his teaching for the rest of his life.

His preaching was highly successful. People flocked to his London chapels, and on Sunday nights there might be hundreds of 'anxious' souls seeking salvation in response to his fervent exhortations. However he became uneasy. His reading led him to ponder on the aim of schism, and as he meditated upon the parable of the wheat and the tares he realised that he ought not to have neglected the work and discipline of his Church because of its unfaithfulness to evangelical truth, for Christ had intended the Christian life to be lived within the Church and to be nourished by its sacraments. No wonder he found himself unable to give his converts 'a home and a discipline ... a nurture and a teaching.'[2]

It was the second decisive moment of his life. He resolved to return to the Church of England (which he had never formally left), and, though there were doubts about his stability, he was allowed to recommence his ministry as an Anglican priest. The next four years were difficult ones as he swung from one extreme to the other; at one moment he seemed the highest of High Churchmen, then he would revert to Methodist teaching again. But he gradually regained his equilibrium, and arrived at that fusion of the Methodist doctrine of conversion with the Catholic emphases on the Church and sacraments which became the distinctive feature of his teaching.

Rev'd Robert Aitken

In 1849 he was offered, and reluctantly accepted, the living of Pendeen in Cornwall, and the rest of his life was spent in this remote and bleak spot amongst rough uneducated people, far from the great towns where he felt he could exercise an effective ministry. Yet these years were amongst the most fruitful of his life, for he had found himself.

Those who knew him in his later years recognised a spirit which was not of this earth. The preoccupations of this world meant nothing to him; God was the only reality and his whole life was lived in His presence. A priest who once spent several months at the parsonage said he did not believe that during this time 'Mr Aitken was (except in his sleep) for five minutes out of the conscious presence of God';[3] and J M Neale was fascinated by his conversation, for he seemed 'to talk as you may imagine St Gregory to have done.'[4] He would often spend six to eight hours daily in church interceding for his people, and before a mission he devoted months to prayer for the places he was to evangelise. Even when travelling abroad, he spent the largest portion of his time alone with God, and a friend noticed that, 'in the woods he would go and meet his Master, returning to his friends with a face of holy joy.'[5] He was by nature a mystic, and to him God was no remote being but an indwelling power in his own soul. A priest who met him about a year before his death could never forget the experience. 'He discussed easily and without restraint many subjects, but all were regarded from the point of view of the other world. In his scheme of life it was evident that Jesus still walked among men. When we rose to separate for the night, it was with a feeling that we had at last been brought face to face with an actual saint of God.'[6]

The little village of Pendeen became a centre of remarkable spiritual power. People were attracted by Aitken's fervent preaching and a revival followed. A fine church, said to be modelled on the ancient cathedral of Iona, was built by the men of the parish to his own design, and the daily service was begun. Charles Bodington never forgot the solemnity of the Sunday communion service, despite its simplicity, for 'the aged pastor was in tears as he administered the Blessed Sacrament to a large number of the rough but earnest miners.'[7] People seeking spiritual help were received at the parsonage and sometimes stayed for several months, and from his study Aitken reached a multitude of souls, most of them personally unknown to him, by means of an enormous correspondence.

His theological position (if one may use so dignified a term) was an unusual one, the result of his personal experiences. Life had taught him two truths: the first, that men needed conversion and a personal relationship with God, the second, that he could not do without the Church and her sacramental life; and though many of his contemporaries regarded the two as alternatives, he insisted that both were necessary if the Christian life was to be lived in all its fullness. Catholic and Evangelical truth were essential to the effectiveness of each other: 'for what is Evangelical truth, but the very life-principle of Christianity? And what are Catholic verities and the sacramental system, but God's loving provision for the greater purity and higher destiny of the renewed soul?'[8] Fruitless controversy had resulted since 'truth has been pitted against truth, and not truth against error.'[9]

He aimed, therefore, at persuading the Catholic party to embrace conversion and the Evangelical and Nonconformist parties to value the sacramental system. But his powers of exposition did not match his insight, and few of his contemporaries were convinced by his arguments.[10]

He was possessed by a longing for Church unity which few could understand, much less share; the thought of unity as the will of God was, he said, 'actually foreign to the spirit of the age.'[11] He believed that there should be one Church to which all Christians should belong, just as in the apostolic days 'every believer belonged to the Church simply because he was a believer.'[12] Believers should be pitted against the world, not against each other. There were times when he hoped that unity might come in his own day. In 1846, for instance, when the new pope had promised to govern the Church by the New Testament and that only, he had been excited at the thought of the reunion of Christendom. He had had his own ideas about a union between the Church of England and the Methodist Church –

and they had come to nothing. But he had never expected unity to come easily, for he realised that 'if unity is ever to be restored, it will only be done by God's special help, and this we cannot expect unless it be done in His own way.'[13]

His banishment to Cornwall did not mean the end of his mission work, for he would escape from 'Old Stoney', as he called Pendeen, to take missions and preaching trips all over the country. He attracted large crowds wherever he went and his mission often created a deep impression on whole neighbourhoods. The secret of his power lay in his burning love for souls. He was oppressed by the thought of the thousands and thousands of men who neglected or defied God and who seemed to have set their course straight for hell. When he came in from walking the streets of London or any other great city, he would groan aloud, the tears running down his cheeks as he exclaimed, 'Oh, these souls. Oh, these souls!'[14] His sense of the intense reality of eternity gave great force to his appeals, and no congregation could remain unmoved. Men sank to the ground to cry for forgiveness. At Hayle, for instance, even the journalist who came to report the services stopped writing, fell on his knees to implore mercy, and was converted. The effect produced by the sermon was driven home at the prayer meeting, or 'after meeting', which followed in the schoolroom, when a final effort was made to bring each soul into conscious union with Christ and to open profession of conversion and assurance. 'Extempore prayer and singing went on continuously while the missioner and his assistants, clerical and lay, women as well as men, moved about amongst the kneeling figures and pressed them to yield to conviction, to unbosom their experience, and to declare themselves as having accepted salvation.'[15] It is easy to criticise Robert Aitken's methods, and many of his contemporaries did so; yet Canon G E Mason, a sober churchman whose words have just been quoted, considered that he achieved 'very great success' by them, though he was critical of their use by some of his assistants. Not surprisingly, a writer on revivals reckoned him the greatest 'soul winner' of his day, and it was fitting that at his death his friends should consider a society for parochial missions the most appropriate memorial they could raise.

Finally, a little must be said about his efforts to revive community life, for although they were unsuccessful, they will be of special interest to the readers of these studies. The impulse to found a community was strongest at the time he was under Tractarian influences. When J M Neale met him in 1842 he was interested in a project for founding a monastery at St Michael's Mount; though this never materialised, he was, by the end of 1843, the head of a little brotherhood in Leeds. Dr Hook, who had brought Aitken to Leeds to found the community, was not very happy about the way in which he was conducting the experiment. He wrote, 'I am uneasy about Mr Aitken. He has fitted up the schoolroom adjoining his church with cells, each containing a bed and a cross; he has some young men with him who have forsaken all; his rule is very strict; he has daily communion; they fast till four every Wednesday, when he allows himself and themselves meat. On Friday they fast until four, and then have fish. In the meantime he, having a family residing five miles away, sleeps in his cell four times a week … his wife complains of his neglecting his six or more children.'[16] In another letter Hook declared, 'As to asceticism it cannot be carried further than there.'[17] The experiment did not succeed. The claims of his family and the brotherhood were incompatible, and it is unlikely that Aitken could supply the stable leadership needed for such a venture. Yet he never lost his desire for community life. A few years later he was thinking of turning his house at Coatbridge into a sort of home for holy living, and in 1872 he still hoped to form a community of young clergy and students preparing for ordination. (He even had four men in mind that might join it.) It was only a dream, but his thoughts and prayers were not in vain, for this aspect of his work was carried out more successfully by his followers.

Although Robert Aitken's personal influence was great, his indirect influence was even greater. He longed for a 'converted' clergy, and he had an extraordinary influence over a number of devoted priests who had been inspired and sometimes converted by him. Canon A J Mason said that he 'poured his Evangelical fervour into High Church vessels',[18] and, strangely enough, a number of these men were High Churchmen. Many of them were Father Herbert's friends. They played an important part in the life of his parish, for they preached in his church, led his missions and conducted his retreats, took his Lent courses and joined in the annual St Peter's-tide celebrations. The lives of the early sisters were linked closely to the worship of the parish church, and so something must now be said about this group of priests from whom they received so much teaching.

In 1854 Robert Aitken preached a great mission in the little church of St James at Wednesbury in the Black Country. It was a High Church parish and Richard Twigg, the assistant curate, who was in charge during the incumbent's absence, was a friend and protégé of that sound churchman, Doctor Hook of Leeds. Twigg is said to have given himself to God while he was still a boy, and he was an exemplary priest, yet the most important convert Aitken made during this mission was Richard Twigg. From this time onwards Robert Aiken was the great influence in Twigg's life. Aitken's ideals became his, and he looked only for God's glory, the extension and unity of Christ's kingdom and the salvation of individual men.

Twigg spent the rest of his life at Wednesbury (he became incumbent in 1856), and Aitken's influence can be seen in the mixed strain of Catholic and Evangelical piety which was so characteristic of the parish. Twigg did not cease to be a High Churchman; in fact he pressed forward with practices then considered 'advanced'. Weekly communion was started in 1855, an altar cross and candles were introduced in 1857, Gregorian tones began to be used in 1862 and vestments were first used in 1866. Yet, at the same time, there was an unexpected Evangelical element in his preaching, and death, judgment, heaven, hell and eternity were brought before men's gaze with an awful clarity as they were urged to make their peace with God. A J Mason declared that he was 'one of the men best qualified by experience of any in England, for the ministry of conversion.'[19] Complaints were made to the bishop because he allowed extempore prayer by laymen in the schoolroom. Sometimes a real blending of the two streams of devotion can be observed, as in the Sunday morning prayer meetings when the steel workers and miners would join together at 6 a.m. to prepare themselves for the Eucharist and to pray for an increase of communicants. Amongst the simple working men of Wednesbury there developed a school of mystical piety centred in devotion to the person of Our Lord, and on Easter Eve they would watch and pray throughout the night as if before the Holy Sepulchre in a spirit more like that of Oberammergau that that of contemporary Evangelical piety.

Twigg was a man of outstanding character, and his teaching and example were bound to attract others. Two of his curates in particular, George Body and Charles Bodington, were imbued with his Catholic Evangelical spirit,[20] and during the seventies and eighties, when Body became a well-known figure, the teaching of the 'Wednesbury School' was brought before a wider public.

Similar in outlook was the great preacher G H Wilkinson, who after outstanding ministries in the north and in London became Bishop of Truro and then of St Andrews. He was not one of Aitken's converts, but had been influenced in his youth by men like Maclagan and Postlethwaite who had been in contact with him, and it was in Postlethwaite's parish of Coatham[21] that he first met Body and Bodington.

Twigg, Body, Bodington and Wilkinson were the most prominent figures in this school of Catholic Evangelical piety, but there were other men of similar views who were associated with them. The names of all cannot be given here, and only some of those who are known to have had some contact with Father Herbert and the early sisters will be mentioned. A J Mason (the friend and biographer of Wilkinson and the author of a book on conversion)[22] clearly belongs to this group. He was the first canon missioner in England, yet was scholar enough to hold a Cambridge divinity chair. Adam Smith was often found in association with the Wednesbury clergy. He was one of Aitken's own converts, (though he never fully adopted his teaching and methods), and worked devotedly for years in building up the life of the Church in the large mission district which later became St John's, Middlesbrough. Some of the Vauxhall curates may also be mentioned. J M Davenport (Mrs Herbert's nephew) who served a long first curacy at Wolverhampton under Bodington, seems to belong to the group, and so does E E Dugmore, who was a relative of Father Herbert's. This priest, who came under Aitken's influence while he was at Oxford, belonged to an Evangelical family; but his Vauxhall curacy and his membership of the Society of the Holy Cross prove conclusively that the Catholic element became an important one in his religion. Norman Dawes, who ran St Peter's mission at Wednesbury, and who entered the ministry under Twigg's influence, could also be reckoned with them. Finally, two men whose associations were with Pendeen rather than Wednesbury must be mentioned. Francis Caudwell, Aitken's son-in-law, was a 'converted man' and yet a definite High Churchman, and William Haslam,[23] the friend of Mother Charlotte (the second superior of CHN) could in his earlier years be described as a Catholic Evangelical. These priests belonged to no definite party and they had no party programme; they were united only by a common experience, spirit and aim; but although there were differences of emphasis in their teaching, certain characteristics may be discerned.[24]

Firstly, their teaching contained elements which were both Catholic and Evangelical, and pronouncedly so, for they followed no nebulous middle way.

They tried to hold together the two aspects of truth: that religion is both individual and corporate, both subjective and objective. Evangelicals might teach that life in Christ begins with conversion, and High Churchmen that it is initiated at baptism, but the Wednesbury men wanted both baptism and conversion. For, although they believed that the Christian is reborn or regenerated at baptism, they also insisted that he must appropriate this new life and make it his own in conversion by a conscious turning towards Christ. They might stress the need for personal religion, but they also taught that Christ had instituted the Church and sacraments and that it is perilous to neglect them, for the Church is the sphere in which the Evangelical experience should be worked out.

Secondly, there is a great stress on reality throughout their teaching. A man like Body might teach sacramental confession, but he did not urge it indiscriminately upon all. 'No one,' he said, 'ought to go to confession except in response to the call of Jesus in the depths of his own being.'[25]

These priests were not interested in rules and precepts which, if correctly followed, would lead men to heaven; they looked for a living relationship with Christ, nourished by the sacraments and developed within the setting of His Church. The flexibility of their teaching may well have been due to their Evangelical emphasis on the Holy Spirit, for they were content to trust Him to lead each individual, little by little, towards the truth.

These Catholic Evangelical priests resembled Robert Aitken in their longing for the sanctification of souls, and it is likely that they doubted the reality of any conversion which did not include a desire for holiness. They became leaders in the spiritual life. They wrote devotional books. (Wilkinson and Body were particularly prolific writers.) They took Lent courses and conducted retreats, and Wilkinson was especially sought after as a spiritual guide.

It is interesting to note how many of these men were involved in the foundation of communities and brotherhoods. Twigg had longed for a brotherhood, whose members would give their lives to the evangelisation of the great towns, and though this hope was never realised during his lifetime, his disciples Body and Bodington formed lay brotherhoods at Durham and Wolverhampton. Caudwell tried to found a sisterhood at Carnmenellis, and it may be assumed that Adam Smith was a friend and supporter of the Community of the Holy Rood since it began at St John's, Middlesbrough. Wilkinson founded the Community of the Epiphany at Truro. He was fortunate in having Canon Body, a man with an 'intimate knowledge of sisterhoods',[26] to help him, and to Wilkinson's relief he became the first warden. Body was also one of the inspirers of the Australian bush brotherhoods, and it should not be forgotten that A J Mason began a little mission college at Barking.

Robert Aitken's longing for a united Church was echoed by the Wednesbury men. They were not much concerned about rapprochements with Roman Catholics and the Christians of the East, but they were anxious about their relationships with their everyday neighbours, the Protestant Nonconformists. Thus one of Adam

Smith's few published sermons was on 'The Union of Nonconformists with the Church', and Wilkinson and Mason were both members of Earl Nelson's Home Reunion Society. When Wilkinson was Bishop of St Andrews he worked hard to bring about a better understanding between Presbyterians and Episcopalians, and he joined with the Presbyterian leaders in securing a special day of prayer for union amongst the churches of Scotland. The desire for the reunion of Christendom was a major theme in Bodington's *Devotional Life in the Nineteenth Century*. Body and Bodington both emphasised the need for unity within the Church of England, and Body was especially known for his moderating influence on the militants of the High Church Party. Mason, on the contrary, had many contacts with churches abroad. He was connected with the Archbishop's mission to the Assyrian Christians, and he took part in discussions with the Church of Rome and with other churches (such as that of Sweden) whose languages he knew.

But it was their devotion to mission work which made these men pre-eminently Aitken's disciples. Although their parishes provided them with abundant opportunities for evangelism, they were not enough for their zeal, and so these priests became pioneers of the parochial mission movement.

The parish of St James, Wednesbury, was closely linked with the rise of this movement. Aitken's mission here in 1854 is often regarded as the first parish mission in this country, and the church proudly regards itself as 'the cradle of parochial missions'.[27] A Wednesbury writer declares that Twigg 'might almost be termed the human author of parochial missions as at present conducted in the Church of England';[28] and the parish undoubtedly produced some of the first and best missioners of the time. Yet the work of these priests in developing the form which parish missions were to take was, in the long run, even more important than their success as preachers. Robert Aitken's missions are sometimes described as 'revival missions'. They can reasonably be described as missions since they were planned and had a definite beginning and ending, and were not simply a spontaneous awakening of the Spirit in answer to prayer;[29] yet they were somewhat formless, depended largely on his personal powers of preaching and prayer and, above all, aroused considerable emotional excitement.

A mission run on Robert Aitken's (or even Twigg's) lines would be acceptable to only a minority of English parish priests. Under Wilkinson and the younger Wednesbury clergy missions began to take a form more in accordance with Anglican ways. The mission in Wilkinson's parish of Bishop Auckland (1865) proved a landmark in the history of the movement. Body, Postlethwaite, Adam Smith, Wilkinson and J H Moore had made a careful preparation for it the previous autumn, and had thought out the lines on which it was to be run. Deliberation marked the whole proceedings. The idea of a Methodist revival was carefully avoided and a special effort was made to guard against unreality and excitement. There were 'after meetings' in the schoolroom with scripture teaching and prayers by the clergy, but they were not 'prayer meetings' and people needing spiritual help were dealt with alone. Names were taken of those desiring confirmation and the mission was followed up carefully with classes. Thus a determined effort was made to link up the ministry of conversion with the sacramental life of the Church. The movement grew rapidly and three years later, when a small conference on missions was held at Wilkinson's house, it was reported that missions had been held at Enfield, Willenhall,[30] Dukinfield, Ratcliffe and Father Herbert's parish of Vauxhall.

It would be wrong, however, to give the impression that the missions led by Aitken, Wilkinson and the Wednesbury clergy were the only ones. By the mid–nineteenth century churchmen were becoming increasingly concerned about the needs of the heathen populations of the slums and of the rough industrial towns, and the necessity for new methods of evangelism was realised. The Ritualists who worked so devotedly amongst the very poor were also pioneers in this direction, and thus there grew up another independent stream of missions which G E Mason[31] connects with Cowley (the Society of St John the Evangelist, Oxford) and St Alban's, Holborn, but which can probably be more correctly attributed to the Society of the Holy Cross,[32] to which many of the early Cowley Fathers and leading Ritualists belonged. It is impossible to deal adequately here with this group of clergy, and it is fortunately unnecessary since they are well described in the church histories of the period, and biographies of the leading figures such as Mackonochie, Lowder, Stanton, Prynne and Dolling are plentiful.

It must be sufficient to note that many of these Anglo-Catholic militants were not ashamed to call themselves Evangelicals, and that they could and did on occasion deliver a simple gospel message which any Methodist might envy. In 1862 the Society of the Holy Cross sponsored its first parish mission at Bedminster[33] led by Benson, Rivington and Lowder, and it was responsible for the organisation of the great Twelve Day Mission to London (1869).[34]

The Mission to London was the first really large mission of the century (120 parishes are said to have taken part and it received a great deal of publicity. It was a focal point in the history of the movement for two reasons: it laid down the lines on which future missions were to be run, and it marked the union of the 'schools of the prophets' of Wednesbury and Cowley-St Albans. Canon Mason thought this union could be dated from the meeting held at Cowley (23 September 1869) to discuss preparations for the mission, for at this conference all strands of the movement were represented. Wilkinson, Body, Bodington, Adam Smith and Father Herbert might be described as Wednesbury men, Mackonochie, Lowder and Randall were Ritualists and Fathers Benson, O'Neill, Prescott and Grafton belonged to SSJE at Cowley. In the mission that followed a real fusion of the two elements took place. For although the mission was organised by the brethren of the Society of the Holy Cross, the Wednesbury men proved to be some of the most effective missioners, and were to be found in the pulpits of the most famous Ritualist churches. Twigg was at St Peter's London Docks, and refused to leave the church for his other engagements because he had so many penitents there; Body was with Randall at All Saints', Margaret Street, and Bodington was at St Alban's, Holborn. Wilkinson, who now had a London parish, was in his own church where he was assisted by W Aitken, Robert Aitken's son.

The Twelve Day Mission and its successor, the Mission to London of 1874, not only brought out the latent powers of the preachers but also popularised the ideas of missions and gave them the imprimatur of authority. By 1877 Wilkinson was afraid they were becoming fashionable, and were in danger of being regarded as the remedy for all parochial ills. In 1878 his friend Bishop Benson appointed A J Mason as his first canon missioner in the country; other bishops followed his example, and Body and Bodington held similar appointments at Durham (1883) and Lichfield (1887). By 1890 the movement had spread so far that 19 dioceses were represented at a conference of diocesan missioners, and within 20 years of the Twelve Day Mission missions had been held in every town of importance in the land.

It must be clear from what has been already written that the Wednesbury clergy and their associates were at the forefront of this movement. And although it is rash to generalise about the relative importance of the parts played by the Wednesbury and Cowley-St Alban's priests without making a more careful investigation of the evidence than has been possible in the preparation of this study, it must be suggested (albeit tentatively) that the Wednesbury men were the 'pacemakers' of the movement. They seem to have been first in developing methods and techniques which were eventually adopted, they had experience and, above all, they had a compelling zeal. Some of the greatest preachers of the mission movement were Wednesbury men. Wilkinson was *the* great figure of the Mission to London (1874) and Body, though only a curate, dominated the Twelve Day Mission. His eloquence led a London daily paper to speak of the new prophet that had arisen: crowds waited to hear his sermons at All Saints and his eloquence moved men to tears. It was said that, 'the effect produced at All Saints, Margaret Street, was compared by a critical visitor to the effect produced by Mrs Mellon's representation in the *Dead Heart* of a mother weeping beneath the scaffold on which her son was to die',[35] and C M Davies declared, 'I certainly never saw such a sight outside or inside the walls of a church as I have seen at All Saints.'[36] It is not surprising that when Body went to Durham he became known as the Apostle of the North, as Twigg had earlier been called the Apostle of the Black Country.

It was against this background that Father Herbert's ministry was set. These Catholic Evangelical priests were his friends and fellow workers, and all strains of the nineteenth-century mission movement met in his parish. The names of Cowley Fathers, Ritualists and Wednesbury men all frequently occur in the parish service registers, and the word 'mission' might be said to be the dominant concept in his thought.

ENDNOTES – CHAPTER 1

[1] No adequate biography of Robert Aitken has so far been written. *The Dictionary of National Biography* contains a short, unsympathetic entry, and there are brief references in histories, and in books connected with Cornwall. The biography of his son, *Memoirs and Letters of Canon Hay Aitken*, by C E Woods, 1938, contains a more adequate account of his life.

[2] Robert Aitken, *Spiritual Vitality*, 1852, p.7.

[3] C E Woods, op. cit., p.66.

[4] E A Towle, *John Mason Neale*, 1906, p.73.

[5] Obituary notice by L Baxter in *The Christian*, 31 July 1873.

[6] C E Woods, op. cit., p.44.

[7] C Bodington, *Devotional Life in the Nineteenth Century*, 1905.

[8] Robert Aitken, *Truth against Truth*, 1851, p.viii.

[9] Ibid; p.vii.

[10] It must be pointed out that Robert Aitken's influence had an unsettling effect on some men. They were unable to reconcile the two sides of his teaching and eventually left the Church of England to join the Roman Catholic or Nonconformist Churches.

[11] Robert Aitken, *The Prayer Book Unveiled*, 1863, p.2.

[12] Robert Aitken, *The Power of Christ's Name*, 1856, p.23.

[13] Robert Aitken, *The Prayer Book Unveiled*, 1863, p.2.

[14] C E Woods, op. cit., p.36.

[15] G E Mason, 'Parochial Missions' in *Newbery House Magazine*, April 1891, p.389.

[16] Pusey House MS, Letter from Hook to Pusey, 20 November 1843; quoted by CPS Clarke, *The Oxford Movement and After*, 1932, p.251.

[17] Pusey House MS, letter from Hook to Pusey, 25 November 1843.

[18] Quoted in C Bodington, op. cit., p.89.

[19] *Memoir of George Howard Wilkinson*, 1909, vol I, p.234.

[20]Neither Body or Bodington had much close contact with Aitken himself, and his influence seems to have reached them through Twigg who helped them both towards the priesthood and who was in close contact with them during the impressionable years of their earlier ministries.

[21]Aitken had taken a mission here a few years previously.

[22]*The Ministry of Conversion,* 1902.

[23]This priest's conversion was influenced by Robert Aitken.

[24]For a full discussion of the teaching of the leading members of this group see D. Vol, *Catholic Evangelicalism,* 1963, pp 43-84.

[25]Quoted from manuscript notes, preserved at the Convent of the Holy Name.

[26]A J Mason, op. cit; vo.II, p.164.

[27]D Vol I, op. cit. p.50.

[28]Quoted in J F Ede, *History of Wednesbury,* 1962, p.311.

[29]For a contemporary ruling on the differences between missions and revivals see the letter by Samuel Garratt in *The Christian,* 14 August 1873.

[30]This was Bodington's parish. Twigg, Body, Lowder of Wolverhampton and Father Herbert are known to have taken part in this mission. Wilkinson also helped with the Enfield missions.

[31]Article on 'Parochial Missions' in *Newbery House Magazine,* April 1891, p.391.

[32]This clerical society was founded in 1855 with three aims: to strengthen the spiritual life of the clergy, to defend the faith and to carry on mission work. Most of the leading Ritualists belonged to it, including a great many of those who were prosecuted in the courts.

[33]This is sometimes considered the first parish mission.

[34]It is sometimes said that the ideas of the Twelve Day Mission originated with the Cowley Fathers (SSJE) or with the clergy of All Saints, Margaret Street; but since many, if not all, of these priests belonged to the Society of the Holy Cross, there is no reason to contest the Society's claim that it organised the mission.

[35]Quoted by G E Mason in *Newbery House Magazine,* April 1891, p.391.

[36]*Orthodox London,* 1876, p.153.

CHAPTER TWO

Father Herbert and His Parish

The life of George William Herbert, the founder of the Community of the Holy Name, was an embodiment of the nineteenth-century mission spirit. From the time of his conversion until his death in 1894 his whole life might be said to have been one long mission, one sustained and earnest effort to bring souls to Christ, and it was his complete consecration to Him and longing to extend His Kingdom which is the key to his whole life and character.

Father Herbert was not a man of outstanding natural gifts; he was, in fact, a very ordinary man possessed of only average abilities. He was not an original thinker;[37] he was not a great leader and, though he was something of a pioneer in parish and mission work, he was not the originator of new ways; he was, however, quick to appreciate their value and to make use of them when he saw them.

Such powers as he did possess were completely given over to the service of God. There was nothing half-hearted about him, and his own total consecration made him impatient of those who were lukewarm. 'One red-hot poker would better kindle a fire than half a ton of warm coke,' he would say, and, 'Training in enthusiasm is training for God's presence.' The 'zeal' which he demanded was defined as 'energetic passion'. The question he would ask in an Advent sermon was: 'What violence are you doing? To self ... to world ... to flesh ... to devil ... to God ...? Does violence at all describe your life?' His subject for a profession sermon was 'whole-heartedness' and he looked for a strenuous and total obedience to Christ. 'Never be content,' he said, 'till you can give Him your whole heart, till you can say, "I love Him more than anything else."'

His self-discipline and sense of stewardship were very evident in his use of material things. He was a wealthy man, but he was also a married man with a family to provide for, and so he did not sell all and give it to the poor. His income was used with great responsibility; money was not squandered on needless luxuries and, rich though he was, he practised little economies, such as using old envelopes for note-taking, which a poorer man would have scorned. He must have spent a considerable sum every year on his parish. An appeal issued in 1894 said that he had 'upheld all its charities, provided for the monetary deficiencies of its schools, supplemented the stipends of the assistant clergy and sustained the organisation necessary in a parish numbering eleven thousand souls,' yet he did not allow his people to believe that they could rely on him for everything. In fact, anyone reading his annual parish letter and charity reports would imagine that the writer was a poor parson who was completely dependent on his friends and people for parish funds. He was careful and businesslike over financial matters, and Sister Elizabeth remembered his telling her that she should always count money given to her, even if it was from her own sister; and, though he sympathised with a sister who had inadvertently paid three shillings instead of three pence for some article and gave her half a crown, she was enjoined to account to her superior for the remaining six pence. The stress on 'accounting' was very characteristic of him.

He was a singularly modest man and had a hatred of publicity. No notices of the church services were ever put in *The Church Times*, for he had no desire to attract strangers and to make St Peter's fashionable. He possessed a positive genius for keeping himself out of the newspapers, even the clerical ones, and a rare contemporary account of one of his speeches gives a very good picture of him as a young man: 'Mr Herbert returned thanks in a modest unassuming speech, in which he gave all the credit for the work to Mr Gregory, saying he had only done what he had been told.'[38]

His gentleness seems to have struck everybody. Men noticed his 'singularly sweet temperament', and not only the St Peter's congregation but all his parishioners spoke of him as 'our gentle vicar.' His daughters could recall many instances of this quality. 'Do you remember,' said Olga, 'when there was a drunken brawl in Millers Lane and he couldn't write a sermon and so went out and found a man and his rather drunken wife fighting under the study window? He picked up her dirty bonnet and tried to clean the dust and muck off it with his hands saying, "I think I'd put it on now, if I were you", and there was dead silence as they all moved off.' Grace Herbert would tell how, when he heard her criticising a clergyman, a serious offence as she well knew, his only rebuke was a smile, and he felt the back of her head, saying, 'Major, you were born without the bump of veneration.' On another occasion a stray cat got into the church and the boys were soon trying to chase it out. His sympathies were with the cat. 'He came to us,' said one of the boys, 'and in a charming manner, asked us not to frighten it. Our whole attitude towards the animal changed.'

His gentleness was the expression of a deep love and sympathy. He saw himself as the father of his people; both the sisters and his parishioners knew him as 'The Father' and his letters to his choirboys always began 'Dear Son'.

He had, too, a special love for the poor. In 1864 he told how St Peter's was the realisation of a dream of his youth. 'He had longed often and often, when newly ordained, to minister in a church entirely free and unappropriated – a church for the poor. He had scarcely dared to think it would be the case, but lo, now he had exactly what he had for years wished for.'[39] He reserved an hour after breakfast for his people, and they would come and tell him their needs. They would wait sitting on a bench in the hall, and his children were taught to find out what they wanted and to report back to him. He told them that by waiting on the poor they were waiting on Our Lord Himself.

Despite his gentleness, he had an iron will. He disobeyed his Victorian parents over his vocation and his marriage – and won. He could even be somewhat puritanical at times, and his disapproval of gambling was so strong that one unfortunate organist lost his job because he was caught playing shove-halfpenny on the vestry steps with some choirboys, but his sternness was chiefly shown towards himself. His family remembered his asceticism, even though it was expressed only in little things, and they would tell how his after-luncheon rest was taken on the floor with a book for a pillow. He always ate very little, often taking only salad and ginger beer for supper, and his wife had to help him at meals, otherwise he would not have eaten enough.

However, the predominating quality in his character was his spirituality. Bodington wrote of his unworldliness, and his daughter Verena noticed his 'spiritual outlook and atmosphere'. He must have been a man who lived in the presence of God, for she said that when he was in a room with others he was often silent, 'but one felt he was surrounded by a holy atmosphere which prevented one from doing anything unworthy in his presence.'

Cavendish House

He was born on 3 October 1830 at Number One, Farm Street, Berkeley Square, and was baptised a month later at the fashionable church of St George's, Hanover Square. His father, William Herbert, was born at Leamington, but had settled in London, where he became a successful builder and architect.[40] George had at least two sisters, Elizabeth and Louise. The family later moved to Cavendish House, on the border of Clapham Common, an historic house which was once the residence of the great scientist Henry Cavendish.

George was an only son and his parents were ambitious for him. He was educated at Eton and then at Exeter College, Oxford, from which he graduated in 1852. Since he only took a pass degree, it may be assumed that he was not academically-minded. He had desired to be ordained from an early age, but his parents hated the thought and did their best to prevent it, for they had other designs for him. Since he was still too young to be ordained, he continued to keep terms at Oxford, though he appears to have spent some time at Pershore, possibly helping as a layman in the parish. According to his daughter Verena, his parents sent him on a 'Grand Tour' of Europe at this time, hoping that he would change his mind about ordination, but since he is known to have been at Oxford or Pershore for most of the time and only a period of three and a half months remained for foreign travel, it seems unlikely that his 'Grand Tour' took place then. If it did, it cannot have been a very 'Grand' one.

Relations with his parents were made more critical by his marriage in 1853 to Miss Louisa Hopgood, for they disapproved of his choice and, when he persisted in marrying against their wishes, his allowance was cut down 'almost to real poverty'.

'But it made no difference,' said his daughter, 'they struggled on.' The reason for his parents' opposition seems fairly clear.

George Herbert was the only son and heir of a wealthy man and his family may have hoped for an aristocratic daughter-in-law with good connections. Miss Hopgood had been born in the City and her father was a silversmith, so that the Herberts might reasonably have felt that their son had married beneath him. But the estrangement between parents and son was probably only a short one, and it may well be that the famous 'Grand Tour' took place soon after the marriage and also served as a wedding trip, for Herbert was absent from Oxford from June 1853 to November 1854 and this would have allowed rather more time for travel.

The interest of foreign scenes did not alter his determination. He was back in Oxford for the Michaelmas term of 1854 and attended the lectures of Professor Heurtley and Professor Jacobson in preparation for his ordination. Early in 1855 he was made deacon in Worcester Cathedral, and his ordination to the priesthood followed a year later. His first curacy was at Pershore Abbey under Doctor Williamson,[41] where he was one of three curates. Pershore was a small market town in an agricultural area. The abbey had several dependent chapelries which were served by the clergy of the mother church and so, for a short time, Father Herbert had some experience of country life. Little is known about his time at Pershore. The first days of his curacy were probably very demanding ones, for Pershore

George Herbert (aged 21)

suffered from cholera during the winter of 1854 to 1855, but he seems to have had time for artistic interests since he and his fellow curate, Frederick Wickenden,[42] together discovered the ancient frescoes on the walls of the Pinvin Chapel, and he restored part of the original painting of the chancel himself. This suggests an interest in church restoration typical of the High Church clergy of that period. His stay at Pershore was short, however, and in 1856 he was back in London as curate to Mr Borradaile at St Mary's, Tothill Fields. Father Herbert was essentially a townsman. He had been born and bred in London and though he later owned a country house at Malvern Link, he seldom used it himself. No doubt he was relieved and delighted to leave Worcestershire for work in a city parish, and he remained at St Mary's until he began his life's work at Vauxhall in 1860.

When Father Herbert went to Vauxhall he was setting his hand to no light task. The new district of St Peter's, which he was to inaugurate, formed part of the large parish of St Mary the Less where Robert Gregory[43] had been working indefatigably since 1853. The population had been 15,000 when Gregory arrived and it was increasing rapidly because of housing developments, so that it was desirable that the parish should be divided. Services had been begun in the little mission church of St Paul and it was here that Father Herbert began his ministry in Vauxhall on Easter Day 1860. Eighteen months later the parish was gazetted – 15 October 1861 – and he, as its vicar, became responsible for all the souls within it.

It is now over a hundred years since Father Herbert went to Vauxhall. During that time there have been vast social changes, and those who have known Britain only since the Second World War can have little idea of what life was like in a London slum in the later nineteenth century. It has seemed desirable, therefore, to say a little here about social conditions in the parish, for it might otherwise be difficult for the reader to understand the circumstances in which Father Herbert and the earliest sisters lived and worked.

The actual area of St Peter's parish was small. It was bounded on one side by the Thames, on another by Upper Kennington Lane (then a road of quiet prosperous houses) and on the remaining sides by Jonathan Street, Anderson's Walk and Vauxhall Street. Although housing developments make it difficult to follow the old boundaries exactly, they can be fairly closely pursued, and it takes but a short time to beat the bounds of the parish. This means, of course, that the area was densely populated. The famous Vauxhall Gardens, originally an aristocratic and expensive pleasure resort noted in eighteenth-century literature, were within the parish, but they had become so degraded that they had been closed the year before the Herberts went to Vauxhall. When Mrs Herbert first saw the parish she could walk down an avenue of fine elms, and the Rotunda, half-ruined, with tattered finery clinging to it, still remained. But the glory had departed and the Gardens were being covered with rows and rows of little houses. Within five years of the sale of the property, the site was built over and the only traces of the famous resort were to be found in the street names. Tyers Street, for instance, preserved the name of one of the lessees of the Gardens, and Gye Street that of a former owner. Glasshouse Street was probably so called because of the famous ballroom lined with Vauxhall mirror glass, and Spring Gardens was an earlier name for the Gardens themselves.

The area must in its earlier days have had a proportion of middle class residents, but this was changing rapidly, and Gregory declared that when he went to St Mary's in 1853 there were scarcely half a dozen people in the parish who did not belong to the labouring classes. This was probably an exaggeration, but it gives a fair impression of the general character of the place. Probably in their later down-at-heel days the Gardens themselves had attracted some undesirable characters. The building of the South Western Railway Line in 1838 and its extension from Vauxhall to Waterloo in 1848 meant that navvies working on the railway would have brought a rough element into the neighbourhood, and the railway goods yard and passenger station would have encouraged an influx of less skilled men from country areas to work as porters and labourers.

The potteries and gas works (erected in 1833) meant extremely good and regular employment for a certain number of men, but they also called for the services of less skilled or quite unskilled workers who earned rather low wages and who were only intermittently employed. Moreover, the smell of gas tended to make the neighbourhood unpleasant and to drive away middle-class residents. Cheap tram and rail fares encouraged mechanics and the more prosperous artisans who worked in the area to move their homes to Stockwell and Brixton, leaving the poorer inhabitants behind, while the character of the neighbourhood was further lowered by an influx of newcomers who had been displaced by slum clearances in Westminster and elsewhere on the western side of the river. As Father Herbert himself wrote: 'Those who are rather better off move away, some to the suburbs where they get new and good houses and cheap rents, and some to the excellent lodgings in the immediate neighbourhood. All these vacant places are filled up by a more destitute class of tenants.' Thus 'in the downward grade of the social scale the district forms a shelf to catch the falling; and those whom the Church uplifts climb to a higher ledge, and other sliding ones supply our losses. We seldom or ever get a bright and well-to-do newcomer to enliven us.' Father Herbert was therefore faced with a parish consisting of the poor, the ignorant, and the uneducated, with no rich and very few better-class residents to whom he could look for help and support and who could be relied upon for example and leadership.

A second difficulty was the fluid state of the population. When Gregory first went to Lambeth he found that the people were incessantly moving, so that before he had visited every house in a street, a considerable proportion of the inhabitants had changed their abode. Father Herbert was faced with the same problem - though possibly in a less acute form, for the social changes mentioned in the preceding paragraphs imply a mobile population. This made it especially difficult to build up the life of the Church, for many of those whom he had carefully instructed would be amongst the families who improved their position and left the parish, while hopeful young men were lost through emigration.

A third difficulty was the poverty. Charles Booth, the social historian, noted that poverty increased the nearer one got to the river.[44] Vauxhall was actually on the river. Even when in full employment, most of the Vauxhall men would have been earning only low wages, and unemployment was common. One of the St Peter's curates, the Rev'd W A Morris, took up the gas workers' cause, lived with them in little rooms in a club he founded for them, and was not only recognised by the men as their leader but had even been the instigator of the gas strike.

Children came breakfast-less to school, and when Charles Booth visited St Paul's School, that expert on London poverty classed its boys amongst 'the very poor'. It is not surprising, therefore, that Father Herbert's reports and annual letters so often contain remarks such as, 'the poverty of the area is ever increasing', and, 'we have this year to contend with a heavier deficiency than ever before.' The annual letter of 1858 referred to a 'year of unusual trial' and stated that the winter had been one of 'great poverty'; 1885-6 was 'a year of great poverty and depression' and these examples could be multiplied. This meant that Father Herbert had to spend a good deal of time and energy in money-raising, for he was morally responsible for the welfare of all his parishioners, and the parish had few resources with which to help its own poor.

Sickness and disease created other difficulties. Being a Thames-side parish, St Peter's lay in an unhealthy situation. Unfiltered sewage was discharged into the river and this resulted in a most unpleasant stench. This was very bad in 1860 when the situation was aggravated by heat and drought, but summer in Vauxhall can never have been other than trying. Lambeth census figures show an average of seven persons to each dwelling, and the tiny houses must therefore have been seriously overcrowded. When poverty and undernourishment were added to these factors, it was only to be expected that the standard of health in the parish should be low. Vestry reports for St Mary's, Lambeth, mention that the very young and very old suffered from chest infections in the winter and bowel complaints in the summer. Scarlet fever, typhus and smallpox were common. It is not surprising that smallpox was 'usually fatal' in 1860, the year the river stench was so bad. In 1865 it was so prevalent that the schools had to be closed. Father Herbert noted in 1866 that there had been much fever around, and that the sister responsible for the parish nursing was unable to help because she had not recovered from typhus herself. This was followed by an outbreak of cholera which, if not so notorious as the epidemic which ravaged East London and Wapping, was sufficiently serious for a special thanksgiving service to be held to mark its ending. Again, Father Herbert's annual letter for 1868 mentioned not only the great poverty during the previous winter but 'the sickness (from which our sisters have severely suffered) in the spring', for the two had had 'a depressing effect upon the general work of the district.' Vauxhall was clearly not a healthy place in which to live.

More important, from Father Herbert's point of view, was the religious situation. Charles Booth, generalising at the turn of the century, noted that religious work was disheartening in areas where material conditions were bad: 'The people, where the standard of life is low, seem to be quite happy in poverty, hunger and dirt, enlivened with drink, and not to be raised to better things, or else the right way to rouse them has not been found.'[45] This is corroborated by Gregory's experience at St Mary's. He declared that 'the special difficulty of the parish that was never really overcome during the twenty years that I was incumbent was attracting the people to Church. They had lost the habit of attending public worship, and it seemed as though nothing would enable them to recover it.'[46] Father Herbert soon found the same difficulty. When he was pleading in 1865 for the provision of a second curate he showed the urgency of the need, saying that during a mission week he had come across a grown person who was ignorant of even the very existence of Our Blessed Lord.[47] He also declared that the reception of the Holy Eucharist had been publicly parodied in one of the streets to annoy an approaching communicant.

This was the environment in which Father Herbert was to spend the rest of his life and in which the earliest years of the Community were passed. It was a slum - but not the worst of slums. Lowder at London Docks, Mackonochie at Holborn and the Southwark clergy had worse conditions to face. There were not the pickpockets' schools of the Crown Street area or the flaunting vice of Ratcliffe Highway, but neither was there the positive life and spirit which those notorious areas possessed. It was grey, grim, grimy and monotonous.

When Father Herbert went to Vauxhall he was a young priest of nearly thirty with five years of pastoral experience behind him. He was rich (at least his parents were) and he was handsome. The world must have seemed to be before him. Yet the world had few attractions for him. He had already evinced considerable determination in choosing his wife and following his vocation against the wishes of Victorian parents, and his deliberate decision to work and, what was more, to live in a slum parish showed that his sense of responsibility and self-sacrifice had already been formed. He was obviously a young man of resolution and also, one suspects, of considerable earnestness. Little is known of his early, or indeed his later, spiritual life, for no diaries, letters or other personal papers survive, but such evidence as there is suggests that he was already a decided High Churchman of the new, post-Tractarian school. His college at Oxford, Exeter, was inclined to be a High Church one and, in his early years at Vauxhall, he associated mainly with High Churchmen. T T Carter of Clewer (Founder of the Community of St John Baptist) preached at the festival evensong which followed the two big events of the early years at Vauxhall, the laying of the foundation stone and the consecration of the new church, and other visiting preachers included such definite High Churchmen as Randall of Lavington, Benson of Cowley and Nugee of Wymering. G Cosby White[48] of the 'advanced' church of St Barnabas, Pimlico, was a frequent preacher and Arthur Tooth, later to be a victim of the Ritual prosecutions, often assisted at St Peter's. Charles Bodington's reference to 'the standard of loyal Churchmanship in which he began his ministry and in which he steadfastly continued to the end of his life', also suggests that Father Herbert was a High Churchman.

His policy during his first five years at Vauxhall substantiates this completely. He began cautiously, for he was far too wise to spring radical, unexplained changes in worship upon his little congregation. When he went to the district in 1860, the usual Sunday services were Matins, Antecommunion and sermon at 11 a.m. , Litany and catechising at 3.30 p.m., and Evensong and sermon at night; Holy Communion was celebrated twice a month; the psalms were chanted. His first step in November was to preach in a surplice (20 years earlier this alone would have caused a riot) and, when this was accepted as normal, the wearing of surplices was also extended to the choir at Easter 1863. His next move was to begin daily service – 14th Sunday after Trinity 1861 – having first preached on the subject. In the beginning only Matins was said, but a daily Evensong was added in 1864. At the same time, the musical side of the services was built up so that on his second Christmas he could write happily, 'Matins and Communion. All fully choral.' By the time the new church was consecrated, Gregorian chant and *Hymns Ancient and Modern* (then considered a High Church book) had been introduced and there had been one or two slight enrichments of the service. For instance, on his second Easter Sunday he wrote, 'decorations in flowers – white bags.' (The 'white bags' were presumably alms bags, which were used for the first time.) All these changes were relatively conservative. The daily service was the hallmark of the Tractarian. Surplices and alms bags were amongst the innovations which C P

S Clarke attributes to the 40s and 50s, while Churton had complained of the enthusiasm for Gregorian chant as early as 1846. Father Herbert's congregation seems to have approved of these changes. It showed a satisfactory response and began to increase so that, on Ash Wednesday 1862, he could write, 'Good congregations', and on Good Friday, 'services all well attended especially six o'clock'; the communicants had already increased from the 19 of his first Easter Sunday to 95 in 1862 and 146 in 1864.

All this time the growing congregation had been worshipping in the little chapel of St Paul in Miller's Lane. It had been intended to replace this as soon as possible with a more worthy building, and one of Father Herbert's main tasks during these early years was the raising of funds for this purpose. Gregory had already acquired a site on which the new church was to be built. This had been given by the owner of the old Vauxhall Gardens, and contemporaries delighted in pointing out that the altar of the new church was built over the place where 'Neptune used to disport', a specially infamous spot in the Gardens. He had also got together trustees who were responsible for the financial side of the work. Money was a major problem, for the parish was too poor to pay for the church itself. But the necessary funds were raised with the aid of outside friends.

On 2 February 1863 Father Herbert wrote joyfully, 'Began clearing ground for new church', and two months later the foundation stone was laid by the Archbishop of Canterbury. The following year (28 June 1864) the church was consecrated by the diocesan bishop, Bishop Sumner of Winchester. Reports of the service vary according to the churchmanship of the paper concerned, but all seem agreed about the splendour of the service – whether for good or ill. Thus *The Standard* wrote with satisfaction that the altar 'was vested in one of the handsomest altar cloths in England',[49] while the less friendly *Morning Advertiser*[50] censured the Bishop for his presence at the ceremony. 'The service,' it declared, 'was most imposing as a pageant. The splendour of the high altar – the thirty-nine priests all receiving the sacrament from the bishop's own hand – the vast congregation – the full surpliced choir singing the responses, and the outburst of the chanted Gloria in Excelsis to a species of Mass music – the silver-haired bishop, with the Order of the Garter on his breast, pronouncing benediction – all gave it the exact appearance of High Mass.'[51] Judged by contemporary standards, both church and service were impressive, and it is not surprising that the venerable evangelical bishop in his sermon pointed out the danger of not using the noble church properly and gave a warning on the dangers of formalism.

Thus by 1865 the parish had acquired a positive character. It was definitely a High Church parish. It had a fine new church and a pattern of dignified liturgical worship was being gradually built up. The growing congregation was being instructed in definite Church teaching in which the sacraments were regarded as of prime importance, and was responding to it. People had begun to trust the judgment of their new priest and to think they knew what he expected of them. The lines on which the parish would develop seemed already clearly marked out.

It was on a congregation of this sort that Father Herbert launched an Evangelical mission; the remarkable thing is that he was surprised at the opposition it met. In order to explain how this came about it is necessary to go back a little, for the remote cause of this baffling situation was – Robert Aitken of Pendeen. How and when Father Herbert first met Robert Aitken is unknown. Bodington says that it was 'in the earlier years of his ministry'.[52] Aitken preached for him at Vauxhall in 1861 and it may be that he had invited him there on a friend's recommendation, in which case this would be the first meeting, or the visit to Vauxhall may equally well have been the result of a previous encounter between the two men.

Whatever the date, the first meeting was an important one since it led eventually to a conversion which affected the whole of Father Herbert's life and ministry', for he was yet another of the earnest High Churchmen who were brought by Aitken's influence into a closer, more personal relationship with Christ. The words used to describe his conversion, 'his soul found repose in Jesus … through the faithful severity of one whom he always venerated as his spiritual father, one who would not let him rest on anything save the One Foundation,'[53] suggest an Evangelical conversion of great depth and sincerity. Thenceforth he was not only a Catholic, he was also an Evangelical.

The actual date of Father Herbert's conversion is unknown, but it seems likely that it was before 1865, though perhaps not long before. Aitken's influence upon him during the next few years must have been considerable, though it is difficult to estimate it precisely, since no correspondence between the two has survived. According to W H Aitken,[54] Herbert venerated Robert Aitken as his 'spiritual father', which suggests a close and affectionate relationship, and, judging by his eager efforts to help the Aitken family, he felt himself under a considerable obligation. Certainly it must have been Aitken's influence, whether direct or indirect, which led him to undertake a mission to his parish. His own experience must be passed on to the souls for whom he was responsible. He must preach the gospel of conversion.

In March 1865, therefore, he announced a mission week. Strictly speaking this was not the first mission held in the parish, for one had been taken in November 1863 by a well-known High Churchman, H W Randall of Lavington. It seems to have aroused little opposition; in fact, it is doubtful whether it made much impression at all. The comments in the services register - 'Monday very full, a decrease until Wednesday, Saturday still less, Sunday full' - do not suggest that much impact was made upon the parish. In 1865 Father Herbert himself was the missioner and took the main evening services which were followed by 'after meetings'. Attention was roused and Father Herbert wrote, 'Even on Saturday night the meetings were well attended.' He omitted to mention, however, precisely why the meetings attracted people, and the reason would never have been guessed but for a few stray references in the Aitken correspondence; for it seems that, though the St Peter's people were roused, it was not to repentance but to anger and opposition. Thus Mrs Aitken could write on 16 March, four days after the end of the mission, 'The Herberts write from Vauxhall that they are amidst the war and tumult of opposition, but yet good is being done. His curate will not countenance him, and some of his choir take their hats and walk out of the church.' Obviously the regular congregation was startled and annoyed by the change in his teaching, probably in the enthusiasm of a new convert he overstated his case, and since they liked their young vicar they laid the blame on Aitken. Father Herbert thereupon called upon him for help, arranged a meeting at which he was to speak, and then had afterthoughts, for Aitken wrote to his wife that, 'Herbert has thrown me all into confusion, insists upon my going to London on Monday,' and then that, 'Herbert thought there was so strong a feeling against me in his congregation for having misled him that I would be anything but acceptable to them at present, but he had invited so many to meet me on Monday that he could not let the arrangement be departed from – his brother-in-law, General Ashburtam etc., etc.'. A difficult situation only served as a challenge to Robert Aitken. He went to Vauxhall a few days later saying that he hoped 'to have some work'. His visit made a most definite impression. On Monday he spoke to a meeting which included some of the neighbouring clergy. 'We had a room full last night,' he wrote, 'about two hundred. And one or two found peace after. Mrs Herbert's niece is now just in the passage from death into life and very sweetly ... '

It may be deduced from this that several of those present were converted and that others were rendered 'anxious', for two days later he was 'going to see people at Vauxhall parsonage' and to hold another meeting in the evening.

The parish was thoroughly roused and it was a question of what the next step should be. Father Herbert's decision was characteristic. He would hold a second mission. In all normal circumstances it would have been folly to have two missions in one year in one parish, yet it proved the right policy at Vauxhall. The minds and consciences of the people had been stirred, first by himself and then by Robert Aitken, but they had not been finally convinced. Thus the second mission completed the work of the first and the November services proved to be very fruitful ones, as the references to 'Good after-meeting' and 'very solemn meeting' show. It must have been through Aitken's influence that he obtained Richard Twigg as his chief missioner, for he does not seem to have been associated with him before. Thus he was drawn into the circle of the Wednesbury School, for Twigg brought with him George Body, who had just left Wednesbury for Sedgeley, and James Malcolmson, who had recently been a curate at Dukinfield (the scene of another of Aitken's great missions). This mission of 1865 always ranked in Father Herbert's mind as *the* parish mission.

From 1865 onwards, Father Herbert can definitely be classed as a Catholic Evangelical. In him, and in his parish, all three strands of the High Church mission movement meet and, what is more, meet before the Cowley conference of 1869. He could be said to be a member of the Wednesbury group. Twigg, Body, Bodington and G H Wilkinson were his friends. With Body he was especially intimate. He stayed at Wednesbury; they preached at Vauxhall and bore the brunt of his earlier parochial missions. He joined them on missions in churches further afield. On the other hand, he did not relinquish his former High Church connections. The St Alban's clergy, especially Mackonochie and Stanton, were frequently at Vauxhall, and Butler of Wantage, Lowder of London Docks, Father

Nihill (a very extreme man) and the Haggerston priests all gave their assistance at times. The names of the earliest Cowley fathers also appear amongst the preachers. Even the devout but eccentric Father Ignatius was welcomed, presumably because of his great gifts as a mission preacher.

As a result of his conversion, Father Herbert's ministry took on a twofold character which many people found difficult to understand. He remained a definite High Churchman, and more, W H M Aitken described him as 'a Ritualist of the Ritualists' and declared that he was perhaps 'surpassed by few, if any, in the lengths to which he went in this direction', yet 'no Primitive Methodist could preach a simpler gospel than he preached, or be more definite in his desire to bring about the conversion of souls'.[55] It is not surprising therefore that he seemed 'the strangest of combinations', as Bishop Ryan discovered when he took a confirmation at St Peter's. Observing the high ritual which obtained in the church, he felt it incumbent on him to put the Gospel as clearly as he could 'lest unhappily formalism should prevail over spirituality' amidst such surroundings. He therefore delivered a charge which was little short of a mission sermon. Great was his surprise on entering the vestry when Father Herbert clasped his hand in both of his, and exclaimed with the deepest feeling, 'Thank God for a bishop that believes in the forgiveness of sins!'

As far as the worship of his church was concerned, Father Herbert went on as he had begun, and it was in the years immediately following the mission that he adopted practices which definitely ranked him amongst the Ritualists. In 1867, a weekly late morning Sunday Eucharist was begun and, for the first time, deacon and subdeacon assisted the celebrant, though the term 'High Celebration' was not used until 1870 and the word 'Mass' does not appear until 1876, and then only in the safe obscurity of the register of services. A daily Celebration was begun about the end of 1870, and in 1871 there is the first reference to a requiem, 'Celebration for Mrs Hughes RIP'. Strangely enough, there is no mention of a procession before the Celebration earlier than 1879. Holy Week was carefully observed. The 'Three Hours' had been introduced as early as 1866, and in 1873 the Reproaches were used for the first time. Four years later, the church was kept open on Maundy Thursday so that the congregation might watch through the night. Even Tenebrae was said in 1894, but no public notice was given of it and it was probably intended only for the clergy, the sisters and the devout. Corpus Christi was celebrated by 1870. The introduction of harvest festivals (begun in 1865) and the Watch Night service on New Year's Eve may have been the result of his friendship with the Holborn clergy. The Watch Night service met a real need, for the livelihood of many parishioners was precarious, and they had much to hope and fear from the coming year. It is not surprising that Father Herbert often commented on the 'large congregation of the very poor' or noticed that the church was 'exceedingly full and very quiet'.

The development of the church services was accompanied by considerable ceremonial enrichment and a desire for all the accessories of worship. This was more likely to arouse opposition than any doctrinal teaching or even liturgical changes, as Father Herbert discovered when he tried to introduce Eucharistic vestments in 1867. At this date they were used in only a few 'extreme' churches; but there had been no legal decision against them and even lawyers employed by the Church Association believed them to be covered by the Ornaments Rubric.[55] Legal or not, Father Herbert's parishioners were apprehensive of such unfamiliar articles, and he had to issue an address to his aggrieved communicants explaining why vestments should be used. Presumably they accepted his wishes since the number of Easter communicants had increased again by the next year. He was unwilling to flout authority, however, and when the Privy Council gave judgment against altar lights in 1868 he accepted the situation temporarily, hoping that the decision would be righted. Incense was not introduced until later. A censer seems to have been subscribed for in about 1891 and Father Herbert's daughter, Mrs McClure, 'had charge of the design, and conformed it to the most ancient models.' It appears to have been used for the first time at Evensong on Christmas Day 1891; but there is no note of the use of incense at the High Celebration, though it was used at Sister Joyce's profession in the church in 1893.

No effort was spared to make the setting of the worship a worthy one. The actual church[56] designed by Pearson and built at a cost of about £8,000 was considered a very successful design and it was favourably noticed in contemporary journals. Built of local brick in the French Gothic style, it was remarkable for its loftiness. At the time of the consecration, however, its interior was somewhat bare. It was especially observed by the critics that the money available had been spent on essentials and that decoration had been eschewed until further funds were available. As *The Building News* commented, 'What has been done has been done thoroughly.' The wisdom of this was noticed at the time, but it must have cost Father Herbert severe self-control. The Victorians loved richness and decoration and Father Herbert was a child of his time.

He longed to see his church look beautiful, yet he did not attempt to do everything himself. The church's needs must be supplied by its friends and parishioners; and he took good care to let them know what those needs were. His earlier annual letters in particular contained lists of items needed for the church. They came bit by bit. In 1866 Father Herbert announced that Sister Eliza had given the four new lights in the apse triforium in memory of her brother and the next letter (1867) mentioned a painting in the apse given by Mr Lancaster. Other gifts followed; but the carving of the capitals was not begun until 1873 and he had to wait until 1879 for his coveted marble altar slab. 'Statues' were mentioned year by year amongst the desiderata, and the font cover, designed by Pearson, had still not materialised in June 1891; in fact several pounds had yet to be subscribed. (This was not surprising, as it was the gift of the church's children and it must have been a big effort for those slum children to save their sweets money.)

Vestments and rich furnishings added to the magnificence of the service. Fine vestments were much sought after. Father Herbert's letter of 1867 mentions the gift of the first (white) set. Special care was taken to follow medieval patterns and Mrs McClure copied the design for a new white chasuble from a thirteenth-century original at Rheims. This seems to have been a very splendid article, for the design, suggesting the tree of life, was of raised gold surrounded by pearls.

The great treasure of the parish, and Father Herbert's special pride, was the oft-mentioned Angel Cope. The material (specially-woven Lyons velvet of undyed silk) had been bought as early as 1884, but the work on it was expensive. Subscriptions languished, and it was not until eight years later that it was actually completed. The embroidery occupied the Wantage Sisters for a year. It was obviously a most expensive item and it is not surprising that a poor parish found it difficult to raise the money. Yet the parishioners were generous to their church and many offerings were made by the guilds. The pulpit desk and processional cross were presented (c. 1867) by branches of the Brotherhood of the Most Holy Redeemer. Banners were given too. Scarlet cassocks for the acolytes and a violet one for the crucifer were introduced in about 1873; cottas seem to have supplemented the surplices around 1888; and servers must have rejoiced in the red slippers which were given by subscribers a few years later.

Friends outside the parish helped too. Miss Lambert of Malvern spent several years over the illumination of the best missal. Mrs Seymour (later Mother Frances Mary) brought back stones from the Holy Land to be incorporated in the altar, and the new altar books were bound in olive and other woods which she had obtained at Jerusalem. 'The exquisite Venetian point lace superfrontal' mentioned in 1877 as 'the gift of a sister' was probably one of her purchases at Venice on her journey home.

Father Herbert was meticulous in his care for everything connected with the sanctuary. He took great trouble over the training of his choir and servers, and choristers had a special admission service. The young servers, who normally wore noisy boots studded with nails, were provided with slippers, and the cope boys wore white gloves to prevent their hands soiling the fine vestments. His love for his church was very great, and a choirboy said that the only time he remembered him being 'proud' was when the Abbé Vignon from Chartres, who had attended the High Celebration, remarked that his choirboys' behaviour was better than that of French boys. 'His face lit up as he mentioned the appreciation,' said the boy.

It could hardly be expected that the impressive services would go unnoticed. Father Herbert's ministry occurred at a time when ritual controversy was strong and bitter. The Church Association had been formed in 1865 to put down ritual; the Public Worship Regulation Act was passed in 1874 with the same object. Many of the leading Ritualists were prosecuted, and several priests were imprisoned. Father Herbert's friend, Mackonochie of St Albans, suffered bitter persecution. It must have seemed unlikely that he would escape himself. Yet he was never actually prosecuted. The church did receive a visit from the Kensitites, but this had an unlooked-for ending. As the unwelcome visitors sat to hear the sermon, they were surrounded by a group of cinderyard women, in case they made a disturbance. The tactics were unexpectedly efficacious. The company of women daily occupied in the filthy work of rubbish-heap sorting was too much for the young men, and one by one they left the church.

Strained relations with his bishop were a more serious matter. When Father Herbert first went to Vauxhall his parish was in the diocese of Winchester. The elderly Bishop Sumner was most kind to him. He consecrated his church and at the luncheon which followed he told the clergy that 'he hoped always to be a friend and father to them', but diocesan boundaries were changed and St Peter's was transferred to the diocese of Rochester. Bishop Thorold[57] (who was goaded on by the militant Low Church party) thought it his duty to show his disapproval of clergy who would not recognise the claim of the Judicial Committee of the Privy Council to decide on the rites and ceremonies of the Church. He declared: 'These brethren of ours are outside the law, and it is their own act that has placed them there. Where I find them I leave them; and what they have made themselves, that I must recognise them to be.' He refused to confirm, preach or perform any official act in churches which would not relinquish certain practices, such as the use of Eucharistic vestments. It was difficult for Father Herbert to withdraw from the position he had taken up, and so his parish fell under the Episcopal ban. No confirmations were held in the parish, and the people never saw their bishop. Candidates had to be sent to other churches, which were consequently so crowded that there was no room for the friends and relatives of those who were not parishioners. (Sometimes as many as five hundred candidates were presented at St Mark's, Kennington, or St Mary's, Newington.) Father Herbert felt this keenly. 'The refusal of the bishop to do the part of a father in God, or allow another bishop to confirm in our church tends to a general disregard of confirmation,' he wrote. The references to 'worry and anxiety' which affected his health in the eighties may well have been partly due to his unhappiness over this matter. However in 1886, Bishop Thorold relaxed his policy, mainly due to the influence of C E Brooke of St John's, Kennington. 'The Church,' he wrote, 'has condoned ritual. I am satisfied of the wisdom of no longer keeping aloof from these men.'[58] In the following year he held a confirmation at St Peter's; it was the first there had been there for nine years.

The Evangelical side of Father Herbert's religion was expressed mainly in his fervent mission work. From 1865 to 1876 there was a mission every year; in 1874 there were even two, for the parish had to take part in the great Mission to London, yet Father Herbert could not bear to relinquish his own Advent mission. Thereafter they were held less frequently; not because he had ceased to find them efficacious, but because of difficult circumstances. The missions were aimed especially at the working men and the really poor, so that bills bore invitations like 'Come to the Mission. Come as you are when your work is done' and 'Come and learn the true way to be happy – to love God, and to feel that He loves'. Father Herbert was determined to get non-churchgoers to the special services, and clergy and workers would join in a good 'hot prayer meeting' before sallying forth literally to compel their neighbours to come in. Mission handbills often carried the note 'No communicants will be admitted to St Paul's schools during the mission unless they bring a stranger with them.' This threat seems to have been put into execution, for tradition relates that just before the beginning of the service he would take the place of the doorkeeper; if he saw any of his own church people attempting to enter the church without bringing someone else with them, he would sternly bar the way, though with a smiling face that seemed to contradict his sternness; 'No, no, my friend! You can't come in without your passport; go out and find some tramp, or coster, or chimney sweep, or someone else of that kind, and bring him with you or I can't let you in.' The appeal was simple and evangelical. The main mission services were followed by prayer meetings in the school which clearly took the form of wrestling with the souls that had been moved. Thus in 1866 Father Herbert could write: 'Meeting more than full. More stayed than we could pray with' and 'Meeting overfull – souls all moved'. A sister singing a hymn at the mission service might find her book taken from her as Father Herbert said, 'Go and pray with that woman over there!' Sometimes there were additional meetings for special groups of people; thus there were services for young men, for young women, for children, and most frequently services for men only. It is noteworthy that in these missions he relied so strongly on the Wednesbury clergy; the services were never taken by the Ritualists, who were asked to preach or take Lent courses. Thus the 1866 mission was led by Twigg and that of 1867 by Bodington, and in 1868 Twigg, Body and Bodington (not to mention Father Ignatius) all assisted. The 1870 mission was taken by Wilkinson, and James Douglas, Body's curate at Kinby Misperton, assisted in both 1871 and 1874. Francis Caudwell, another 'Aitkenite', took the mission in 1881. This suggests that he found the Wednesbury men were the most effective missioners.

A mission was no flash in the pan, an annual effort after which everyone relaxed until the next one came round again. Father Herbert understood and loved souls too much for that. Those moved by the missions were not necessarily ready for the worship of the parish church, and so special services and classes were provided for them. These began as early as September 1865, for a newspaper of that date reported that: 'There are meetings held in the district to which the poor can come in their working clothes; and when they are sufficiently instructed to value the privileges of worship, they attend the hearty congregational services in church.'[59] One of the results of Twigg's great mission in 1865 was a Sunday night prayer meeting which was still being carried on in 1893, and presumably the 'Advancement Class' mentioned in 1867 was for those who had been touched by a mission and who needed further help and instruction. In later years a permanent winter mission led by one of the parochial clergy was set up in St Paul's schools. There were also special missions to meet particular needs. For instance, in 1867 an evening centre for the very poor was set up at Cliff's potteries and was inaugurated by special tea meetings: for cinder-sifters, dustmen, etc., the first evening, the next night, for navvies, and for mothers on the third night. This mission included a night school two evenings a week as well as a Wednesday devotional meeting and a Sunday morning Bible class for men which Father Herbert was still taking years later.

In 1880, there was a special mission to navvies. Father Herbert also followed the contemporary practice of dividing the parish into 'districts', each under a 'visitor' who tried to become personally acquainted with every family in her streets. Thus a really determined effort was made to reach every individual in the parish.

He was far from content with converting his people; he wanted to lead them on in the way of sanctification. He realised how difficult, if not impossible, it was for them to live Christian lives in the midst of such pagan surroundings. The society of Christians in circumstances similar to their own could, he saw, be a source of strength to them, and so he instituted the system of guilds which was such a feature of the parish. The aim of the guilds was to stimulate the faith and form the lives of beginners in the Christian life. Though there were many of those societies – in 1893 there were fifteen in addition to branches of the Confraternity of the Blessed Sacrament and the English Church Union – they had mainly the same purpose and served simply to separate the ages and sexes. Their names, often quaint to modern ears, were intended to 'awaken enthusiasm' and 'kindle a spirit of loyalty'. Christian Soldiers was a name which doubtless appealed to boys and Comrades of the Cross may have inspired young men, but it is difficult to see why The Pierced Side and The Pure Offering were considered especially suitable for women, and The Children of Divine Grace were not infants but young women in service or business. Needless to say, the Holy Name was represented by several wards, and there was also the company of the Holy Name for men. A few guilds were formed to meet special needs. The Ward of St Peter, for instance, was founded for the poor boys working in the potteries who attended St Peter's Mission School, and the guild of the Holy Redeemer was for sidesmen. Obligations of membership varied from guild to guild, but they usually included attendance at certain services and at a monthly ward meeting which often included a tea.

It was difficult for the poor in the overcrowded homes of Vauxhall to find a quiet place in which to say their prayers. Father Herbert was therefore very insistent that the church should always be open so that they could pray there. On Good Friday 1864 he noted that, as usual, the church was open all day and, 'a good many availed themselves of the opportunity'. Lent notices would end with the information: 'The church is always open for private devotion.' He realised that it was not enough to leave the door unlocked; the church must be comfortable and inviting. And so, when St Peter's was being built, he paid special attention to the heating system so that he could be sure it was always warm and welcoming to those who slipped inside.

Fr Herbert

Father Herbert's longing to help men advance in holiness made him one of the pioneers of the retreat movement. The first Anglican retreat had been held at Oxford in 1856.[60] It was soon followed by others, and in 1868 T T Carter could write that retreats were being held in 18 to 20 places every year, some of them being for laymen.[61] Father Herbert wished his people to have the advantages of a retreat, but he seems at first to have had rather vague ideas as to what a retreat should be, for he intended Twigg's stirring mission of 1865 to serve as a retreat for his communicants. But he soon discovered that retreats and missions were two separate things, and in 1867 the first retreat was held. It must have been one of the first *parish* retreats in the country, and is especially interesting for that reason.

One hundred and fifteen people gave in their names to attend, but many of them must have had to go to work, and only a fraction can have been present the whole time. The retreat lasted for two full days with a preliminary address on the previous evening. Services and meditations were in church. Secular and unnecessary conversation was to be avoided, but there was no rule of silence, and since there was no provision for meals, and long stretches of time had to be spent at home or in church, the quietness of the retreat would have depended largely on family cooperation.[61] Four years later, when the next retreat was held, there were several developments.

This time there was an outside conductor (C Bodington), and though the word 'confession' was avoided, the clergy were available in the vestry at specified times. Retreatants were also urged to make resolutions in writing and to offer them at the final Celebration. Strangely enough, there was not another retreat for 15 years, though towards the end of Father Herbert's ministry there was an annual 'retreat or quiet day'. By this time the difficulties of home distractions had been realised and the sisters had come to the rescue, so that he could write (1890): 'Our own people at 141[62] kept the day very strictly, not speaking a word, but employing their vacant time in reading. The sisters charged two and six to those who could afford it and one shilling to the poorer.' Retreats had obviously become a normal part of parish life, a creditable effort for a nineteenth-century slum parish.

The spiritual and ecclesiastical sides of Father Herbert's ministry were undoubtedly the most important to him. But they did not exhaust his work. The nineteenth-century parish church was a centre for social and philanthropic activities, and in a slum area like Vauxhall it often became responsible for a number of dependent institutions which arose to meet the needs of the people. Father Herbert therefore found himself responsible for a network of institutions and organisations which required attention, help and often financial support. He started with one big advantage, however. Robert Gregory was a most energetic worker and he had already laid the foundations of many important parochial works, and something approximating to a parish centre had been planned. Thus around the church and parsonage quite a complex of buildings grew up.

The first of these was the soup kitchen, already established before Father Herbert's arrival. The provision of nourishing soup to those in need was a normal part of parish routine, and proved a costly item in the accounts. From this kitchen the 'twopenny dinners' for schoolchildren must also have been supplied. Above the kitchen was a useful clubroom for meetings.

In the same block was the orphanage.[63] This building was a home for middle class girls (especially daughters of the clergy) who were trained to support themselves as elementary school teachers. It was not, strictly speaking, a parochial institution. The building had been given by Mrs Lyall, widow of a Dean of Canterbury; the management and maintenance of the institution were the responsibility of Miss

Gregory, Robert Gregory's sister, and, for a time at least, he was the chaplain. The girls were apprenticed as pupil teachers in the parish schools, however, and to that extent formed part of the parish. Some years later a home of a different type was founded in nearby Gye Street.[64] Here the girls did laundry work and were trained for service. Mrs Herbert interested herself in the work and was always anxious to get situations for the girls. Yet a third home (another orphanage) was opened about 1877 by 'a lady'. It was 'nearly opposite the church' and, strictly speaking, outside the parish, but Father Herbert mentioned it in one of his annual letters, which rather suggests that the children must have attended St Peter's or been under his care.

The biggest responsibility of the parish was its schools. When Gregory went to St Mary's in 1853 he found nothing but a Sunday school (in which the children would have learnt to read the Bible) and a tiny Dame School for a parish of 15,000, for as yet there were no State Schools. The need for more schools was urgent. He soon established schools for both boys and girls, and a site next to that intended for St Peter's Church was also acquired, so that by the time Father Herbert came to take over the daughter parish the new school buildings were well forward. A year later, St Peter's Schools were opened by the Bishop of Winchester, and the parish celebrated the event with a monster tea-party. These schools, however, only catered for the children of his more affluent parishioners, for the fees charged were sometimes as high as a shilling a week and could only be met by small shopkeepers and well-paid artisans.

The first attempt to help the really poor children was made by Sister Eliza, who began the 'Penny School' from which St Paul's schools (opened 1869) later developed. These schools were always a heavy charge on the parish. The children who attended them were 'of the poorest; hungry, poorly clothed, and ignorant'. They had to be fed at the soup kitchen and helped with boots and clothes. Children from such a background were, not surprisingly, 'weak in capacity' and did not show up well before government inspectors. This meant that the schools' grant was low, for the system of 'payment by results' was being applied to education, and the authorities expected as much from these children as from those from comfortable homes. The Education Act of 1870 created difficulties for both St Peter's and St Paul's Schools, for it was followed by the establishment of one of the undenominational Board Schools in the neighbourhood. This school tended to draw off children, so that the Church schools, which had been built at considerable expense, were not full. This was galling since the Board Schools were only supposed to fill up gaps in the voluntary system. A Nonconformist minister, the Reverend Murphy, seems to have led the Board School crusade and raised objections to the ritualistic practices at St Peter's (the school children attended the church), so that in 1874 even the pacific Father Herbert became embroiled in the correspondence columns of *The Times*. In a sense one can hardly blame Mr Murphy. Father Herbert was not really interested in education as such and, as Mr Murphy suspected, his main object was to ground the children in Church teaching. He went so far as to call Church schools, '*the* only bulwark of Christianity' and accused Parliament of creating a new sect called 'undenominationalism'. The schools were indeed another form of mission agency, a fact which was not missed by the unsympathetic Charles Booth in his report on the parish. 'The doctrinal training begins with the schools,' he said, 'and it is hoped that the impress made may remain. It is an individualistic system. Every child who attends the day school learns thoroughly the doctrines which are regarded as of such vital importance; and the fact that no child is ever withdrawn from this teaching raises a hope (not I think likely to be realised) that through the children the parents also may be reached.'[65] When the church was planned, a special aisle for the school children was provided; and St Peter's schools adjoined the church and vicarage, so that the connection between church and school could hardly be missed.

One other educational institution was connected with the parish – an Art School. Gregory had realised that there were large numbers of young mechanics in the neighbourhood, many of them employed in Maudslay's steam engine works, who needed to draw better in order to set out their work. He established an evening Art School, and this grew so rapidly that a permanent building was soon required. The foundation stone of the new school was laid in 1860 at a great ceremony, which attracted a good deal of notice since it was the first public act of the Prince of Wales after his coming of age. The Archbishop of Canterbury and three bishops were present, and the Bishop of Winchester and Father Herbert officiated at the special service. The school proved a great benefit to the neighbourhood and was soon taking full-time students. It was especially valuable to those working in the potteries and Mr Doulton, who was one of the managing committee, was persuaded to recommence ornamental earthenware productions, for which Lambeth had once been famous, in order to provide work for its pupils. Thus the famous Doulton ware had its origin in the school and its pupils. The Art School formed part of the complex of buildings around the church and Father Herbert was one of its managers, but it was a purely secular institution, and one feels that of the numerous educational enterprises of the parish it was the one which interested him least.

In addition to the day schools, efforts were made to provide elementary education at evening classes. It is difficult to discover how many of these there were and where they flourished, for they were much less formal affairs than the regular Church day schools. In the sixties Sister Gertrude conducted night schools three times a week, and The Standard mentioned evening schools for men, women and children in 1865.[66] St Peter's Mission school, begun in 1873 in two rooms in the High Street, provided classes for poor boys from the potteries. It was later transferred to new premises where the Boys' Club was opened.

It is not surprising that drunkenness was one of the great problems for the parish. When life was drab, grim and bitter the temptation to escape from its dreariness by intoxication could be overwhelming. Moreover, as the author of 'The Missionary Aspect of Ritualism' pointed out,[67] the colour, bright lights and cheerfulness of the gin palace could be as big an attraction to those living in squalid surroundings as the liquor itself. In 1877 Father Herbert founded a temperance guild, but it was not enough to ask men to take the pledge without offering them an alternative place of entertainment, and so in the following year the Men's Institute and Boys' Club were opened, with a coffee palace under the same roof. The clubs seem to have flourished, so it may be assumed that they met a real need. Yet excessive drinking must always have been a problem. At one time, Father Herbert issued a special Christmas pledge headed 'How to keep a really Happy Christmas', and the fact that St Peter's kept (1882) so unliturgical an observance as Temperance Sunday suggests that drunkenness was still a major problem. It probably remained so throughout his ministry.

The communities founded by Father Herbert must be mentioned at this point, since they arose to meet parish needs. The story of the sisterhood will occupy the remaining chapters of this study, but the little Brotherhood of the Holy Name must be discussed now. By the 1860s brotherhoods were in the air. The needs of the great towns led men to look for new forms of mission agency, and many felt that the answer was to be found in brotherhoods. By a brotherhood was meant a group of men living a simple community life, bound by no vows, and devoting themselves to mission work. Quite a few were founded, and in 1876 Father Herbert, who was usually abreast of the thought of the time, followed suit. Unfortunately very little is known about this venture. On 21 October, a house (11 Harleyford Road) was blessed for the brothers, and on 30 November they were formally admitted. The superior was Brother Clare, who probably belonged to a family which was very active in parochial work[68] and there were two more members, Brothers Lambert and Bouser. Technically speaking, the brothers were not religious. (Father Herbert hoped that a first order for men would also eventually be founded.) Since they devoted only their spare time to corporal and spiritual works of mercy, it may be assumed that they continued their work in the world. A few examples of their mission work may be mentioned. In 1878 they gave addresses to children at the permanent winter mission, and in Lent 1880 Brother Clare took one of the actual mission services. Their work probably lay mainly amongst the men and boys, since they were anxious to build a house next to the Men's Institute.[69] It is unlikely that the brotherhood continued long after 1880, though the actual date of its dissolution is unknown. None of the other brotherhoods founded at this time succeeded and, like the Brotherhood of the Holy Name, must be reckoned an experiment that failed.

When Father Herbert died, some the newspapers pointed out that, with the exception of the sisterhood, his life's work had been mainly confined to his parish. *The Record* stated that 'it was in his heart to live and die amongst the poor of Vauxhall',[70] *The Globe* wrote that he had for a long time past 'seldom been heard of outside his own parish',[71] and *The Church Review* remarked that 'he cared little to see strangers' and described him as 'a stay-at-home priest, rarely heard of outside his parish'.[72] On the whole they were right. His main work was at Vauxhall; he was essentially a parish priest. Yet it was not the whole truth. For, in his earlier years his influence and activity extended far beyond Lambeth.

It was as a missioner that his most significant outside work was done. The number of missions he took part in was not, by modern standards, large.[73] However, in his earlier years missions were regarded with considerable suspicion by the majority of the clergy and to hold one at all was a brave, pioneer effort. For this reason the earlier missions at Vauxhall itself had significance for the Church at large as well as for the parish.

In 1868 he took part in his first outside mission, at Willenhall in Staffordshire, where Bodington was rector and Twigg, Body and Wilkinson were his fellow missioners, and a few weeks later he was seen at the Rugeley mission in the same county. Throughout the 1870s he was actively engaged in outside mission work, and he helped with three more missions in the 1880s. Thus his main work was done at a time when the mission movement was in its formative stage. His influence was considerable. He was one of a limited number of priests who had practical experience of missions, and he seems to have been recognised as an authority on the subject. Thus he was one of the 12 priests invited to the Cowley conference to discuss arrangements for the Twelve Day Mission, and he gave an address at the retreat day held at St Barnabas', Pimlico, for the clergy taking part. He was asked as an 'experienced missioner' to take part in the conference about after-meetings, which was held before the Mission to London (1874), and four years later he was present at another St Paul's conference which, under the chairmanship of G H Wilkinson, discussed the training of missioners.

Although Father Herbert was not a great preacher, he undertook a certain amount of outside work. He preached mainly in local churches and for the Confraternity of the Blessed Sacrament, though he did once deliver a sermon in St Paul's Cathedral. His earlier preaching engagements were often in support of causes such as The Additional Curates Society, The Surrey Churches Society and the Association for Augmenting Southwark Benefices, which all appealed to his mission sympathies. His literary output was small. His *Notes of Catechisings* was published in 1884 and a posthumous volume, *Notes of Sermons*, was edited by his son. The annual addresses which he gave to The Company of Christian Mothers were privately printed, and he seems to have compiled an Altar Manual, though no copies of this can be traced. It was fitting that his one really valuable publication should be the little book, *Suggestions for a Mission Based on Several Years' Practical Experience by Two Parish Priests*, which he wrote in collaboration with G H Wilkinson, and of which many thousands were sold.

He did valuable work in training the younger clergy. During his long ministry at Vauxhall many curates came under his influence. None of these became famous, though the name of W H Longridge, who joined the Cowley Fathers, is still remembered for his work in popularising Ignatian retreats. What is, however, interesting is the number who left for the foreign mission field, of whom the most outstanding were B T Atlay (Archdeacon of Calcutta) and N Dawes (first Bishop of Rockhampton). To these should be added the name of W T Gaul (Bishop of Mashonaland) who was a member of the St Peter's congregation, though never a curate there.

Father Herbert's death on 14 November 1894 was sudden, having been preceded by a heart attack as he was preaching at Evensong a few days before. His health had, however, been undermined a good ten years earlier; in his annual letter for 1883 he mentioned that he had been away more than half the year suffering from a weak heart, and his trip to the Nile did not completely restore him, for the following year he was away for nearly three months. Hard work and slum conditions were no help to a man with a weak heart and it is not surprising that he should die at the relatively early age of 64. His death was marked by a great outburst of public sorrow. A perpetual watch was kept in the church and the Office for the dead was said daily. On the funeral day the outside of the church was literally blocked with people and the police could hardly clear a pathway for the long procession, three hundred strong, which accompanied the body to its final resting place. On the evening before the burial Canon Dugmore, a relative of Father Herbert's and a former Vauxhall curate, preached to an immense congregation on the text 'I was not disobedient to the heavenly vision'. There could be no more fitting words with which to sum up his life.

ENDNOTES - CHAPTER 2

[37]For an appreciation of his thought see A M Allchin, *George William Herbert: Some Aspects of His Teaching*, printed at the Convent of the Holy Name, Malvern Link, 1965.

[38]The Church Review, 1 July 1865.

[39]Ibid.

[40]In the 1861 census returns William Herbert is described as architect of the Board of Inland Revenue. He built a good many houses on the Grosvenor Estate including most of Gillingham Street, and he built – and is said to have designed – the block of houses in the Strand opposite Charing Cross Station. His wharf and sawmills were on the Grosvenor Canal, Pimlico. He had a natural taste for art and his extensive fortune allowed him to become a considerable buyer of pictures and sculptures.

[41]A former headmaster at Westminster School.

[42]Later Canon Wickenden. He was the friend of H W Benson who became Archbishop of Canterbury.

[43]Dean of St Paul's 1890-1911.

[44]*Life and Labour of the People of London*, series I, vol. I, 1902, pp.277, 290.

[45]Ibid, p.285.

[46]W H Hutton, *Robert Gregory*, 1912, p.61.

[47]*The Church Review*, 1 July 1865.

[48]*The Oxford Movement and After*, 1932, p 164.

[49]*The Standard* 29 June 1864.

[50]*The Morning Advertiser* 1 July 1864.

[51]*The Record*, 23 November 1894.

[52]Ibid.

[53]Ibid.

[54]Ibid.

[55]The use of vestments was not included amongst the charges in *Martin v Mackonochie* in 1868 because the great lawyer Stephens believed them to be legal.

[56]For a full description of St Peter's Church see T P Bumpus, *London Churches Ancient and Modern*, series II, 1908, pp.276-280.

[57]C H Simpkinson, *The Life and Work of Bishop Thorold*, 1896, p.119.

[58]A G Deedes, *Charles Edward Brooke*, 1912, p.137.

[59]*The Builder*, 2 September 1865.

[60]This is the usually accepted date, though it is sometimes claimed that the first retreat was held in a parsonage in Kent in 1855.

[61]'Retreats' in Shipley, O., *The Church and the World*, vol, III, 1868, p.433.

[62]The Mission House.

[63]Opened 24 June 1862 by the Bishop of Oxford.

[64]This home was in existence in 1871.

[65]Op cit. series III, vol 4, 1908, p.43. Charles Booth's visit was made a few years after Father Herbert's death, but the policy of the school seems to have been continuous.

[66]26 August 1856.

[67]'R F Littledale' in O. Shipley, op. cit, vol I, 1866, p.39.

[68]An Edward Clare ran a mission to the potteries lads and D Clare was made sacristan in 1867.

[69]They actually settled at 69 Upper Kennington Lane. The house was blessed 1 December 1877.

[70]23 November 1894.

[71]17 November 1894.

[72] November 1894.

[73]The parish services registers show him absent on missions at Wolverhampton (1871), Liverpool (1873), Gravesend (1875), Bradford (1876), Manchester (1877), Tynemouth (1878), and Horbury (1879), and there are further references to St Paul's, Great Portland Street (1865), Newmarket (1888) and Mildenhall (1889).

CHAPTER 3

The Earliest Sisters and Mother Charlotte

Unlike many of the early sisterhoods, especially the first – Holy Cross, Park Village West – the Community of the Holy Name was never really planned or founded. Dr Neale had deliberately founded St Margaret's, East Grinstead; Miss Lockhart had intended to start a sisterhood (Community of St Mary the Virgin) when she joined Butler at Wantage; Harriet Brownlow Byron believed she was called to found a community (All Saints sisters) when she commenced her life in Margaret Street; but no one ever deliberately began the Community of the Holy Name. Father Herbert, it is true, is reckoned the Community's founder, yet he never consciously planned the formation of a sisterhood; and though Mother Frances Mary is accounted its foundress, she was in fact the third mother and had nothing at all to do with its earliest years, for the Community of the Holy Name was never really founded at all; it just happened.

An entry in an old number of the *St Peter's Parish Magazine* gives the clue to the beginnings of the little community. 'In the year 1862, or thereabouts,' it says, 'a novice came to work in the parish of St Mary-the-Less and in the newly formed district of St Peter, Vauxhall, as parish nurse. After a year or two, she wished to become a confirmed sister. With one or two others, who desired to devote themselves to God, she then lived in lodgings in Brunel Street.' The student of church history pauses in dismay before that statement – 'a novice came to work in the parish.' Surely the writer has made a mistake? He must have meant that a lady came to work in the parish, felt the call to a dedicated life and asked to become a novice. But this was not so. The strange statement was correct. The very first member of the Community of the Holy Name was already a novice when she arrived at Vauxhall.

Charlotte Gertrude Ronalds, or Sister Gertrude as the novice was called, had an attractive and compelling personality. Her original, pioneering disposition was only what might be expected from a member of the talented Ronalds family. Her father, it is true, had followed the conventional career of a city merchant, but his brother, her uncle, Sir Francis Ronalds, of Kew Observatory was the first inventor of the modern telegraph, and another relative, Edmund Ronalds[74], was a chemist of sufficient eminence to be noticed in the *Dictionary of National Biography*. It is not surprising that with this background Sister Gertrude refused to accept the conventional life of a Victorian lady. Her desire for a life of service led her to Wymering, where the Community of St Mary had been established in 1859 by the Reverend

Sister Gertrude

George Nugee. Nugee has been described by Peter Anson as 'one of the most bizarre and original personalities of the second phase of the Anglo-Catholic Movement'.[75] He was a man of enthusiastic temperament, with a taste for the dramatic, and his ideas were hardly suited to the sober churchmanship of his time. He was not content with the 'Sarum Use' which satisfied all but the most extreme of his contemporaries, and the ceremonial at Wymering church was an eclectic version of the Roman rubrics devised by Nugee himself. His longing for a reunion of the Roman, Orthodox and Anglican Churches led him to become secretary of the Association for the Promotion of the Unity of Christendom and he is believed to have been one of the members of the ill-fated Order of Corporate Reunion. It is clear that a sisterhood founded by such a man could hardly fail to be 'extreme.' Sister Gertrude cannot have spent more than three years at Wymering, and it may well have been less. The Sisterhood ran an orphanage and a middle class school, but its main work seems to have been nursing, and she may have gained her own training there. One wonders why she left. She probably found Nugee's enthusiastic temperament congenial, and since he remained her friend and adviser, it is unlikely there was a serious breach between them. Possibly she found life at Wymering too restricting. She decided to give up her connection with the Sisterhood, but not to abandon her religious dedication; this was quite in accordance with contemporary teaching,[76] and so she came to Vauxhall in 1862. Nugee may have suggested this himself, for he seems to have been acquainted with Father Herbert and he had preached for him in Lent 1862. At first she was attached as a nurse to an institution known as Lady Page Wood's Mission, but she soon extended her activities so that she was teaching night school three days a week and running guilds. A reference to 'Sister Gertrude's Christmas Tree' shows that by January 1863 she was already well-established. Her personal sweetness and piety gave her an extraordinary influence over young people. Sister Gertrude did not remain alone for long. In June 1863 she was joined by her friend Eliza Rogers (later Sister Eliza), a young lady still in her twenties.

Sister Eliza

Eliza had been born in the Wiltshire village of Alvediston, though she had lived more recently in Scotland. She had begun her work amongst the poor of Dundee at an early age under her friend Dr Forbes, the energetic High Church Bishop of Brechin, and she had also worked at Edinburgh and Crieff. The two friends lived together in lodgings in Brunel Street, where they may have been joined at times by one or two other ladies.

The thought of a sisterhood began to fill their minds more and more. The first step was taken in February 1865 when the two friends gave up their lodgings and took a house, 21 Brunel Street. Then, on Easter Eve, Eliza was clothed as a novice.

Three months later, Sister Gertrude, who was now sure that she wished 'to become a confirmed sister' (in modern terms, to be professed), took her vows in St Peter's Church in the presence of the Coadjutor Bishop of Edinburgh. The Community had begun.

For 18 months the two sisters pursued their uneventful life together. Then on St Stephen's Day 1866 their new home, Eldon Lodge, in Upper Kennington Lane, was blessed. Two days later, an older woman, Mrs Charlotte Maris Broadley, was clothed a novice. With the arrival of a third member community life became a reality.

Mrs Broadley had had a rather different background from that of the other two sisters. She came of an Irish family, though she had spent much of her earlier life in Jamaica, for an uncle who had settled there begged to be allowed to adopt her as she was so like the only daughter he had lost. In 1833 she married the Reverend William Broadley, an island curate, and after a few more years in Jamaica which tried both her health and her conscience, for the prevailing vice and licence caused her great distress, they settled in Cornwall where her husband became curate of Cury and Gunwalloe. Shortly afterwards he was incumbent of the new district of Carnmenellis, a bleak moorland mining village some miles from Redruth. The church was as yet unbuilt and there was much to be done in the schools and parish. All Church work was made especially difficult by the strong Cornish Dissenting tradition, and husband and wife found plenty of scope for their energies. They remained at Carnmenellis until his death in 1855.

The years at Carnmenellis were important ones of the religious development of both Mrs Broadley and her husband. Until this time her religion, though probably genuine enough, had been neither deep nor personal. The removal of the Broadleys to their new parish in 1843 led to a great spiritual crisis in her life. As she and her husband were crossing a bleak desolate moor in their gig, the horse suddenly took fright, bolted, dashed the carriage to pieces and threw its occupants violently to the ground. Mr Broadley was only shaken, but she was severely bruised and one leg was broken. They were alone on the moor and all he could do was to drag her gently to the side of the road and leave her while he went off for help. He had to go about two miles and was away nearly three hours. She was left in great pain and loneliness, but in her distress she cast herself with all the power of her will upon God and realised, as never before, His nearness, mercy and pardoning love. When her husband returned, instead of the moans he dreaded to hear, he found her happy and thanking and praising God. In after years she used to say, 'The breaking of my leg was the conversion of my soul.'

It was not her complete conversion, however, though Mrs Herbert in her little book *Mother Charlotte*[77] gives that impression. It seems that some months later her happiness died away and that for some years her experience meant little to her. Then help came. Her husband had been 'awakened' by a sermon of Robert Aitken's at Baldhu in about 1851. He tried to forget it, but after his friend William Haslam was converted he endeavoured to pass on the message to his old friend. Mr Broadley was clearly somewhat afraid of his changed views. He declared that he trusted in his baptism and was quite unwilling 'to cry for mercy as a common sinner'. One day Haslam decided that he ought to try to convince his friend again. When he arrived at the parsonage gate he saw hoof marks which suggested that Mr Broadley had just gone out. However, he rang the bell. Mrs Broadley asked him in and seized the opportunity of consulting him about her own religious perplexities. His account of their conversation is couched in old fashioned Evangelical phrases, but its import is clear. He taught her not to trust in any feelings but in Christ Himself. 'I at once pointed her to passages of Scripture, where we are told that we have forgiveness of sins through the blood of Jesus, and I put Christ crucified before her as the object of faith. I told her that, as certainly as the blood of Jesus had been shed, there was mercy and forgiveness for her. I said: "I believe it, and have forgiveness: and you may have it too, not because you feel happy but because Jesus died." She did believe, and we rejoiced together.'[78]

A few months later her husband had a similar experience. He announced his conversion to his congregation the following Sunday and a revival followed in the parish. Its spirit seems to have been that of Cornish Methodism. 'The power of the

Carnmenellis Church

Lord overshadowed the place, and there was as usual a simultaneous melting of hearts all over the parish, and a running together of the people to hear the Word, and what is better, to obey it. Then followed a true Cornish revival with full manifestations, and Mr Aitken came to preach. The fire was burning and shining before; but when this mighty man stirred it, it rose to a tremendous height. The excitement of the parson and people was intense, and hundreds of souls were added to the Church, who had been brought from the death of sin into the life of righteousness.'[79] Just one example must be given of the atmosphere at Carnmenellis at this time. When a missionary meeting was held in the parish, the attendance was so large that there was scarcely room for the people to stand in the church even though all the seats were removed. 'Ere long the missionary meeting had to be turned into a prayer meeting, to the astonishment of the missionary and the consternation of the less enthusiastic clergy present, one of whom afterwards stated that "the atmosphere at Carnmenellis was warm, exceedingly warm".'[80] Carnmenellis had joined Pendeen, and Baldhu as a centre of the revival fervour seems to have lasted throughout the two and a half years which remained of Mr Broadley's ministry. No doubt much good was done and many souls were brought to Christ, but the revival had its limitations. Excitable local peole depended too much on their feelings and they were not really incorporated into the life of the Church. Despite the ministry of 'converted' clergy, they began to fall away, and eight years after Mr Broadley's death Francis

Caudwell could complain that there was 'Methodism in every house' and that there were seven meeting houses in the parish.[81]

The revival at Carnmenellis has been described here because it was a factor in Mrs Broadley's own religious experience. It shows that she did not belong to the pure High Church tradition but should be placed within the orbit of Robert Aitken. His disciple William Haslam was the agent of her conversion and that of her husband, and there seems to have been a close friendship between Robert Aitken himself and the Broadleys. But like many of his followers, she was as much a Catholic as an Evangelical. Her husband appears to have been a High Churchman before his conversion, and no doubt she held the same views as he. As the excitement of the revival died away, her churchmanship must have returned, but balanced now by a deeper, more personal spiritual experience than she had known before.

In 1855 she lost her husband. Mr Broadley was a man of enthusiastic, energetic, impetuous temper. Outwardly eccentric, he was generous and warm-hearted, much beloved by others. Yet her marriage cannot have been an easy one. His unstable temperament and the fits of depression to which he was liable in the spring and late autumn must have been very painful to one of her clinging, sensitive disposition, and his death in tragic circumstances was inevitably a great shock.

It was only to be expected that she should leave the scene of her great grief, for she was not a Cornishwoman. Yet surprisingly, she stood firm. She felt that God had led her to Carnmenellis and that she ought not to move without a clear leading of the Holy Spirit. She built herself a little house, Tranquills Cottage, close to the church, intending to spend the rest of her life there, working amongst the villagers. Then came a call for help. A sister, 20 years younger than her, from whom she had been separated since her childhood, was left a widow with children needing help and training. Mrs Broadley's duty was clear. She left her peaceful cottage and the work she loved for the less congenial London suburb and devoted herself to the care of her nieces and their mother.

Mrs Broadley became acquainted with Father Herbert sometime in 1866. Her sympathies were aroused by the needs of his large poor parish, while he realised that her devotion and spiritual experience had fitted her for the task of training others in mission work. He therefore asked her to join his little community. She was made a novice on Holy Innocents' Day 1866 and professed six months later, as it was felt that her age and experience made a long novitiate unnecessary.

The whole future of the community depended upon Sister Charlotte, though of course this was not realised at the time. It seems desirable therefore to say something about her character at this point. She was first and foremost a woman of prayer. She loved especially to pray in the early hours of the morning and neither pain, nor cold, nor disabilities could rob her of her early prayer and the Offices she loved. Prayer was not just a comfort to her; it was a weapon and a work. She was a woman of great modesty and purity of character who shrank from realising the existence of vice in others. Her own conscience was so tender that she would suffer any pain or inconvenience rather than disobey its slightest warning. If anything, she was over-scrupulous, for she would almost torture herself in examining the purity of her motives. She was always ready to ask pardon, however slight the offence she had given. 'I wish Mother Charlotte would not ask pardon,' indignantly reflected an associate, 'for if an inch represented her offence, the fault on the other side was yards long.'[82] A sister who had been away for a long time found that 'the Mother's greeting was to throw her arms around my neck, and ask my pardon for any rude or unkind words she might ever have been guilty of towards me'.[83] Sensitivity and sympathy predominated in her character and this meant that some things were great trials to her which would have been trifles to one of more robust sensibility. Thus, when a relative once suggested that some plan of hers was the result of subtle worldly policy, she was not indignant, as most would have been, but tears streamed down her face as she tried to detect whether she had really harboured so unworthy a motive.

Mother Charlotte

Her ardent spirit made her an ideal mission worker. As a sister said, 'In season and out of season she never failed, but named the Precious Saving Name to all her voice or pen could reach. Every inmate was faithfully dealt with, as were also the visitors, the poor, the tradespeople, no-one were neglected.'[84] She could not visit the dentist without speaking to him about salvation, and a sister accompanying her to the clock-mender was surprised to hear her gently, but firmly, question the tradesman, quite an old man, about the state of his soul. Her genial, cheerful manners attracted many who would otherwise have turned a deaf ear to religious subjects. A friend said, 'I used to bring people to the St Peter's teas when I knew she would be there, on purpose that she might say a word to their souls; because I felt they would take from her what would have offended them in anyone else.'[85]

Her sensitive spirit was never intended for leadership. She leaned on others and longed too intensely for sympathy to gain the calm mental equilibrium essential to wise and successful rule. 'If God has called you to rule others, my sister,' said a wise priest to her one day, 'you must learn to live alone: it is the fate of all who rule.' 'Oh don't give me so hard a precept!' she replied. 'I can never obey it.'[86] The advice was necessary. She could pour herself out for others, but not rule them. Her zeal was also liable to surpass her prudence. For instance, her longing for prayer was so great that she sometimes roused the sisters at two or three in the morning in her anxiety that they should be up in time. This was unwise when some of them were adjusting themselves to a new life and all had a hard day's work ahead. Yet, she was called to leadership from the start and the duties of her position undoubtedly brought her suffering and sacrifice. 'What battles I have had in this little room,' she once said, looking round the small oratory at Eldon Lodge. 'Every plank of the floor is marked by some internal struggle.' It must have taken every ounce of courage she possessed to make her persevere through the years ahead.[87]

One may ask whether Mrs Broadley had any knowledge of sisterhood life before she entered the Community. The answer is, probably just a very little. Francis Caudwell had begun a sisterhood at Carnmenellis for the poor mine girls soon after he became vicar. This had six probationers, that is, novices, in 1861, but he seems to have had difficulty in finding a superior for them and in 1864 the house was taken over by the Devonport sisterhood. Mrs Broadley was deeply concerned in everything affecting the parish and retained her cottage even when she was living in London, so she must have known something of the sisterhood. It was only a small house, however, and even when it had been taken over by the Devonport sisters, its life would not have been developed enough for her to have learnt much from it.

When Mrs Broadley entered the Community it consisted of only one sister, one novice, and one associate sister. The first three associates were admitted on the same day as herself. Her arrival seems to have encouraged the others to go forward, and on 8 January 1867 the first chapter meeting, then called council meeting, was held and a simple revised rule was adopted.

The most pressing need was for a superior. Sister Gertrude had been the first superior, but her appointment had ended the previous Easter, and she was anyway temperamentally unsuited to the office. And so only 10 days after her clothing - and she had no postulancy, poor Sister Charlotte was 'requested to take the management of the house in the same way as Sister Gertrude has taken it since Easter', presumably as a sort of acting superior. On 1 April she was elected superior, though she was not actually blessed as mother until three weeks after her profession on 5 July 1867.

Mother Charlotte's position was a difficult one, as the infant community was in a state of great instability. It must be stressed that the early sisters believed themselves bound by their profession to a dedicated life, but not to life in one community. Opposite the minutes of the first chapter meeting is the following memorandum: 'Sister Gertrude has undertaken to stay till Easter 1867, Sister Eliza till Christmas 1868, Sister Charlotte till Christmas 1867.'

No one undertook to stay for more than two years. (Sister Eliza and Sister Charlotte were only novices, however.) The suggestion of instability in this entry was fully justified. By the end of January Sister Gertrude wanted to leave immediately, and by 3 June 1867 she had gone, leaving only Mother Charlotte and Sister Eliza. But worse was to follow. Sister Eliza was unsettled too, and matters came to a head two years later when Father Herbert declared that since Eliza had been for a long time 'very unsettled in her allegiance to this sisterhood, and having several times spoken about joining some other house', she should 'either throw herself heartily into the well-being of the house and seek to remedy its defects through the council, or resign her connection with it to work as a sister elsewhere'. Sister Eliza declared that she could not stay in the 'unamended' sisterhood. The changes she desired seem anyway to have involved the participation of a certain Mrs Robins and her daughter Sister Gertrude and, since they felt it best to join a large community, Sister Eliza decided to leave Vauxhall and to continue her dedicated life in the Community of St Thomas at Oxford.

This proved to be the crucial point in the community's history. It now consisted of only one professed sister (Mother Charlotte) and a lay novice, the future Sister Emma (clothed 30 January 1868). The financial position must also have been insecure as Mother Charlotte's resources were modest and Sister Emma presumably had little or nothing, so that the withdrawal of Sister Eliza's annual contribution of £150 must have been a serious loss. At this point the council minutes cease. There was little use in continuing formal meetings which consisted only of Mother Charlotte and Father Herbert. For nearly four years the minute book is blank.

Sr Mary

The remarkable thing is that the little community was not dissolved. Mother Charlotte remained firm. It must have been a hard thing for her to stand alone, but her strong faith in God and her sense of duty sustained her, and the Community owes her a great debt of gratitude, for without her constancy it would never have survived at all.

Gradually numbers increased. Sister Emma was professed as a choir sister in 1870, and later the same year Sister Mary was clothed (professed 25 March 1872). In 1871 Sister Ellen became an associate sister. She transferred to the novitiate in 1872 and was professed only a year later. Two other associate sisters, who were admitted in 1873, were later professed as Sisters Elizabeth and Margaret Mary. In 1875 Sister Eliza asked to return and was readmitted that summer. In the same year two lay novices were clothed. The community, though small, was beginning to grow and seemed to hold the promise of life in it.

Barely a year later, however, it suffered another loss in the resignation of Mother Charlotte, who not only relinquished her office of superior but withdrew from full community life. For some time it had been clear that the burden of responsibility was too much for her. She was no longer a young woman and her health was seriously deteriorating. She had been obliged for some time to give up her Bible class, and her failing strength made her shrink from seeing strangers and visitors. She felt that God was calling her to a less laborious position, and that, without relinquishing her religious vocation, she should retire to a quiet country place and devote herself to the care of her nieces. She did not actually resign from the sisterhood, however, and the sisters often stayed with her in her country cottage, but she was now living apart and could no longer be called on as an active member.

Sr Ellen

Sister Ellen was elected mother in her place (30 June 1876). She had been associated with the Community since 1868, though she had only been actually professed three years when she became superior. She had had the advantage of a short training at the East Grinstead sisterhood (18 August to 28 October 1875) which had been intended to fit her for the office of assistant superior. For three years she quietly shepherded the little household until the leader who was so badly needed had been trained for her office.

Before turning to the period of Mother Frances Mary's superiorship, it seems useful to consider how far the Community's life had already developed. Numbers had increased considerably. By 27 June 1879 (the date of Mother Frances Mary's election as superior) there were nine choir sisters, two lay sisters, four novices and two postulants, making a total of 17. These were supported by at least 13 associates (there were probably more) and seven associate workers. There may have been some associate sisters also. The Community had therefore grown large enough to have a real life of its own and to put some order into that life. A simple rule had been drawn up, and the offices of mother superior, assistant superior, novice mistress and sacristan had been instituted. In 1874 the Community moved to its first permanent home, 141 Upper Kennington Lane, which had been built for it by Father Herbert. Mission work had begun in the Midlands and a penitentiary had been opened at Malvern. Thus the Community was already something more than a parochial institution.

One may ask, 'What part did Father Herbert play in the establishment of the community?' Although he is called its founder he had never deliberately planned a sisterhood. He was an ordinary parish priest and not a specialist in monastic spirituality, and he had no expert help to give. Did he, in fact, contribute anything to the life of the community? The answer is an emphatic 'yes'. Without Father Herbert it would never have survived, for he provided that element of stability which the sisters lacked. Above all, he was always there. Throughout the critical early period he was the *de facto* superior, and his influence penetrated every aspect of the sisters' lives. He was the spiritual father of the house. All inmates were under his guidance and could consult no other priest. He preached at clothings and professions. He was a member of the chapter (then called the council) and like the superior he had two votes. This could be important when numbers were small.

141 Kennington Lane

Although domestic matters were the superior's province, there was a right of appeal to the priest. No work was to be undertaken unless appointed by the superior or the Father and appeals about hours of work could be made to him. He appointed the sacristan and novice mistress and selected the assistant superior in conjunction with the mother. Sisters in charge were appointed by the priest, mother and assistant jointly, and they also decided all arrangements of oratories. Father Herbert was also concerned with the practical side of the Community's affairs. He took over the lease of Eldon Lodge when Sister Eliza left and he built the mission house to which they afterwards moved; he signed the house accounts and they were only laid before the chapter when he thought it necessary. He came to the rescue when the money box was stolen and there were bills to be paid. He even decided quite trivial matters. For instance, no newspapers were to be allowed in the house without his permission, and no books were to be lent out in the district 'without the approval of the Father'. This detailed attention to all the affairs of the sisterhood was absolutely necessary at this stage. The little community would have disintegrated without his support, and he may therefore reasonably be considered its founder.

It is proposed to end this chapter with some short biographical notes about the early sisters, for they were the foundation stones on which the community was built, and their personalities were an important factor in its development.

Unfortunately very little is known about some of them, and so they will not all be mentioned by name here. Firstly, something must be said about the later lives of the original three members: Sisters Gertrude, and Eliza and Mother Charlotte.

When Sister Gertrude left Vauxhall she returned to Father Nugee's influence. She seems to have gone first to the All Saints sisterhood and then to the Home of Compassion in the City Road. She afterwards settled herself at Manchester where she became superior of a house run by the Wymering sisterhood. The sisters worked in the parish of St John the Baptist, Hulme, and Sister Gertrude was soon busy nursing the sick, visiting and teaching in the night schools. A soup kitchen for 50 poor children, a clothing club and guilds for married women and young girls were also established. After seven years she moved to Marpole, and this was followed by periods at Beaconsfield and Berkley. Then Father Nugee suggested another good work, a house of rest for poor needlewomen, and so she removed to Herne near Canterbury. The home never materialised, but instead she had the boys from Watford School and children from the Royal Masonic Orphanage, Wandsworth, for their holidays. This work continued after she moved to

Broadstairs. The last three years of her life were years of sickness. This did not prevent her giving the children a party her last Christmas, but immediately afterwards she had a relapse from which she never recovered and she died 2 October 1894 after a life filled with devotion and good works.

Despite her defection in 1869, which she always deeply regretted, Sister Eliza was one of the real foundation stones of the Community. After her return in 1875 she was unswerving in her loyalty to it and untiring in her work. She was a stalwart character and was quite undiscouraged when the Roman Catholic population of Glasshouse Street showed its disapproval of Anglican sisters by pelting her with mud as she passed to and from her work. Her concern for the really poor children of the district led her to establish the 'Penny School' from which the St Paul's Schools later developed. She was not satisfied with being a mere amateur and soon held a government certificate which she had earned in the parish schools. At the same time, she was one of the sisterhood's most valuable mission workers. No case was too difficult or too hopeless for her to undertake and marvellous victories of grace were accorded to her. She had a wonderful influence with men and the Guild of Apostolic Witness was the outcome of her working men's Sunday Morning Bible Class. Her kindly, helpful disposition must have drawn them to her. Thus, when a ladder broke and a man had a bad fall at the brewery near the mission house, Sister Eliza went to the rescue and gave what first aid she could. The man's way of showing his gratitude was rather unfortunate, for the next Christmas there arrived a barrel of beer addressed to Sister Eliza, who was a very ardent teetotaller. Her generosity must have endeared her to many. Once she even removed her flannel petticoat to give to a poor woman, an act not commended by her superior. She was a woman of intellectual energy and to her last hour she retained a deep interest in all affairs affecting the Church and the poor. Her breadth of knowledge earned her the nickname of 'The Encyclopaedia'. When her health broke down in 1886, she took to writing. She contributed articles and poems to *The Gospeller* and other religious periodicals. The proceeds of her *Legend of Dahout and other Poems* were given to the Grahamstown Cathedral fund. She had had a great desire to offer herself for foreign mission work and, though she decided that home missions had the stronger claim, she retained her interest in work overseas. She was a strong supporter of the Bloemfontein mission and organised a working party and promoted intercession for it. For a short time she was the sisterhood's first novice mistress. Her last days were spent at the Community's home at Parkstone, and it is touching to read how her generous spirit was evident to the very end, for, when her mind was wandering, her one anxiety was that the poor incurable children were not being properly fed.

Mother Charlotte lived on for six years after she retired from community life. At first she went to Parkstone in Dorset where a former Vauxhall curate, the Reverend E Dugmore, was vicar, but she soon returned to her beloved Carnmenellis and remained there until her death in 1882. Here she lived a life of devotion based, as far as possible, on that of the sisters. Every morning she rose early for an hour of solitary prayer in the church, though there was no service and she was the only worshipper. At midday she returned for another hour, and she spent much time in devotion in her own home. The curate of the parish said he only knew her absent once from a Celebration in three years. He often remonstrated with her about coming out so early in the winter mornings but, with tears in her eyes, she would say, 'I must come, if I am to live.'

Her concern for the spiritual welfare of the parish not only remained but increased. Despite her modest resources she had already purchased the advowson of Carnmenellis and assigned it to trustees, and built a vicarage. One of her first cares on returning to the parish had been to open a Sunday School, with the help of her nieces. But the great desire of her last years was to provide for the spiritual needs of an outlying village called Four Lanes. The only place available for worship there was a rather dilapidated room over a carpenter's shop and her long experience of mission work taught her that a mere preaching room was never adequate. 'You will never be able to teach the people reverence for God,' she said, 'until they have a church suitable for the worship of God.'[88] She set herself to raise the necessary funds, denying herself in every way so that she might give more to the work. The doctors might say that it was necessary for her and her family to go to the seaside; 'But the church is more necessary,' she would answer. A pony carriage would have been a great convenience to her, yet she denied herself this luxury so that she might give more. No unnecessary shilling was spent and she lamented to her bishop that with all her care she could not live on less than £80 a year. 'I have been forced to dig rather deeply into capital,' she wrote, 'but I do not regret it, I so long to see souls brought in and trained for eternity.'[89]

Her efforts were rewarded. On 4 April 1881 the bishop consecrated the little

Mother Charlotte's Grave

church. Her own gifts had been munificent. She had promised £500 towards the building, but this subscription was afterwards largely increased, and she had endowed the living with £2,300 and built a house for the vicar. Even the frontals and nearly all the choir surplices had been made in her house. From this time her health steadily deteriorated. A postscript to a letter telling of her joy at the consecration ran, 'My old pain is so severe, that I cannot write as I would – indeed I can seldom finish a letter without suffering; but my time is nearly over.'[90] Mental suffering was added to her physical distress for she feared 'the passage of death', though not death itself. The peace and joy she had continually experienced in communion with God disappeared and were replaced by fears and perplexities such as she had never known before, and this spiritual conflict was a heavier cross than any pain she had to bear. But the day before she died she told Sister Ellen that she had seen Our Lord in a vision or dream (she did not know which) standing very close to her. The realisation of His nearness dispelled her fears. Now she asked simply, 'Shall I soon be home? The darkness is gone, and it is all light!'

Sister Emma, the fourth woman to join the Community, will not be discussed here, for she later became mother superior and her story will therefore be told in the following chapter.

Sister Mary (Mary Hodgson) was already 46 when she entered the sisterhood, though she was to be a member of it for 37 years. She has been described as an aristocratic, loving old lady. Even when she was bedridden she received the novice sent to help her as if in her drawing room. She kissed her hands for a thank you and was always tranquil and patient. When an old sister, she spent much of her time in intercession, for she said that all she could do for her sisters was to pray for them. The sacristan sometimes found her praying in her stall when she came down to open chapel before Lauds. Sister Mary was told that she really must not come down early as it was not safe at her age, but, though she replied meekly, 'Very well, dear mother,' she was liable to forget the injunction in her zeal.

Sister Ellen's earlier life has already been described and there is little to add to it. She became assistant superior again after her three years as mother. She was a great friend of Mother Charlotte and had been sent to her when she was dying. Father Herbert mentioned 'sweetness, gentleness and unselfishness' as the dominant qualities in her character.

Sister Elizabeth (Harriet Elizabeth Linker) was a different type of woman. She must have been a courageous character, for when Father Herbert warned some of the early sisters of the risk of losing their money in the sisterhood, it was she who replied, 'There's always the workhouse, Father.' She became mistress of St Paul's Girls School in 1873 shortly after becoming an associate sister, and it seems likely that she was the assistant mistress previously, in which case she had been educated 'at one of the best training colleges'. She was clothed as a novice in 1874 and held various offices in the community, including those of novice mistress (lay) and assistant superior, and she was sister-in-charge of the Home of the Good Shepherd and of the New Brunswick and Vauxhall mission houses. She always retained a deep affection for the Good Shepherd girls and when she was an old sister would spend every Friday as a retreat day in intercession for them.

Sister Faith Louisa (Louisa Caroline Helder) was born at Clapham. She was one of the Community's first associate sisters and was already 50 when she joined the sisterhood. She held the offices of novice mistress, assistant superior and sister-in-charge of the London house, but is mainly remembered as Mother Frances Mary's companion on her tour of Switzerland in 1883.

Sister Grace (Kate Margaret Barlow) was born in London in 1852 and was 25 when she entered the Community, of which she had previously been an associate. She became the sisterhood's expert needlewoman.

Sister Louisa Mary (Louisa Robson) was an interesting character. She was born at Holtby Hall in Yorkshire in 1825. Her family was wealthy, and she must have been an enterprising young woman for she became one of Sister Dora's nurses at a time when nursing was not a usual occupation for a lady. She became an associate sister in 1876 and was in charge of the Wolverhampton house until she entered the novitiate in 1877. She was a great mission sister, and after her profession was often in charge of mission houses. A sketch book of hers still exists which was compiled around 1850. It provides evidence of her interest in architecture and landscape if not of high artistic powers, and one sympathises with the note she added in her old age: 'Never taught to draw or sketch. Be gentle when you criticise.'

These first sisters were brave women, since they gave up comfortable homes for hard lives in slum conditions. Their reward was not even a stable community life; it had to be learnt by trial and error. Inevitably there were some errors, but, more important, there were faith and courage. 'Be gentle when you criticise.'

[74]Edmund Ronalds was either Sister Gertrude's brother or cousin. The family, which came originally from Scotland, had settled at Brentford, where St Laurence's Church contains memorials to many of its members.

[75]For an account of the Wymering sisterhood see P.F. Anson, *The Call of the Cloister*, 1964, pp.376-8.

[76]For a sketch of the life of this unusual man see ibid., pp.91-103.

[77]Louisa Herbert, *Mother Charlotte*, n.d. p.10.

[78]W Haslam, *From Death into Life*, n.d. p.150.

[79]Ibid., p.151.

[80]Obituary Notice of Mother Charlotte, *Western Morning News*, March 1882.

[81]Letter from Frances Cauldwell to Dr Pusey, quoted by R M Caitling in *Old Cornwall*, vol. V, no. 2, 1961.

[82]Ibid., p.24.

[83]Ibid., pp.24-25.

[84]Ibid., p.25.

[85]Ibid., p.16.

[86]Ibid., p.26.

[87]Ibid., p.28

[88]Ibid., p.34.

[89]Ibid., p.36.

[90]Ibid., p.36.

CHAPTER 4

Mother Frances Mary

If Mother Frances Mary had a motto it must have been 'Efface yourself'. It is almost incredible that she has managed to hide herself away so successfully. Although she was the third mother, the contribution she made to the community's life was so important that she has always been called its foundress, and the decisive development of its life is believed to have stemmed from her. The Jubilee booklet of 1915 declared what 'a great treasure' she was to the Community. Everyone agrees about her importance. Yet when a community history came to be written in 1950, it was found that so little was known about the mother foundress that even her family name had been forgotten. She had hidden herself too well.

There were two reasons for this. The first was her humility and sense of unworthiness. Her ideal of a sister's life was so high, and her sense of what was due to Christ so strong, that praise seemed almost mockery when compared with 'what others have done, with what brides of Christ *ought* to do in His strength'. There was a touch of St Teresa in her gratitude for 'the covering He so often seems to throw over our unworthiness, veiling our faults from the eyes of others'. Secondly, she was afraid that she would lose what she had been given if she displayed it. She was thinking of the story of King Hezekiah when she wrote, 'Our enemies are ever watching for an opportunity to carry off to Babylon the gifts we bring to Bethlehem, our talents, our work, our powers mental and spiritual are safe only when hidden, little displayed and dwelt upon even to ourselves. They must be guarded day and night until we can lay them in sacrifice at Jesus' feet.' This explained her desire that her life should be a hidden one. The amazing thing is that her sisters and friends were content to let it remain so.

Some facts about her life have since been recovered, but they are still few. Her family background can be reconstructed tolerably well, but there is no personal material available until 1875. Copies of some invaluable letters of travel survive for this year, though even these cover a period of only five months. There are few references to her after she entered the Community, apart from a handful of business letters and some brief entries in the chapter minutes, and though some notebooks containing meditations and instructions have been identified as hers, they provide little biographical material. It will be realised, therefore, that this study of her life must of necessity be uneven and full of gaps, and often blurred and uncertain.

Louisa Frances Macdowell Grant was born at Beverley in Yorkshire on 8 March 1831. But she was a Scot through and through. Her father was William Macdowell Grant of Arndilly, the son of Captain David Macdowell of Garthland and Castle Semple, who had taken the additional surname of Grant on his marriage to Mary Eleanor, the heiress of Arndilly. The Macdowells were of ancient, even royal lineage, being descended from Balliol and Montrose and related to others of the most ancient Scottish nobility. A claim to royal ancestry was also made by the

Grants. Her mother was the Honourable Eleanora Frazer, a daughter of the fifteenth Lord Saltoun. Thus on both sides she came of old Scottish stock.

She must have spent much of her early life in Scotland. Her father inherited the Arndilly estate on his mother's death in 1832 and, though the family may have spent part of the year in London or Edinburgh, they lived mainly on their property. Thus she grew up in lovely, if remote, surroundings. Her father's estate, which has been described as one of the most beautiful in Scotland, lay on the borders of Banffshire and Elginshire, the house and the greater part of the property being in the parish of Boharm.

Arndilly House

There was no real village and the nearest towns, Keith and Rothes, were six miles away, and Elgin thirteen. The estate was extensive and included a large acreage of woodland. The countryside was given over entirely to agriculture and forestry and there was no industry; even spinning, the support of poor, unmarried, cottage women, had declined rapidly with the introduction of machinery. Fish and game abounded. The coast was not far distant and in the spring and autumn violent winds swept in from the sea, but the parish was said to be healthy despite the frequent rain and the cold, moist climate. Arndilly House had been well-placed, however. The mansion was built on an eminence where centuries earlier had stood a church; what had once been the glebe now formed part of the lawn. Woods surrounded it on three sides and on the fourth it looked over the Spey, which here spread out into a broad pool, and then beyond to the Belinnes. Behind it, or rather around it, for it was in a recess of the mountain, loomed Benagen. Pictures of the house which still survive show it after the alterations made by her uncle, but it must always have been a substantial and imposing mansion. Thus the graciousness of her home and its beautiful surroundings, the silence of the woods and countryside and the tremendous sense of space must all have made their impression on her early consciousness.

Life in her remote Highland home was balanced by contact with a wider world. Visits to other country houses were part of the usual social pattern. She had many relations amongst the Grants and Frazers, at whose country seats she would have met distinguished and interesting people, and one at least of her aunts had a London house. In fact she hardly needed to go outside her own family to acquire that knowledge of men and the world which came so instinctively to her. The Grants, for instance, had many foreign contacts. Her grandfather, David Grant, had been well-known as a naval officer and had spent many years in government service in Jamaica where he became acting Governor. Two sons who had followed him to Jamaica had died there. Her grandmother seems to have owned property in the West Indies and her uncle Hay Grant, who had followed a commercial career in those islands, had taken an active part in slave emancipation. The family had also army connections. Her aunt Eleanor married General Macdowell and her uncle, Lord Saltoun, was a distinguished general described by the Duke of Wellington as a 'pattern to the army both as a man and a soldier'.[91] (Surprisingly, he was also a great musical patron.) The family was also in touch with public affairs, for Lord Saltoun had sat in the Lords since 1807 as a representative Scots peer and one of the Frazers was in government service at Somerset House. Hay Grant, on his return to Scotland, had stood for the county, but he had not been elected and did not stand again.

There is little to say about the parents. Her father, William Grant, appears to have been a somewhat dullish country laird, interested in hunting but in little else. Her grandfather had improved the estate, but it seems to have slipped back under his son, and at his death the house needed many repairs. One suspects he lacked both the ability and the attractiveness of his father. In 1849 he overtired himself with hunting and was seized with cholera, dying only eight hours later. His sudden death had important consequences for his family. It had always been understood that his daughters would succeed to the property, but when the entail was examined the legal authorities decided that the succession belonged to his brother, Hay Grant, and the estate would not pass to the girls until his death. This meant that Mrs Grant and her daughters, May and Fanny (the future Mother Frances Mary), had to leave Arndilly. Thus not only had they to bear the sudden loss of their father but also to leave their beautiful home. May settled her life by marrying Ronald Stuart Menzies, the son of a neighbour, three months later. Fanny must have joined her mother in a new home. Three years later Mrs Grant died and she was left parentless at 21.

It has not been possible to discover where she lived during the following years. A young, unmarried woman did not usually live alone, so she probably joined one of her relatives. One or two slight references suggest that her home may have been in Edinburgh. But wherever she lived, she probably led the conventional life of a young lady. Quite likely she travelled abroad and spent some time in London, though even this is conjecture. For the next eleven years nothing is known of her.

On 5 November 1863 she was married in Edinburgh to Edward William Seymour, a grandson of the eighth Duke of Somerset. Her husband was a widower and considerably older than herself. The family had naval connections and he had entered the service himself, retiring with the rank of commander. He appears to have lived a quiet life as a country gentleman, acting as justice of the peace and deputy lieutenant for his county. In 1826 he also served as High Sheriff. But he took little active part in public affairs, whether national or local. He had settled in the tranquil little market town of Crickhowell in Breconshire and for the next 13 years Fanny's home was Porth Mawr, a modern mansion at the west end of the town, built on the site of the Herbert family's old castellated dwelling, whose picturesque turreted gateway of the fifteenth century still remained and served as the entrance to the new house.

As yet nothing has been said about her religious faith. It is, of course, impossible to write about the development of her interior life, as there are no personal writings available, but something can be said about her religious background. Her family was traditionally Episcopalian, but the nearest church was fifteen miles away, so that they are unlikely to have attended it regularly. Her grandparents seem to have been genuinely religious people; in their time the service was read at home on Sundays and her parents may have continued this practice. The New Statistical Account of Scotland (1845), however, states that the Episcopalians of Boharm generally worshipped in the parish church, so that she may have attended Presbyterian services, though there is no trace whatsoever of Presbyterian influence in any of her later writings.

The vital religious influence within the family was a surprising one. Her aunt, Wilhelmina Grant, who had been one of Robert Aitken's most devoted friends and helpers, became his second wife. The family accepted the marriage and, although Aitken and his wife and children lived in far-away Cornwall, they paid long visits to the Scottish relatives. Thus the conventional aristocratic Gordons, Grants and Macdowells had the claims of religion as a spiritual reality thrust upon them. They did their best to respond, but try though they might, they could never live up to Robert Aitken's standards. He doubted whether kindly Mrs Gordon was 'really converted to God', and he clearly disapproved of General Macdowell's frivolity in spending his time curling on the lake. He wrote from Garthland (the Macdowell's home), 'It is an awful house full of worldly company and worldly ways.' Yet the Macdowells were doing their best, and a few weeks later he was considering going to Scotland again since Mrs Macdowell was 'very anxious that I should meet the ladies of *high quality* who are awakened in some measure and whose conversion would greatly startle the west of Scotland and help the Word of God'. His influence (whether direct or indirect) did have its effect. Fanny's sister May, for instance, was eventually converted. In 1856 Aitken was writing to his wife, 'I would not think of going to May. It is lost time and lost money, and far too much of both,' and, 'I hardly think you will be justified in going to visit May. There seems to be very little prospect of doing any good.' Yet in 1863 he was rejoicing that 'the heiress of Arndilly' had 'found peace'.

There was an especially close relationship between Robert Aitken and Fanny's uncle Hay Macdowell Grant, who became Laird of Arndilly on the death of her father. Landowner and aristocrat though he was, Hay Grant became one of the greatest lay evangelists of his time. The description of him as 'a man of the world transformed by grace into a man of the world to come'[92] is hardly accurate, for he was always a genuine Christian, though his religious practice was unobtrusive. Probably his own phrase 'a closet Christian' sums up the position best. But in 1856 Robert Aitken held a series of revival meetings in the neighbourhood of Arndilly and Mr Grant was forced against his will to carry on the work. When he made his first convert he said, 'Now I am thoroughly committed; and God helping me, from this time forth, whether in season or out of season, I will as I have opportunity, teach and preach Jesus Christ.'[93] He became completely devoted to spiritual work. He concentrated at first on his own estate and the surrounding countryside, visiting from house to house, holding meetings at night, and often walking through heathery and swampy moors the whole day. The following day he preached in the open air for the first time. His work had soon extended all over Scotland and he became one of the leading figures in the revival of 1859 to 1860. Later he worked in the south also. But preaching was only part of his ministry. He believed it his duty to speak about their souls to everyone he met, and one can only imagine what this meant to a man who had the instinctive reticence of his class. He made it a rule to 'speak' to all who came to Arndilly, and when he was travelling, or visiting in country houses, he approached everyone from maid to mistress. He 'spoke' to Miss Burdett Coutts, the great heiress, though his courage failed him when he was faced with Princess Edward of Saxe-Weimar.

He once said that he had 'spoken' to 1,500 people in three months. 'Show your colours', became his motto; and through every letter ran the same message, 'Speak a word for Jesus in all ways, at all times and by all means.'[94] Everything was consecrated to Him. The hunting stables at Arndilly were turned into a hall which would seat 150 people, and believers from the neighbouring churches used to meet here on Sunday nights to pray for their parishes. The house itself was given over to the service of God. The excellent shooting and fishing became baits for the spiritual fish he hoped to catch. Invalids were invited for the Arndilly 'season' to try the effects of rest and the fine air, and in later years the park was the scene of open-air meetings at which nearly 3,000 people might be present. His teaching was centred on Jesus. Haslam noticed 'how visibly he had to do with a living *person*, and not merely with doctrinal truth'. 'His prayers,' he said, 'were ever like direct speech to one who loved him and stood by his side.'[95] His whole spirituality was summed up in his last message to his friends: 'Tell them' he said, 'that I have proved it now in my own experience; the world fails and friends fail, and the body fails, and the mind fails, and everything fails, but Jesus never fails. This is my testimony. In the midst of all my suffering, one thing has supported me – JESUS never fails.'[96]

Aitken's influence probably reached Fanny Grant through her uncle Hay and her aunt Wilhelmina Aitken, for it seems unlikely that there was much direct contact between them. When Aitken was on his way to a mission at Newport in 1871 he stayed with her at Porth Mawr. 'I had a most loving welcome from May and Fanny,' he wrote. 'May is very clear on first principles and Fanny sees eye to eye with me every way.' This quotation makes his relationship with the sisters reasonably clear. He was known to them and was probably venerated by them, but there cannot have been much close contact, otherwise he would have taken their religious beliefs for granted. The fact that Fanny saw 'eye to eye' with him shows her sympathy with the more Evangelical side of religion.

At the same time she was a definite churchwoman. This aspect of her faith probably developed quite early. Her letters of 1875 make the 'Catholic' nature of her devotion very clear, and it was far too natural and spontaneous to be that of a recent convert. The convent library contains a copy of *The Constitutions and Canons Ecclesiastical of the Church of England* which was given to her in 1853, and it is unlikely she was reading such a book unless she was already influenced by Tractarian teaching. Thus it seems likely that she had accepted High Church principles when she was quite young.

Life at Crickhowell must have become increasingly quiet as her husband grew older. There are few details available about her at this period, but just two points can be made. Firstly, her friendship with the Herbert family must stem from this time. Grace Herbert thought they became acquainted through the Mitchells of Llanfechfa, friends of the Herberts, who lived fairly near the Seymours. They had certainly met by 1870. It is not to be wondered at that a close friendship developed between those who shared a similar faith and outlook, and by 1873 Father Herbert, who did not often leave his parish, was staying at Crickhowell. The letters she wrote two years later show that she was on most affectionate terms with the family, and knew the parsonage, church and sisters well. She became an associate of the sisterhood too, though strangely enough the date of her admission has not been preserved.

She was probably occupied in much spiritual work during these years, but details remain of only one of her activities, the Company of Christian Mothers, which she founded in 1870. This must serve as an example of her mission work at this time. The Company was a society of upper-class women who joined in intercession for each other's children. The link between members was almost entirely a spiritual one, though there was an annual chapter at Vauxhall which enabled them to meet one another. The Company is especially interesting as an embodiment of the Catholic Evangelical spirit. The Evangelical stress on personal religion is shown in rule four: 'That mothers ... first give their own hearts to the Lord, so shall they be able to teach their children from personal knowledge of His redeeming love,' and the mission spirit may be seen in the Advent resolution 'to make some real and active effort for the conversion of souls to God'. This was balanced by a Catholic emphasis on the Eucharist. The Company's special devotion was to the Blessed Sacrament; there was to be a monthly intention for the Company at the Eucharist and its litany was to be said, if possible, at a Celebration. It is interesting to see that Mrs Herbert, Mrs Body and Miss Bodington were all members. Mrs Seymour was secretary of the Company until she entered the sisterhood, and her own mission spirit was shown by the number of her relatives and friends who joined it.

In 1874 her husband died, leaving her a widow at the age of 43. She had no children and no responsibilities. She was rich. She could have chosen an easy, cultured existence, yet the call to a dedicated life pressed itself more and more strongly upon her, and two years later she joined the sisterhood.

The year before she entered she went on a pilgrimage to the Holy Land with two friends, Celia Davenport (a niece of Mrs Herbert's) and Kate Whitehead. This was no whirlwind tour, but a leisurely affair which took nearly eight months, and included visits to Rome and Egypt on the outward journey and time in Damascus and Constantinople on the way home. Fortunately all three travellers wrote back lively letters to Vauxhall. These give a vivid picture of Mrs Seymour and they are the main source for the description of her personality which follows.

The first quality which strikes the most casual reader of the letters is her humanness – humanity is too cold a word to apply to so vivid a person. She was not naturally indifferent to the things of this world. The travellers' accounts include quite frequent payments for the 'trois glaces et gateaux' with which the ladies refreshed themselves in the midst of their European sightseeing. She enjoyed the hot coffee their monk guide brewed for them on top of Sinai, despite the awe-inspiring associations of the mountain, and she was not indifferent to the fact that their cook was 'a marvellous artiste under difficulties.' Her account of a fast-day dinner at Bethlehem with its greasy soup, sardines and fried eggs can only be described as rueful, and though the friends politely told the monk waiter that they had had a very good dinner, she ends up frankly, 'I confess I was so hungry I didn't sleep for hours.' She did not minimise the disagreeableness of early rising in the desert, 'At 4 o'clock Vincent's voice is heard at (the) tent door "Madame c'est quatre heures" and Madame answers more with lips than with heart "Merci Vincent." On a sharp frosty morning it is *not* pleasant.' She was not indifferent to clothes either. She loved the Zion nuns, but thought very poorly of their appearance, for she wrote, 'They wear the most hideous bonnets I ever saw and collars even uglier than our own.'[97] She noticed the sweet scent of the leaves their camels munched and the wild creatures they met. She loved natural beauty, especially the colours of the sunrises and sunsets, and she was excited by the vivid Palestinian flowers.

Mrs Seymour inherited her father's love of horses, and she must have been a first-class rider. The prospect of schooling a tricky little cob appealed to her, even though he was 'so undisciplined in his dear little character'. She was delighted at the idea of riding astride. She said she had wished to do it since she was a girl, and had urged it because it was safer in the hunting field. She almost suggests that she had hunted herself.

At the same time she was a woman of high intelligence. This is shown by the shrewdness of her comments, the penetration underlying her witty remarks and the succinct brilliance of her descriptive writing. She had been endowed with a good brain, and her natural abilities had been developed by travel and by association with able, cultured and important people. She had visited Italy at least once before 1875 and knew residents in Rome; she had travelled in Switzerland; she could hardly have failed to know France. Probably she knew much of Europe well, though she had never visited the East until her Jerusalem pilgrimage. Her letters show she spoke fluent French and Italian. The education she received from her family circle and from the society in which she mixed has been already mentioned, and is further illustrated by remarks in her letters which show that she dined with the consul (General Stanton) at Cairo, met the Jerusalem consul at a tea-party and knew the wife of one of his predecessors. She had useful introductions to the heads of the Palestine Exploratory Expedition too, for she and her friends were no idle sightseers and they carefully studied the sites they visited. Details of her formal education are lacking, but it must have been a good one, and her reading was sometimes surprisingly stiff and technical. For instance, Neale's *Translations of The Primitive Liturgies,* which she was reading in 1868, was an unusual book for a lady to have been studying. She did not sketch, though her friends did, so presumably she had no artistic gifts, but she could appreciate art as her remarks on the sophisticated loveliness of the mosque of Omar show. She certainly appreciated music, and a passage in Sister Faith Louisa's diary of a Swiss tour suggests that she could play. Thus a picture emerges of a travelled, cultured and highly intelligent woman.

It could be wrong to think of Mrs Seymour as a purely intellectual woman, however. She was no cold, detached scholar. Imagination and enthusiasm were conspicuous elements in her character. When she visited historical sites she loved to imagine herself back in the past. At Pompeii, Cecy read to her from Bulwer Lytton's *Last Days* so that they could realise what had happened there, and she was disappointed at being unable to visualise the Colosseum at Rome. The sight of Christian skeletons in the catacombs filled her with excitement: 'Fancy seeing a man who may have been converted by St Ignatius,' she wrote. She expected others to share her ardour, and thoroughly approved of their monk guide who 'was a delightful enthusiast himself ... and seemed to love his mouldering bones'. Her letters show she was a woman who reacted instinctively to scenery. 'Its barren desolation on every side and flinty hopeless character has an oppressing, depressing effect upon one as speaking so literally of a wilderness of punishment.' The grandeur of Sinai overwhelmed her with a sense of sin and made her long for the Eucharist with its reconciliation between God and man. On the other hand, the intense silence of the desert gave her great joy because of its feeling of aloneness with God. She reacted in the same way to human situations, particularly dramatic ones; thus she identified herself completely with the tragic scene of a conscript train leaving the station: 'The grief of the passionate Italian nature left behind was thrilling,' she said, and it was hours before she could forget it and cease praying for the sufferers.

It is clear that she was a born leader. Celia Davenport was a strong character, but there was never any question who was the head of the party. It was Mrs Seymour to whom the manservants looked instinctively; it was she who made all decisions, and who was appealed to in all difficulties. At times of danger or perplexity she was calm and clearheaded and acted decisively. For instance, when she and Miss Davenport were in the midst of a difficult descent of Sinai and their monk guide disappeared and darkness came down, she was quite prepared to send their Arab off for food and wraps and to spend the night on the mountain. Fortunately this proved unnecessary, for he brought back helpers who set the undergrowth on fire, and the travellers eventually made the descent in the light of the burning bushes. Another night their dinner was disturbed by the sound of a fearful brawl between their Christian and Muslim servants. A

Sinai

Turk rushed in, 'and pushed nearly into my soup an appalling face, bathed with blood, with his mouth wide open to show me where the blood came from.' She behaved with complete composure, refused to interfere in servants' quarrels and got him to leave the tent. When necessary she could show considerable physical courage, which cheered her more fearful companions. The precipices around Jericho tried Kate and Cecy considerably, and Cecy admitted that she had hindered their journey by dismounting to walk several times. Yet she reported that 'Mrs S. did not seem to mind a bit'. Perhaps her native mountains had given her a head for heights. She seemed undaunted by the difficult climbing amongst the mountains of Lebanon, though she did admit that the ascent of Sinai involved them in some 'dreadful climbing'.

When they were in Egypt she and Cecy started out together to visit the mummy palace of Cheops, but so difficult and unpleasant was the undertaking that 'Cecy gave in directly and returned to the blessed daylight' and only Mrs Seymour completed the expedition. Her sense of humour and her cheerfulness inspired the others and kept the party together. This was sometimes sorely needed, and it is doubtful whether the other two would have had the courage to surmount their first painful experiences of desert travelling if it had not been for her example. Kate admitted that it was 'impossible not to feel a sinking of heart sometimes', and declared that Cecy's heart had 'failed her more since she heard of there being serpents in the desert'. They both felt 'very blank' at the thought of the increased strain which lay ahead, and all were overdone with fatigue. Yet somehow or other Mrs Seymour preserved her cheerfulness, so that Kate could write, 'Mrs Seymour is wonderful, her courage and energy never fail.' Probably her cheerfulness was due as much to her will as to her nature. Once they were in real danger when they were detained in the midst of the desert at a place called Nakel amongst Arabs who were described, as a 'savage, malicious and revengeful race'. Yet she wrote, 'Fortunately we are determined to be happy under all conditions.' It was no doubt her determination to be happy which kept the party calm.

The preceding paragraphs may have given the impression that she was a physically strong woman. However, this was not so. The fatigue of constant travelling was too much for her, and neuralgia was an old enemy. Yet Celia Davenport's prophecy in Egypt that though Mrs Seymour was 'much knocked up' she would outdo herself and Kate was realised. Her determination was stronger than her physical weakness. Her attitude to the first terrible days of camel riding shows her spirit: 'Give in with Sinai in front of one – not I. For Sinai or Jerusalem, any discomfort purely personal and for the present only, is worth bearing.' Her letters from Jerusalem tell of her love for the city, how she was tempted to make it her home for two years, and how leaving it 'was like a human parting'. Yet she confessed afterwards to Mrs Herbert, 'I wonder how I got thro' any writing at all there or thought of anything; the place, dear as it was to me, suited me so poorly I have rarely felt so little up to anything, whether work or play, or so determined the stupid body should not be master.' But she waited until she was away amongst the cedars of Lebanon before she admitted her weakness.

She was obviously a most attractive woman. However, to use this word gives a very inadequate and superficial impression of her personality, for she possessed an uncommon depth of character. Her religion must have been very deeply grounded for it was so natural, almost instinctive. She saw everything very simply. Christ was the centre of her life and she judged everything in relation to Him. When she reached the East she became very sensitive to the Muslim world around – and hated it. She was pained by the boats flying crescent flags at Alexandria because they advertised the supremacy of Islam, and she made a point of getting up early to go to Church the next day. A letter from Bethlehem showed how glad she was to be in a village without a mosque. Their journey was a real pilgrimage and not just a sightseeing tour. When they

Via Dolorosa, Jerusalem

visited the church of San Clementi in Rome, they were shown what was believed to be the site of St Clement's own house, where no doubt 'assembled and debated and prayed Saints Peter, Paul and Barnabas!' She had to kneel and pray. 'Wet though it was, one could not remain standing. In so holy a place one bit of loving worship must go up.' When the travellers reached Bethany they had been six hours in the saddle, but they dismounted and walked, each alone, in silence, into Jerusalem; and since they arrived in Holy Week the ladies deprived themselves of sightseeing until Easter, spending their time in their rooms and in the Church of the Holy Sepulchre. She was determined to spend Easter Eve there too.

Despite the hardships involved, 'weather outside' (snow, wind and lightning) and 'neuralgia in, stay away I could not. A great longing took me to watch for Easter at the Sepulchre the one only time in life I could do it.' She obtained permission to watch, but only on condition that she was shut in the church for 13 hours with nothing to eat. Even she remarked that this was 'rather formidable', for her watch had to begin at 6.30 p.m. on Saturday evening and the Celebration at the English Church was not until 10 a.m. the next morning. But she was undaunted, for 'there is no limit to supernatural help, and tho' terribly fatiguing, no doubt, a very blessed watch it was: and almost a dream of wonder at times to recall this wonderful reality of where I really was allowed to be.'

The churches they visited gave her many extra opportunities for prayer, and she wrote to Father Herbert from Rome that she could give him many a 'loving prayer' and that 'we go into so many churches – opportunities are showered on us'. When they were travelling through the desert she spent an hour or two daily with her Bible. The friends attended the local church services whenever possible, even when they were at inconvenient times and in incomprehensible languages. But they could not receive Communion in the Churches of the East, and English chaplaincies were few. Thus Mrs Seymour's greatest hardship was to be deprived of Holy Communion. She had longed for it in the desert, and even Jerusalem seemed unbearable without it; for though there was an English church, Celebrations were infrequent, and they were conducted so irreverently that she wrote of Easter Sunday, 'Of our Church here and of the Blessed Sacrament the less said the better. I could have cried bitterly that within three minutes of Calvary we alone among Christians despised and insulted His Eucharistic Glory.'

Her devotion to the Holy Name was a very real part of her religion long before she entered the Community. Sister Elizabeth used to tell of a visit they made together to a monastic church in Switzerland; it was in this church, she told Sister Elizabeth, that she had prayed long ago, and written out an act of dedication to the Holy Name and slipped the paper between the back of the altar and the wall. The community's dedication to the Holy Name was due to her also. The sisterhood had originally been dedicated to Saint Peter, and it was a letter she wrote while still only an associate which caused its name to be changed to the Mission Sisters of the Holy Name. This devotion explains the many little references to the Holy Name in her letters, and her disappointment at not finding it in the catacombs.

Her vocation to mission work was striking. It was something she simply took for granted. Perhaps this is not surprising considering her family background. She could understand a hermit or hermitess 'whose light was not mission work' being utterly happy alone in the desert, but it was not for her. She thought poorly of Christians who made little effort to convert the heathen. Thus she approved of the Latin monks of Bethlehem – 'plenty of conversion work there among the natives (none by the Greeks which is sad)'. She was dissatisfied with the Orthodox monks of Sinai who had civilised their Arab servants and dependants, but had not tried to convert them in case it led to quarrels with neighbouring tribes, for she wrote, 'I am afraid we put the good Sinai monks down for an idle lot.' She felt that if she were a Roman Catholic she could settle down at Jerusalem with the Zion nuns 'who convert many natives', and she spoke approvingly of their 'straightforward mission work'. She did not neglect the opportunities which came her own way, and the letters record a conversation on religion with a Coptic boy, while during her watch at the Holy Sepulchre, 'God gave me graciously some Apollos work to do.'

The breadth of her sympathies is interesting. She was no insular Anglican. The three friends took part in the worship of the Churches of the places they visited, and showed a lively interest in their doctrines and ceremonies. Mrs Seymour was most at home in the Roman Catholic churches. (She was probably already familiar with their worship from her previous continental travels.) There are frequent references to her attendance at Mass, and she also went to Vespers, Benediction and Stations of the Cross. The Franciscans at Tiberias even said a special Mass for them. At Bethlehem she joined in a procession. 'The Latin monks were kind to me,' she wrote, 'gave me a book and candle and invitation to procession for hymns and prayers at all the Holy Places as it was the eve of Palm Sunday.' She persuaded their monk guide to lead them in a *Pater Noster* in the Roman catacombs, and she hated being unable to communicate at the Holy Sepulchre. However, she was not uncritical and wrote from Egypt that she wished the Roman

Catholics preached more Evangelical sermons, 'specially in this place which used to be called "The Evangelical See".' Her contacts with Roman Catholic religious were particularly interesting. She made friends with two friars on board the Alexandrian steamer – one lent her a book on the Holy Land and the other offered them the hospitality of his Jaffa convent, so their relationship must have been a cordial one.

The travellers paid two visits to the Sisters of Nazareth, but their real friendship was with Les Filles de Zion, a congregation founded by Father Ratisbonne for work amongst the Jews. Mrs Seymour managed to get a long and interesting conversation with him and the three ladies paid many visits to the convent, becoming 'thick friends' with the sisters who shed the 'their little private ways' and invited them to their country home at St Jean de Desert. Mrs Seymour was frequently to be found at Benediction in their chapel. She seems to have been interested in the Eastern churches before her pilgrimage, for she mentions that she had visited the Syrian patriarch in London, but was less at home in their churches than in the Roman ones. The Greek monks at Sinai treated the travellers with every courtesy, altering the hour of Mass to allow them extra rest, and showing them the monastery treasures. She described their service as 'warm and very devotional' but she was unhappy about the state of the Greek Church in Jerusalem. The Armenian service she described as 'very like the Roman only altogether less reverent and refined', but she liked the poor and simple Maronites of Lebanon and described their service as bright and devotional. She was interested in the Copts of Egypt, but unfortunately her reactions to their worship have not been preserved.

Mother Frances Mary

The travellers arrived back in London at the end of August 1875. Fourteen months later Mrs Seymour entered the sisterhood. She must have resolved to do so before she undertook her pilgrimage, for some of her remarks are unintelligible otherwise. The reference to a temptation to make Jerusalem her home for two years 'could one do two things at once' suggest that she had already reached a decision. Kate and Cecy said 'sans adieu' to Jerusalem, but she had no thought of returning. In fact she was determined to spend Easter Eve at the Holy Sepulchre because it was 'the one only time in life I could do it'.

She may have visited the continent again during the following year. According to Community tradition she had spent some time studying the life of French convents, and she made copies of their rules. She is unlikely to have made such an expedition before her husband's death, but it would have been a natural thing to do before she entered the Community, and it may explain why she waited another year before doing so.

She was received as a postulant on All Saints Day 1876. The Community realised that it had been sent an exceptional soul, and one well-fitted to become the leader they so badly needed. But she had first to learn the life herself, and the Vauxhall sisterhood was too small and inchoate to give her a thorough religious training. She was therefore sent to East Grinstead soon after she had entered (2 December 1876), and though she returned for her clothing she spent almost the whole of her novitiate there. It is difficult to overestimate what she must have gained from living in a well-established sisterhood. Judged by contemporary standards, Saint Margaret's was a large community. Great conventual buildings in the best Gothic style had been begun in 1865 and these could hardly fail to impress Novice Frances Grace (as she was called), who always loved the picturesque. The peacefulness and stability of her environment must have been a big contrast to noisy Vauxhall. Even more important was life in a well-ordered novitiate under the experienced novice mistress, Sister Benedetta Josephine. In April 1877 she was fortunate enough to be in one of Father Benson's retreats. The bright and kindly Mother Alice understood the difficulties of novices and the gentle, peacemaking chaplain, Father Alison, must have made the convent a very pleasant place, so that her time at East Grinstead was probably a very happy one.

It was soon over. On 9 January 1878 Sister Emma fetched her home and on 2 February she was professed. Her responsibilities soon began, for she was made assistant superior the next month. It is interesting to note that, whereas in the past decisions were frequently left to the warden and mother, they were now referred to the warden, mother and assistant superior, for the Community depended on her judgement from the first.

On 27 June 1879 she was elected superior. The choice seems to have been a foregone conclusion. At the chapter meeting Father Herbert simply pointed out that Mother Ellen's term of office was about to expire, paid 'a warm tribute to the merits of her rule' and then asked the sisters to elect her successor. The question of re-election was not even raised. Sister Frances Mary was unanimously elected. She was the obvious choice and she remained mother until her death, being re-elected three times.

It is difficult to write adequately about her work as mother because, as usual, she has successfully hidden herself. It is possible, however, to summarise briefly the main contributions she made to the Community's life. Firstly, she was responsible for much of the work on the Community's Second Rule and Constitution. This was, of course, the work of the Community as a whole. It was begun before she was professed and the final section was not completed until after her death. However the work was mainly carried out during her time in office, and her influence must have been all important, for even when she was a novice the chapter gave permission for her to be consulted about important alterations in the Internal Rule. The Second Rule and Constitution proved inadequate and was replaced in 1899

Orphanage Children

by more comprehensive formularies, but it formed a necessary stage in the Community's development and helped to shape its life at an important time. Secondly, there was considerable expansion in the Community's work during her time as superior. Another mission house was opened at Emscote, and though this was closed a few years later, it was only in order to take up work in the slums of Birmingham. A house was opened at Wednesbury and the expansion of the community's work which followed within a few years of her death, including the little orphanage at Malvern Link, the mission house at St Paul's, Walden, the home for incurables at Parkstone and the first overseas work in New Brunswick was only possible because of the foundations she had laid.

Even more important was the widening of the community's interests which took place at this time. It was her influence which led the sisters to take up penitentiary work. She gave the house at Malvern Link in which the Home of the Good Shepherd was established, and much of her own time was devoted to the home. The work expanded greatly during the next 10 years, and though the Leamington penitentiary which was undertaken in 1880 had to be relinquished a few years later, the refuge at Worcester was retained. Moral welfare work, as it is now called, had become a real part of the Community's work by the time she died, and it has remained so ever since.

Probably the most important decision she made was concerning the removal of the mother house to Malvern Link. This was decided upon in January 1887, and the house was blessed the following August. The move was a vital one. Father Herbert had envisaged a parochial sisterhood whose *raison d'etre* was mission work at Vauxhall. The Community had, in fact, established houses elsewhere, but its work was still centred on one London parish and the greatest concentration of sisters was there. This was not good for the Community because, as Professor E R Hardy has pointed out, sisterhoods organised around local interest and work seldom developed.[98] The establishment of the mother house at Malvern was important therefore, since it made it clear that the sisterhood was no longer a parochial institution.[99] Secondly, the community was set free to develop along its own lines. Father Herbert's influence and support had been essential in the early days. However his thoughts and energies were largely devoted to his parish, and he had little knowledge of the Religious Life. Under Mother Frances Mary the sisterhood had begun to acquire a better understanding of its own life, and the move to the country set it free to develop this in its own way. Thirdly, noisy

Vauxhall was not the best place for training novices. It is easy to exaggerate the rural charms of Malvern,[100] but it did offer a greater quietness and seclusion than were obtainable in a slum mission house.

Moreover, Malvern had many points in its favour. The Community penitentiary was already established there, and Mother Frances Mary must have known the neighbourhood well. The local clergy were friendly. Mr Newbolt at the Link had been one of Butler's curates at Wantage, and the sisters were already working in his parish. Newland with its almshouses was a centre of spirituality. Although the saintly Mr Skinner had retired, his successor, Mr G Cosby White, was a man with considerable experience of sisterhoods, and he became honorary chaplain to the sisters in 1880.[101] At West Malvern, Frederick Eichbaum[102] was in charge of the orphanage and the Clergy House of Rest[103] with its pioneer retreat work. Thus the sisters were sure of spiritual help.

Although Mother Frances Mary was a woman of deep spirituality, she was also extremely practical. A priest noticed that she had 'a marked capacity for such secular business as must always fall on the ruler of a society'. Thus she was not above concerning herself with the material interests of the Community. She was a wealthy woman herself and her gifts to the sisterhood were considerable. The villa which became the convent and the houses which were turned into the penitentiary were her gifts to the Community. This was important, for it meant that the sisterhood now had a home of its own. (The Vauxhall mission house was the property of Father Herbert.) During her lifetime she gave substantial financial support to the penitentiary, and at her death she seems to have left quite a large sum to the sisterhood. This was a great help to the Community as it had little or no endowment, its mission work was unpaid and all expenses had to be met from the incomes of the choir sisters. Many of her personal treasures found their way to the convent too. The fine sapphires and diamonds in the best chalice once formed part of her jewellery, and the paintings she brought with her included a Perugino.

Yet her greatest gifts to the Community were spiritual ones. The depth of her inner life and the power of her example meant more to the struggling little sisterhood than any material help. It was noticed at her death that 'her generous heart, her deep wisdom, her unfailing devotion' had been the main strength of the community and its works. But though people might talk of her 'beautiful example' they omitted to leave an adequate record of it, and so it is impossible to give a picture of her in her dealings with the sisters. Her teaching on the Religious Life will be discussed in the next chapter, for it contains no personal details and belongs more properly to the life of the Community.

Only one thing can be said with safety: her life in the community was not an easy one. The subject Father Herbert chose for her clothing address was 'Obedience through suffering', and though the suffering he discussed was limited to that which came through obedience to the rule, his choice seems to have been prophetic.

The life must have been costly even on a physical level. She was not strong when she entered the Community and it was unlikely that a Vauxhall slum would improve her health. In 1883 she was so ill that she had to go abroad with Sister Faith Louisa for over two months. Even after six weeks' holiday the pair were 'intent on performing in two days what in average tourists is a matter of five hours', and they regarded this as 'a bold expedition', so she must have been very weak. Three years later Father Herbert's charity report referred to 'the severe illness of the mother superior', and some (undated) retreat notes ask for prayers for 'your mother in her present distress'. Thus it seems likely that she suffered from ill-health throughout the latter part of her community life. This suggestion is reinforced by the words of the Reverend WC Boulter who said, 'It pleased God to send her a long and painful illness, but He also gave her the grace to bear it with singular humility and patience.'

Her sensitivity cost her dear. She had initiated penitentiary work and was outstandingly successful at it. Yet some aspects of it were very painful to her. This is shown by her sorrow 'that as religious and mission religious especially we must know more of evil than other women'. The contact with sin, even with coarseness, was grievous to one who was so close to God, and it was probably her own experience which made her realise so vividly the suffering caused to Christ through contact with the sinful hearts of men.

Hardest of all were the demands of the life itself. Some words of hers expressing the inevitable loneliness of those who accepted a religious vocation seem to depict her own experience. 'We are out of harmony with the world thro' which we pass to our Home – our message unheeded in the streets. Even those who love them (religious) best, who up to a certain point have most sympathy with them, cannot go on now, cannot understand their vocation – often think they are wrong and deluded – self-deceived in following the star. They must go on alone with God.' A radiant faith shines out in her earlier letters, but her retreat notes suggest this was not hers for ever. '"Where is He that is born king of the Jews?" A sad question when asked by those who had left all to seek Him. Where? They thought the star would never fail them and now it is hidden by a cloud.' Again in speaking of the cross it seems to be her own experience she is describing: 'Perhaps you too in past times have looked forward to long hours of ecstatic prayer,' she wrote, 'to sensible sweetness, peace and consolation in the Religious Life – and have found out your mistake. Learn from His own words – and from His dealings with His mother, to expect as *proof* of His best and closest love – desolation, labour, humiliations, tears, anxieties, disappointment and sufferings. With Mary hold out your hand to receive His gift a daily cross.' But her courage never failed and she accepted completely whatever God should send, as her words to a novice before profession show: 'And for the future, I know that endless temptations may come about me – that my profession is but a fresh beginning of the storm – of bearing the cross. That to correct and amend me Thou mayest give me even more – probably far heavier – crosses than I have ever known – more than I have dreamed of – today – tomorrow – all my life long. I do not make conditions. I do not ask to see my way – one step enough. All my future "I commend into Thy hands" and I resolve to take it back from Thee as Thou wilt not as I will. So only wilt Thou accept the gift I bring, the gift of myself in union with Thy and my Beloved.'

Malvern Link Convent 1892

Yet it would be wrong to end this chapter on a note of sadness. For, though life may have brought the cross to Mother Frances Mary, she hid it carefully from others. What her friends remembered were 'her wide sympathies, her sanctified common sense, her prudence, her powers of looking forward, her bright cheery manner' of which they 'had daily evidence'.

Her life in the Community was not a long one for she died on 11 August 1888,[104] less than 12 years after she had entered it. At the beginning of 1888 she had told the Community, 'This will be a good year for us because it has the threefold number of the Holy Name.' No doubt it was a joyful year for her since it meant her entry into the life of eternity, but it was a sorrowful one for her sisters, and it is not surprising that it was 'with breaking hearts' that they sang 'Jesu, Dulcis Memoria' to her as she was dying.

[91]Quoted from J Macveigh, *The Scottish Family History*, n.d., Vol III, p 401. Lord Saltoun had distinguished himself at the defence of Hougomont (when he had four horses killed under him), had served through Sir John Moore's campaign and was at the battle of Corunna. He had been a member of the Walcheren expedition and was present at Quatre Bras and Waterloo. Later he served in China during the Opium War.

[92]Quoted from H Johnson, *Stories of Great Revivals*, 1906

[93]Mrs Gordon, *Hay Macdowell Grant of Arndilly*, 1877, p.43.

[94]Ibid., p.318.

[95]Ibid., p.288.

[96]Ibid., pp.381-382.

[97]That is, uglier than those worn by the Vauxhall sisterhood.

[98]For a discussion of the Community's penitentiary work see infra.

[99]Quoted in P F Anson, op. cit, pp 574-575.

[100]The Vauxhall house still had a privileged position, however. The mother had to spend several months there every year, and the novices were supposed to spend 'a part of their probation' in the London house.

[101]In Mr Newbolt's time (Vicar of Malvern Link 1877-1888), the population of the parish was about 3,000. A map in the Worcester Record Office shows that many houses had been built along the main road near the convent as early as 1858.

[102]The brother of Mother Emily, foundress of the Sisters of the Church.

[103]The House of Rest was originally established at Malvern Link in what became St Saviour's Guest House. It is likely that the former novitiate wing of the convent was used as the orphanage. Both institutions later moved to West Malvern.

[104]She died within the octave of the Holy Name at the hour of consecration.

life and experience of grace, your enlightened conscience, and lastly, the Holy Scriptures, are placed in your power as well-proved artillery and armour for your warfare against sin and Satan.' He told the sisters that they were especially called to bear witness to Christ with their lips. Example and intercession were not enough. He felt that if the grace of God was really in their hearts it would be manifested by their words. It was perilous to keep their spiritual riches to themselves. They were to ask themselves, 'Are we *receivers only* of His goodness or do we dispense as stewards the manifold grace of God?' For, 'one *word* from a heart full to overflowing is but a crumb of the riches we enjoy and yet it may be the means used by the Holy Ghost in the turning of a soul from the darkness of ignorance to the light of the life of God. *One word,* one sentence, one passage of Holy Scripture, has again and again caused a soul to stop, to think, to repent or to believe, and so been the cause of its conversion ... Woe be to us if we close our lips when we should open them for the good of others.' Yet words alone were not enough. The sisters must be instruments of conversion through whom Christ's power could reach souls. It was through their voluntary embracing of the cross that God could touch others. 'You need the holy cross,' he said, 'to carry out that vow. With it alone will you have power with souls ... You must stretch yourselves on the cross in preparation for your mission work. You must not come down from the cross while you are engaged on it. You must exalt the cross while, like Heraclius, you abase yourselves. And when your work is over, you must glory in the cross of apparent failure, leaving the results to God the Holy Ghost whose work it is to save ... The cross must be in the heart – the heart must be in the cross ... such is your motto and such must be your life.'

All mission work was to be done in the power of the Holy Name. Thus he declared in 1877 that, 'This Holy Name is the great weapon of warfare and instrument of conversion which the mission sister in this community wields against the powers of darkness and ignorance, and which she skilfully employs as she adds stone by stone to the fabric of the spiritual temple of her Lord.' He laid great stress on the audible pronunciation of this Name, and insisted that it should be spoken regardless of surroundings. No distinction of social rank should cause the sister any nervousness in uttering it. 'The same force of tender love must move her to breathe the Name which is above every name to one as to another. She must lose all consciousness of the earthly surroundings in the sense of the pricelessness of the treasure with which she is entrusted.' He felt that the future of the Community depended on devotion to that Name: 'O may this community when we are entered into rest, *remember* the Holy Name. Each sister, as she comes in, should *remember* what her own people have done before – should *remember* it is the special heritage of the house. In proportion as this Name is *honoured* and *loved* and *reverently used*, souls will be *gathered* in, and they shall give thanks unto Thee O Lord.'

It is clear that the type of mission work Father Herbert was looking for was impossible unless it was deeply grounded in prayer. For he was not demanding activity for its own sake; he was looking for lives surrendered to God through whom He could act. Prayer was to be the pervading spirit of the whole life, for 'the sister must not only pray in order to live – but must live to pray'. He was sure that the recitation of the Divine office was an essential part of the sisters' life. He told them that it was a temptation to think that the time spent on the daily Offices would be better employed in 'prayers and meditations more adapted to elicit earnest devotion towards the person of your Lord, or in petitions framed to express your more particular or community needs'. He seems to have regarded the recitation of the Office as a way of fulfilling the obligations of the three vows. Obedience was shown in a willingness to join in the prayers and praises of the Church rather than use 'self-selected prayers and subjects of consideration'. Poverty was also expressed because God spoke to the soul through the words of the Office, supplying its need, and demonstrating its dependence upon Him. Chastity (or charity) was supremely shown in the recitation of the Office because the sisters praying in their oratory became 'the voice and lungs' of 'all who are absent and who cannot ... yet pray for themselves'. They were to say the creed on behalf of all believers, the confession was to be made on behalf of all penitents and sinners, and the psalms were to be said for 'those unconverted souls to whom the language of praise and thanksgiving and joy is a hieroglyphic they cannot understand'. But their love must range even wider. They must pray and praise for all animate and inanimate creation, they must unite themselves with the adoration of the angelic host, and in the 'Gloria Patri' join in with the ever blessed and holy Trinity in the joy which was God's before all things were created'. On such foundations was the Religious Life of the Community laid.

Once Mother Frances Mary had been elected as superior, new influences came to bear upon the sisterhood. She had received almost the whole of her religious training outside her own community, and though Vauxhall and East Grinstead had certain characteristics in common, such as a devotion to the Holy Name,[106] there was considerable difference in their ethos. St Margaret's had been founded by Dr Neale, a brilliant man of ardent and impulsive temperament, a great scholar whose studies embraced the Eastern as well as the Western Church. His outlook was less 'Church of England' than that of many other successful founders such as Carter of Clewer and Butler of Wantage. He had died ten years before Mother Frances Mary went to East Grinstead, but his spirit lived on in the teaching and devotions which she learnt in the novitiate. Great stress was laid on devotion to Jesus in the Blessed Sacrament. It is believed that the convent was the first place in England in which the Sacrament was continuously reserved,[107] at least as a centre of *cultus*, and by 1859 Neale had familiarised his sisters with the rites of Exposition and Benediction which he regarded as the logical means by which the dishonour endured by our Lord among His creatures could be repaired. This teaching made an indelible impression on Mother Frances Mary – and it had one serious drawback, for she had been taught to express her devotion under the forms of a spirituality which was not that of her own community. Furthermore, she was a woman of deep, almost passionate, feeling which found its expression in the rather florid phrases of late nineteenth-century piety. This means that her writings are unpalatable to the modern reader, and makes it more difficult to perceive the significance of her contribution to the inner life of the community. Yet the importance of her teaching can hardly be overestimated.

Before considering it in detail, it may be useful to sum it up in one word; depth. Mother Frances Mary's teaching was not at variance with Father Herbert's, but it went much further. It was more profound. For Father Herbert was not called to the Religious Life himself. He was a married man, a priest devoted to the care of his slum parish and the work of an evangelist. He did not know the life from within, and he could not be expected to realise all the implications of a Religious vocation. But Mother Frances Mary lived the life which she had to teach to others. She was led in ways of prayer which were not his. She knew the demands God would make of the sisters if they were to be true to their vocation.

Even a casual reader of her notebooks cannot fail to be struck by the completeness of the sacrifice which she takes it for granted that the sisters must make – and will desire to make. Several times she compares profession with death in the absoluteness of its break with the world and its values. Thus she could write, 'The religious dies with Him, and makes the Holy Sepulchre to be her bridal home. She dies to the world. She dies to earthly love. She dies to independence and liberty. She dies to herself in every possible way.' She knew God would never be content with any partial giving. It was not until the Magi had opened all their treasures, the whole of their store that they could begin to offer. The sisters might bring much or little, but if they kept anything back, He would turn away from their gift. The offering, once made, must be given completely, to be used solely as God pleased: 'We leave our oblation at the foot of the altar and we know not how God will use our gift. Perhaps very differently from what we hoped. They (the gifts) may seem to us almost wasted when we had hoped they might do some great thing for God. It matters not. They are **His**, not ours now, and God has never yet allowed Himself to be outdone in generosity. They are well bestowed. They are safe tho' He is silent on His altar throne.' This sacrifice was to be consummated in martyrdom: 'For us what remains – but offering our lives in sacrifice to be martyrs if so He wills it ... All is finished by your profession. Then and there we joyfully anticipate death and live henceforth only to be sacrificed at His dear pleasure. He accepts us unworthy tho' we be, among His martyrs.' Few of her sisters could reach the heights she set before them. Nonetheless her teaching was badly needed. It was essential that they should recognise and seek to realise the ideal to which she pointed them, even if they could never completely attain to it. For the weakness of the Community lay in the incompleteness of the sisters' giving. They all desired a dedicated life, but for some it must still leave room for their own choosing, and if it threatened to assume forms of which they disapproved, they would pursue it elsewhere. They were prepared to give, but only in their own way and with reservations. Thus in insisting on the need for total consecration Mother Frances Mary made one of her greatest contributions to the Community.

She considered the three vows under several aspects. They might be taken to increase the sister's usefulness in the world (that is, to enable her to do her work for God more efficiently); they might be taken as a means of embracing a more perfect state and of perfecting the soul; or they might be taken as an act of reparation for the opposite sins. But these were all subsidiary interpretations. The vows were really important to her because they made the sister more like Jesus.

She had a deep and passionate love for Christ. She longed to be identified with Him and so she wished the circumstances of her life to resemble his. Thus she treasured the three vows, not only as a means of binding her more closely to God, as Father Herbert taught, but as a way of making her life more like the incarnate life of Jesus. This interpretation was cherished by the Community and it has passed into the present rule which still states that it must be 'the aim of every sister to be conformed to His likeness'.

She welcomed poverty because of our Lord's earthly poverty. A favourite title of hers for Him was 'The Poor King'. She laid more stress on external poverty than did Father Herbert. She would choose poverty because Christ, who had all the riches of heaven, had chosen it: 'A religious, the more poor on earth, becomes the more like her Lord ... The more poor and empty, the fewer little treasures a religious has, so much the more is she the bride of the Blessed Sacrament and of Him who there is poor ... The more she gives up so much the more can she say ... "O God Thou art my God".' She considered that poverty, though conferring apparent weakness, was more powerful than wealth. She saw it not only as a power for personal sanctification 'but as God's great chosen state, to be a power to move the world'. Her interpretation of internal poverty closely resembled Father Herbert's, though it was carried deeper so that she could define it as 'the resignation of the possessions of the soul'. Friendships, praise, influence, success in work, approval of superiors unduly sought, the consolations of God Himself, were all given to Him by the vow of poverty.

It was the relationship with Christ which she stressed when she was discussing the vow of chastity. Father Herbert had seen chastity as the freeing of the sisters to become spiritual mothers. She emphasised the vocation to be 'brides of Christ'. For her the essence of chastity lay in consecration to Jesus Christ. As in earthly marriage the bride took her husband's rank, whether lowly or great, so in profession the sister must imitate the life and partake of the mind of her Lord. Her life must be like His in its hiddenness, its endurance and its perseverance.

The sister's obedience was to be fashioned on that of Jesus. In 'The Infant Jesus a Model for Religious', she meditated on the completeness of His obedience: 'Now – He will not move except in obedience to His creature – He sleeps – or wakes – at Mary's word. He is passed from her arms to the embrace of Saint Joseph – perhaps on to others also. He is clothed and unclothed and has no will of His own. His life in the Bethlehem stable is perpetuated in the tabernacle – in the Blessed Sacrament. Still has He no will but our will – Still no choice but ours "I can of mine own self do nothing." How could the sister, in return, do less than obey Him utterly? His obedience compelled hers. 'Will you not now do His will, who has so long been content to do yours?' As He had obeyed without reserve, so must she. Thus she could say, 'May God make my external obedience to be fashioned after the model of our Lord's. May it be the gift of all my faculties of soul and body as entire as His. May it be yielded instantly because it is to be the sacrifice of a ready mind ... And ever as to God not to man. Accepting the voice of even a fallible superior – even one whose faults are not hid – as so far God's own voice and command, that

I must imitate Him who comes down to the Consecration of the most unworthy and most faithless priest.'

But likeness to Jesus was not enough. The sister could never be content until she was one with Him. Jesus must not only be 'Best of all' but 'All and only'. There could be room for nothing but Him. She was to find all her joy in Him, 'in His presence, His conversation, His caresses, His will and service.' She was to be a Eucharist with Him, not only offering Him, but by virtue of her union with Him, giving herself as a living sacrifice, taking upon herself His burden, sharing His sorrow in the ingratitude of men. It was to be a literal union of hearts. 'We have *taken away* the Heart of God. It belongs to us, more than to Himself... We must give Him ours in exchange. The result is the two hearts are one, perfect union.' Like the bride in the *Song of Songs*, 'She says nothing of him as belonging to her – she thinks not at all of herself except for His service. She lives not to *enjoy* Him, but to *serve* Him ... She sees herself only as a resting place for Him who once "had not where to lay His head".'

It was in this context of union with Christ that Mother Frances Mary placed her teaching about mission work. It was to be the outcome, the natural fruit, of a burning love for Jesus and zeal for His glory. Because she loved Him so much, the sister must make Him known to others, so that He might find a worthier resting place than her own heart. It was useless for her to go forth by herself; she could only go with Him, for without Him she could do nothing. His love must overflow from her heart to all the world. For 'we are made so to abound and be made more than full, that we ought to flow out with Jesus, over all creation, that God may be "all in all". And we should desire this to be brought to pass, not less in everyone else than in ourselves, because we ought to have so hearty a desire along with God, that everything good should be given to all. There is no clearer mark of union with the Word than thus without any straightening of internal breadth to converse in common love, giving all things, filling all things with Jesus – that nothing may remain without its full share. Thus so far as in us lies, we try to fill heaven and earth and all that therein is with our love, which is God, for "God is love".'

Such were the ideals which were set before the little community by its founders. However, it must be remembered that they were ideals, and the ideals of individuals. It cannot be assumed that they reflect the thought of the whole community. It is necessary to turn also to the official records to see what they say about the community's life and object.

The first reference to the spirit and purpose of the Community is to be found in the second part of the First Rule (April 1867). The clause runs as follows: 'That in order to build this house on a deep religious foundation for the purpose of instructing and training souls for the work the Lord shall appoint, none shall seek admission hereinto who have not made up their minds to give up all for Christ's sake and live a mortified self-denying life, forgetting their own in ministering to the wants and cares of others. A sister's life should be the copy however faint of the dear Lord in His active and contemplative life, for this and each sister shall have a special time allotted to her each day for meditation and prayer.' Even here the object of the Community is not plainly stated, it is only implied. But certain points are clear. Firstly, the sisters were intended to lead the 'mixed' life as the reference to Christ's active and contemplative life shows. Secondly, the building up of the Religious Life of the house was of primary importance. The training of the sisters' souls must be put first, otherwise they would be unfit for God's work. Prayer must therefore be an important element in their lives. Thirdly, they were to be filled with the spirit of self-sacrifice and their lives were to be modelled on Christ's own. Finally, they were to be engaged in 'ministering to the wants and cares of others', though the exact form their work would take was left undefined; it would be that which 'the Lord shall appoint'.

There was no real uncertainty about the nature of the Community's work, however. For when in 1876 Mother Frances Mary (then an associate) suggested changing the Community's dedication from St Peter[108] to the Holy Name, it was because she considered the former inappropriate to the Community's special work. The letter she wrote to Father Herbert gives such a clear expression of the spirit of the community at that date that the most important section of it must be given in full: 'My principal reason,' she wrote, 'is that the name of a community should bear ... some allusion to its own special work ... Much help may be got out of a name, whether for encouragement, or for sense of responsibility. Now in whatever work we are now engaged, or whatever may become thro' God's blessing, the various works of our house in the future, we are all – from yourself downward, desirous that one spirit should pervade the whole; the direct mission spirit; the carrying the Holy Name of "Jesus, Saviour", definitely to each soul with whom sisters or associates have to do. Alliance with St Peter's name does not help much here. Even St Andrew's name would help more; but best and most helpful of all might be, to be dedicated in *title* as well as in spirit, to carrying the dear Name of our salvation to others. To be thus devoted even by our title to speaking the Name of Jesus, Healer and Saviour, to the soul sick, and *not* to lift it from the heart to the lips, ought surely to come home to each worker as a contradiction. While you live and while the present generation of sisters and old associates live, we may hope and expect that the direct spirit of the house will live too; but should it, now or later from any cause decline, let our very name rise up in witness against us, and be a weapon ready made to the hand of those who would seek to lead us back into the old paths.' This letter shows that the community considered that its spirit was a 'direct mission spirit' - and an aggressive one at that, and its object the conversion of individual souls to Christ. The emphasis on witnessing with the lips should also be noted, for it is very characteristic of this early period and illustrates the more Evangelical aspect of the community's heritage.

This letter must have expressed the mind of the whole community, for on 7 August 1876 its dedication was changed to the Holy Name. Soon afterwards the sisters were considering the embodiment of their special dedication in 'a fourth promise', and in July 1877 they all agreed to make the additional promise by which they bound themselves to use every means in their power 'for winning to Jesus the souls for whom He died'. The object of the community was at last expressly stated. It was: 'To honour the Holy Name of Jesus in the strength of union and in the fervour of a devoted life: By winning souls to Him and by helping associates in their religious character and work.' The aim of the life was still essentially the same as expressed ten years earlier, and consecration to Christ was placed before all else, but the form of the sisters' work, previously unspecified, was now defined as the conversion of souls. As time went on these two main objects of the Community, the honouring of the Holy Name and the winning of souls to Christ, were expressed more fully, but they have never been substantially altered. The clause about helping associates has been dropped, however, and the emphasis on witnessing with the lips, which was prominent in the early rules, has gradually diminished.[109]

It should perhaps be mentioned here that some slight changes have been made in the name of the Community. Since about 1932, 'Community of the Holy Name' has replaced 'Mission Sisters of the Holy Name' in everyday use, and the full title is now 'Community of the Mission Sisters of the Holy Name of Jesus'. Strangely enough, there is no record of the change, but it was probably connected with a revision of the statutes which was carried out at that time.

The community's interpretation of the three vows has developed considerably over the years, and they now involved much stricter obligations than when the early sisters took them. This is largely due to the insistence on stability. When Sister Gertrude was professed in 1865 she presumably took the traditional three vows of religion. (The actual formula has not been preserved.) But she did not believe that these vows bound her to live in a particular community. She seems to have regarded her profession as an act of *personal* consecration, binding her to a life of a particular quality. It is clear that other early sisters, such as Mother Charlotte and Sister Eliza, understood their vows in the same way, and this interpretation was generally recognised by the Anglican communities of their day. A sister writing in *The Church and the World* (1867) could say that profession bound a sister to the Religious Life for ever: 'She can never again return to an ordinary life in the world.' Yet, 'After her profession, a sister is not bound to remain for life, however, in the same sisterhood. She is free, it is believed, in all orders, to leave at any moment. The Religious Life she *cannot* leave, any particular religious house she may.'[110] This was so generally recognised that, to give one example, a sister who had been professed at East Grinstead and had left it to work with the Devonport sisters in London, was considered a fit person to become the prioress of yet a third society, the Benedictine nuns of Feltham. This interpretation was clearly accepted by the Community's constitutions of c. 1878. These made it clear that the three vows were of lifelong obligation, but they took it for granted that a sister might leave the community. In that case she had to give up her cross and 'the distinctive garb of the community', but was to retain her ring and an 'unmistakable sisterly dress'. Furthermore, the council had the right by a four-fifths vote to request a sister to leave, but she might not 'without great moral fault be sent empty away'. It is significant that the cause of her dismissal might be something less than a 'great moral fault', and that it was reckoned that another sisterhood might be willing to receive her.

This flexibility was a good thing at the time. The first Anglican community had been founded only twenty years when Sister Gertrude was professed. It was important that those involved in the revival of the Religious Life should not be bound too strictly, for there was no fund of inherited experience to draw on. Mistakes might be made about vocations, and there was no provision for dispensation from the vows. Moreover, the actual life of the community might change as the sisters' conception of their vocation developed, and a woman who entered in the early days might find herself faced twenty years later with a stricter pattern of life than that to which she had believed herself called.[111]

But what was right in the first days was not so for ever afterwards. It was impossible to build up a stable community if the sisters did not believe themselves wholly committed to it. Moreover, as will be shown later, the vows could not be observed strictly if stability was not required. The sisters became increasingly aware of its importance, and the draft constitutions of c.1890-94 laid it down that the contract between the sister and the community was a lifelong one and could not be severed without grievous sin on either side. It was not enough to keep the vows; they must be kept in the community in which the sister was professed. It is virtually certain that stability was made obligatory by the constitutions of 1899, but since no copy of these survives, this can only be assumed.

The interpretation of the vow of chastity seems to have been the one in which there was least development. It was also the vow least affected by the obligation of stability, for it was always assumed that it involved a lifelong renunciation of marriage. The paragraph on Purity in the Second Rule remains (with some alterations) at the head of the section on Chastity in the present rule, though much has since been added to it, and the vow of chastity as taken in 1888 is identical (apart from a few purely verbal changes) with the present one.

The vow of obedience, however, became a very different thing when it had to be observed for life within one community. Obedience without stability meant very little, for if a sister found life in her own community difficult, or if she disapproved of the way things were done, she was free to go to another sisterhood. It would have been difficult to live her dedicated life outside a community. Presumably her obedience would have been given to a (self-chosen) spiritual director.[112] Thus, the obligation of stability made a real difference to the meaning of the vow of obedience.

The interpretation of the vow of poverty has seen considerable development. When the earliest sisters spoke of poverty they meant an outward austerity of life, a sharing in the hardships and privations of the poor. One of the early sisters used to exclaim in her old age in Malvern: 'Poverty! they don't know here what poverty is!' She said that in the early days food was bought almost daily from the local shops – one sister bringing in a loaf of bread and a packet of rice for the next day, for instance. This may have been partly in order to do as their neighbours did, but it was also because money really was short. A postulant received in Mother Charlotte's time exclaimed at the coarse brown (unbleached) calico sheets on her bed, and received a silent rebuke when the mother removed them for her own use and provided better ones for the newcomer. On the other hand, the sisters were not poor in the sense of possessing no property. The Second Rule provided that any income which remained over after the sister had made her contribution to the expenses of the house[113] must be disposed of annually to relatives or to charities sanctioned by the priest. Even as late as 1888 the question put to a novice at profession was: 'Dost thou henceforth (apart from any contribution to this house while you remain in it, or for the necessaries of life elsewhere, renounce all worldly substance for the benefit of the poor, widows, orphans or other needs of Christ's Church'. Thus capital was clearly not disposed of. Other evidence shows that the sisters exercised considerable freedom in the use of their property. They made many gits to St Peter's Church. Sister Mary (professed 1872) caused great perplexity to a novice trained in later ways when she gave her a shilling 'to spend in your district'. Sister Marion could remember how Sister Louisa Mary (professed 1878) had her own private nurse-attendant in her old age, and she deduced that she must have been one of the early sisters who retained a 'peculiar' (a sum of money for her own use) with which she paid her wages. It was right when they were under no obligation to stay in one community for life, that the sisters should retain their incomes, for otherwise they would not have been free to leave. But, as the life of the Community became more settled and the need for stability was recognised, the sisters were made aware of their inadequate interpretation of the vow of poverty. Therefore the constitutions of 1899 ruled that sisters might not hold private property, though it was understood that those who had entered under the old constitutions were allowed to remain as before, if they wished.[114]

In later years there were two changes in connection with the vows. Firstly, the actual profession formula was remodelled. This originally consisted of only a verbal 'promise and vow'. It had not made the sister's obligations to the community really clear and it was doubtful whether it was adequate from a legal point of view. In 1944 this was replaced by a more precise formula, which was signed as well as read aloud at the profession service. The second change came with the introduction of temporary vows in 1954. These were to be taken for a period of three years with a possible extension for a fourth year. It was emphasised, however, that when the sister was professed she desired and intended a lifelong dedication.

ENDNOTES - CHAPTER 5

[105]A schism in the Community was therefore very serious because it not only imperilled its own existence, but was a scandal to the world.

[106]For instance, the Litany of the Holy Name was recited at East Grinstead and the 'Jesu Dulcis Memoria' was sung every night.

[107]This refers, of course, only to the Church of England.

[108]The Community was originally known as St Peter's Mission Sisterhood.

[109]The best example of this may be found in Internal Rule 1. 'Let the sisters remember while embracing intercession as the best means of furthering their special dedication that it is of primary obligation to bear witness to others with their lips as well as in their lives to the power of the saving name of Jesus.'

[110]Ed: O Shipley, article on 'Sisterhood Life', p.189.

[111]This may have happened at Devonport. See TJ Williams, *Priscilla Lydia Sellon*, 1950, pp.191-193.

[112]Marion Rebecca Hughes, for instance, who is believed to have been the first sister in the Anglican Church, took the vows of religion in 1841. Yet three years later she could write: 'I saw Dr Pusey and resolved to fulfil the obligations I had made to live a life of obedience by having him as my director as well as spiritual father.' (*Mother Marion's Diary*. vol. I, p.29. Records of the Society of the Holy and Undivided Trinity.) Thus it did not occur to her until 1844 that her vow involved her in as much as obedience to a director.

[113]Each choir sister was expected to give £50 a year, or £100 if she had it, to the expenses of the house.

[114]Although the actual statutes have not survived, their ruling about poverty is quite clear, thanks to information from other sources.

CHAPTER 6

The Devotional Life of the Community

A community leading the mixed life will express that life naturally in two ways, worship and work. The first of these ways, worship, will be discussed in this chapter. But before the development of the Community's pattern of worship can be examined, something must be said about its chapels. The chapel is the setting for the worship, and it is especially important in a community which lays the emphasis on prayer in chapel rather than in the cell.

According to tradition, the sisters had their own oratory from the earliest days, and it is certain that there was one in 1866 when Eldon Lodge was taken over. Father Herbert was careful to provide a chapel on the quiet side of the building when the mission house was built in 1874, and this was large enough for 54 people to squeeze into when the house was blessed.

It would be interesting to know what those first chapels looked like. No details of the very earliest ones are available, but fortunately two photographs remain of the chapel at the mother house at Malvern Link as it was in the early 1890s. The chapel was formed from two rooms thrown together (later used as the library). The small, heavy wooden altar (later used in the Lady Chapel) stood in front of a projecting chimney piece. Behind it hung a heavy dossal, decorated with a large velvet cross from the angles of which sprang four stylised flowers. On the inevitable gradines stood a realistic crucifix, two angel figures, two large candlesticks (the candles decorated with armorial badges), two seven-branched candlesticks and five vases of flowers. Altar cloths and a heavy lace superfrontal completed the furnishings. The altar was provided with 'wings' of heavy cloth trimmed with velvet and the walls behind it were hidden by curtains. It stood on a raised platform with three steps which were partially covered with carpeting. A litany desk was placed immediately in front of it and chairs for sisters, facing forwards not choir-wise, were set on either side of a central aisle. Unfortunately the photographs show only the centre of the room, so any statues or pictures which may have been put in the corners cannot be seen. Despite the elaboration of the altar furnishings, it was a simple chapel (judged by contemporary standards) and the hangings have a somewhat amateurish, homemade look. There is a temporary air about all the arrangements; the chapel is obviously a converted room and not a specially-erected building. It seems that it was small and cramped too, and could never hold the whole Community, so it is not surprising that when the sisters were considering what form their memorial to Mother Frances Mary should take their thoughts turned to a chapel.

The Community was fortunate to secure as its architects Messrs Bucknall and Comper.[115] On 9 June 1891 the foundation stone was laid by the Duke of Newcastle 'with ceremony', and about 100 invited guests watched the proceedings from an elevated platform.[116] It had been hoped that the building would have been completed in a year, but it was found advisable to make the permanent cloister to connect the convent with the Home of the Good Shepherd at the same time, and this and other reasons caused a delay of many months, so that the dedication was put off until the retreat time of the following year when most of the associates of the Community could be present. Thus it was not until 6 June 1893 that the chapel was dedicated.

Dedication of Malvern Chapel

Since the dedication day was one of the great events in the Community's history, a fairly full account of it will be given here. It caused immense excitement at the time; the tension and elation of the occasion can be sensed even now in Canon McClure's account.[117] Five hundred guests had been invited, but fortunately only about half of this number were present at the ceremony, and even these taxed all the resources of the neighbourhood, for rooms had to be found for those who must sleep the night. The day beforehand people poured in: 'Sisters from all parts, some of whom had not visited the mother house for three years, associates of the community, honorary chaplains and priest associates, ladies who were to join the retreat, workers from St Peter's, relatives of the sisters, servers from Vauxhall to assist at the dedication, our crossbearer from Dorchester, all thronged in and offered willing help in final preparations. The whole village here was stirred and many offers of hospitality came to the mother.

'Going down to meet fresh arrivals at the station, we were stopped by the postman, who eagerly asked the hour of the service next day, and what chance there was of admittance. It was whispered that provisions would run short with such an influx of visitors, and extra supplies had to be sent for from Worcester, six miles away. The hospitality of the sisters seemed unlimited. The mantle of Prior Whitborne, the 'good housekeeper' who 'fed many', seemed to have fallen on them. In the midst of receiving her endless guests, the Reverend Mother stopped to order that a meal should be given to some poor children, peapickers, who had tramped in from Ledbury, fifteen miles, and had slept all night on the common close by.'

No effort was spared to make the service as splendid as possible. Vestments, including the famous angel cope, were despatched from Vauxhall; choristers came from Newland and Fairfield churches; Lady Beauchamp sent flowers and evergreens. The acolytes were 'boys from the Reverend E N Dew's school who thoroughly understood their work' and the servers came down 'specially from St Peter's. As he considered that there was no generally authorised office for the dedication of a church, Father Herbert suggested that an ancient one should be used, and so a special translation was made from the old Latin pontifical of Archbishop Bainbrigge of York. Canon McClure declared that 'all were struck with its solemnity and beauty'.

The day itself was hot and sunny. At 2.30 p.m. the long procession, singing psalms, set out to make the circuit of the chapel. At each door and at the foundation stone special prayers were said, and after the warden's solemn entry into the building the actual act of dedication was made:

'Forasmuch as the Lord God of Israel instructed His servant Moses to prepare a tabernacle where His Name shall be honoured and in after time did commend the fervent desire of David to build Him a house; and nothing doubting but that He has put it into the hearts of these sisters by His Holy Spirit, to set apart a fitting place to His Glory – we, therefore, dedicated this chapel in honour of Almighty God, and under the invocation of the Holy Name of Jesus, in whose praise it is built – that here the sisters may daily honour Him whose Name they adore, that here devout women may resort in the quietness of retreat, that here penitents may find mercy, and that all who gather within these walls may learn more and more of the power and pity, the meekness and majesty of His Holy Saving Name.'

Inside Chapel at Dedication

The dedication of the altar then followed. 'Jesus Dulcis Memoria' was sung while it was vested, and Father Hollings SSJE gave an address dealing with the vocation of mission sisters from a historical standpoint. The hymn 'Urbs Beata' was sung and the service proper concluded with the very solemn blessing given by the warden. Even then the ceremonies were not quite over, for there were six priest associates to be admitted. Then the guests (some 240 of them) were received on the lawn by the Reverend Mother and Mrs Herbert, and tea was served in the community room.

At the time of the dedication, and indeed for many years later, the chapel was much plainer than it became later; in fact it was somewhat bare and austere. The walls were of natural stone and there was no reredos. At the dedication service the altar had a 'temporary canopy of red velvet, with side curtains, "costers" of green', but like so many 'temporary' things the canopy remained for some time. The altar furnishings, unlike those of the old oratory, were very simple and consisted only of a crucifix and two brass candlesticks, though frontals seem to have been soon added. The roof was unpainted. The windows were plain glass and the sanctuary steps were uncarpeted. The stalls were only of deal, so their plainness was disguised by green cloth covers with long fringes which had to be tidied by unfortunate novices. A simple reading desk was placed where the pulpit later stood and a litany desk occupied the second sanctuary step.

The austerity of the chapel was due to poverty; there was no money to spare for decorations. It was with difficulty that the sisters scraped together sufficient funds to pay for the building, and though the estimate of 'over £4,000 pounds' was not high, it may not have included the cloister. A debt remained which was not cleared until 1896. However gifts and legacies enabled the Community gradually to complete the chapel. Since all additions and alterations were made with the advice of the original architects, the result was a beautiful and unified building.

In 1906 the altar was enlarged and a reredos in stone and alabaster was added in memory of the founder. It had always been intended to add one when funds were available.[118] Three years later it was gilded and coloured at the expense of Father Herbert's son. About this time the sisters' stalls were completed.[119] In 1924 an associate gave the hanging pyx over the high altar. The architect had suggested one as early as 1892, but it was many years before it could be added. Yet it was worth waiting for. Its workmanship was exquisite, and the two men who had made it could hardly tear themselves away from it, for they said they would miss it so much. In 1925 the south window was given by Sir Charles and Lady Ellis in memory of their daughter, Novice Inez. Eighteen months later the great east window was dedicated. At about the same time the walls were whitened; not everyone agreed with Comper about this, but he declared that the Benedictines of Downside Abbey had made the same outcry but were well pleased with the result, and so were the sisters. Mother Agnes Mary said that it gave the chapel a look of breadth and drew out the beauty of the proportions and the gracefulness of the arches. At the same

Hanging Pyx

time it emphasised the colours of the sanctuary ceiling which had been just decorated in blue and gold. In the following year, 1928, the window on the north side was given by Miss Glennel. All these windows were designed by Comper.

It is difficult to obtain much information about the private prayer of the early sisters. The First Rule laid down that 'each sister shall have a special time allotted to her each day for meditation and prayer', and her weekly timetable was to have 'the hours for work and devotion' marked in it. The Second Rule was more specific; every sister was to have at least half an hour for meditation and prayer with an additional quarter of an hour before Compline for prayer and self-examination. The meditation time was later (probably about 1899) increased to three quarters of an hour; and half an hour for spiritual reading and at least a quarter of an hour for private intercession, were provided for. In 1889 a devotional rule was adopted. This consisted of a prayer to be said on rising and retiring (later the Community ejaculation) and certain memories which were to be said when two or more sisters were together in one of the common rooms at certain specified hours. These were called 'The nine hours in union with the nine angelic choirs.' Thus at 10 a.m. the sisters joined with the angels, and prayed for purity of heart, at 11 a.m. they united themselves with the archangels in praising Christ, and so on. Some sisters can still remember saying these prayers. They are not observed now, though they lingered on in the novitiate for some time.

The need for special times of quietness and prayer was recognised from the first. The rule of 1867 provided that before a novice was clothed 'she shall take three days retreat for communion with God and her own soul as to the life she is about to enter – shall keep silence, attend the Church services, if possible receive Holy Communion and have no intercourse with any but the priest and superior or one appointed by her.' Strangely enough, neither the First nor Second Rules made any mention of retreats before profession. They must have been made, however, for notebooks full of addresses for profession retreats exist in Mother Frances Mary's hand. One set, entitled *Calvary and the Blessed Sacrament* gives a complete programme. The retreat began at Vespers and continued for seven full days. Three meditations were made each day in addition to Bible reading, three periods of spiritual reading, intercession and two 'visits' to the Blessed Sacrament. Intentions for Communion and subjects for self-examination were provided. These early retreats called for considerable mental and emotional exertion and for much self-examination (and thanksgiving) and the making of many detailed resolutions. Retreat days for each sister were provided for in the Second Rule, which laid down that a sister might have a retreat day each month and must not take less than one day in two months. In 1896 a retreat day a month became obligatory. Rather surprisingly, the early records show no provision for community retreats (as distinct from retreat days for individual sisters). Yet such retreats must have been held. A reference in the Vauxhall registers shows that the Reverend T Bates took a retreat for the sisters in June 1881 which lasted from Monday to Friday. They had probably been begun some time before this. Later, two community retreats were held each year, one at Epiphany and one at Holy Name-tide, but it was not until 1917 that it was decided that sisters must 'make every effort to attend both'. The Advent and Lent retreat days were also often conducted, and sometimes the chaplain general might go to branch or mission houses to take them there. These days were unconducted in later years and the pattern of community retreats made much simpler.

Details of the earlier clothing and profession offices are few and far between. The earliest extant form for the reception of a postulant dates from 1888 and is quite similar to the present one. But in the very earliest days a sermon was always preached and notes for many of these survive. Thus, when Kate Barlow was received in 1877, Father Herbert preached on 'The Three Characters', stressing obedience to the call of God. The earliest clothing of which there are any details is that of Sister Elizabeth in 1874. The service seems to have taken place at seven in the morning and the actual admission preceded the Communion service; there was a sermon and a hymn and after the celebration the 'Nunc Dimittis' was sung. At Sister Susanna's clothing three years later the 'Veni' was sung and psalm 122 (with an antiphon) was chanted during the habiting of the novice; there were two hymns and, of course, a sermon. The time and details of the service have varied from time to time. The central core of the office of 1888 was retained in the subsequent, though simplified. Clothings later took place after Vespers. The earliest profession was, of course, Sister Gertrude's in 1865. This took place in St Peter's Church at 9.30 a.m. She made her vows kneeling on the altar step and received a blessing from the coadjutor Bishop of Edinburgh, who also celebrated. There seem to have been nine communicants, but there must have been many more people present in church, for the profession is said to have made a great impression on the parish, and thirty years later there were still a few who could remember seeing 'Sister Gertrude married to the Church'. Judging by Sister Ellen's profession in 1873, the profession office was normally followed by Holy Communion and an address. The service was at 8 am and, like all professions except Sister Gertrude's and Sister Joyce's, took place in the sisters' own chapel. A copy of the profession office as used in 1888 still survives. It was more elaborate than later ones. The office still preceded the Eucharist, a hymn served for the introit, there was an address after the creed, and during the ablutions the Te Deum was sung. It was not until Sister Joyce's profession in 1893 that the profession took place within the actual setting of the Mass. Other changes have been made over the years, and the introduction of temporary vows made further alterations necessary. A new service was first used in August 1954, and in 1957 an additional office for the making of life vows was adopted.

ENDNOTES - CHAPTER 6

[115](Sir) Ninian Comper was then a young man at the beginning of his career. He was already engaged in building the chapel of the convent of St Margaret at Aberdeen (dedicated in 1892).

[116]The ceremony had been fixed for Whit Tuesday but had to be postponed owing to the death of Earl Beauchamp who was to have laid the stone. The duke and the earl were both prominent Anglo-Catholics.

[117]Canon McClure was Father Herbert's son-in-law.

[118]It is interesting to see that the reredos erected in 1906 was quite different from that shown in the plans of 1890. These show a high reredos placed immediately under the east window with the Virgin and Child as central figures.

[119]The oak canopies in the two west bays were not added until 1939.

[120]This was a usual sisterhood practice. A little later, sisters who had mothers' meetings were also excused.

[121]These were presumably used at Vespers only.

[122]Op.cit., pp.336-337, note 1.

[123]Ibid., pp.430-431.

[124]For instance, reservation was begun at the St Alban's mission house at Birmingham when Dr Gore was bishop (1905-1911). The altar and tabernacle were his personal gift. (G D Rosenthal and F G Belton, *So-called Rebels*, 1930, p.4)

CHAPTER 7

Rules, Constitutions and Organisation

This chapter will be concerned with the structure and organisation of the Community: it might well be called its constitutional history. The subject is a rather involved one for two reasons. Firstly, many of the necessary documents are missing, and others are undated. The material available is therefore inadequate and difficult to use. Secondly, the Community was once a most complex organism. The question 'What is the Community – of whom does it consist?' would have received different answers at different times. If the present constitutions were consulted the reply would be: 'The Community consists of a mother superior, professed sisters and novices', but in 1867 the sisters would have said: 'The Community consists of confirmed (i.e. professed) sisters, probationer sisters (novices), serving (lay) sisters, sisters associate, associates and postulants'; while in 1878 there would have been yet another answer: 'The society consists of professed sisters, choir and lay..., novices, choir and lay ... postulants, associate sisters, associates and associate-workers.' In the early 1890s, a third order, the Servants of the Holy Name, would have been mentioned too. Thus any discussion of the Community's constitution must include an account of all the grades within it. The rules and statutes of the first order will be discussed first, however, for it is the only order which still remains, and the other grades always depended upon it.

When J M Neale submitted the draft of his rule for the East Grinstead sisters to Butler of Wantage he received the following reply: 'My impression is that you have too many (rules), especially for a beginning. Rules should shape themselves as the work goes on and need occurs. With good people, such as sisters of mercy are likely to be, one can risk a little and wait to buy experience.'[125]

It is unlikely that the Vauxhall sisters ever heard this wise advice, but they instinctively followed the same policy. The first extant rule was accepted in 1867, and it was not until 1899 that the rule and constitutions which form the basis of the mid-20th century ones were passed. The intervening period was a time of continual experiment and change as the Community discovered by trial and error the path it should follow.

The first rule which exists is a very simple one. The first part of it was accepted on 7 January 1867, and on 1 April an additional set of rules was also passed. These were clearly intended to supplement the previous ones, and for convenience the two sets of rules will be considered as a unity and referred to as the First Rule. Although this rule was very rudimentary, it provided for most of the essentials of community life. The government of the sisterhood was vested in the chapter (called council), which was to consist of the sisters then present, those subsequently professed, and the priest. It was responsible for 'organisation and management', though in domestic matters the superior could act alone. A skeleton timetable was provided with fixed hours for Offices and meals, and there were short but definite silence times. Provision was made for the financial needs of the house by the rule that sisters should pay £50 a year, £100 if they had it, towards domestic expenses. No proper procedure was laid down for elections, but the length of the postulancy and of the novitiate was fixed; thus there was some attempt to regulate the admission of new members. Other rules dealt with domestic matters such as silence places and reading aloud at dinner. Provision was also made for a weekly reading of the rule and breach of rule. This First Rule was, of course, far from adequate. Its most glaring defect was the omitting to provide for the election of a superior and to limit her term of office, but this was remedied a few months later.

The history of the rule during the next ten years or so is extremely obscure. Additions or alterations were frequently made at chapter meetings, so that it grew slowly and gradually. It seems probable that a good many changes were made during the difficult years 1869-73 when no chapter meetings were held. The rule was possibly rewritten, certainly extended, and an additional General Rule was probably drawn up.

The next extant rule (or rules) seems to have reached its present form in about 1878 and the years following. It will be referred to as the Second Rule. The very existence of this rule is a mystery, for there is no mention of its adoption by the chapter,[126] yet its whole form is different from that of the First Rule, so that it is not just an expansion or rewriting of the earlier one. One would expect to find it mentioned in a chapter minute, for it is clearly no mere draft, but the rule actually binding upon the Community. It is not profitable to discuss the complexities of the matter further, however, especially since the solution is likely to be a simple one. The early Community was not very businesslike (it once even forgot to elect a superior), and most probably the proper formalities were simply omitted or forgotten.

The Second Rule regulated the life of the Community for about twenty years, so a little must be said here about its contents. The format of this rule was unlike that of those which came before or after: it was not so much a rule as a collection of rules.[127] Firstly came the constitutions. This section showed a considerable advance on the corresponding sections of the First Rule. The superior's term of office was limited and more detailed provision was made for elections. The existence of a minor council which could deal temporarily with unimportant matters was recognised, and the offices of assistant superior, novice mistress and sacristan were regulated. The explanation of the Community's work was shown by rules which provided for the formation of branch houses, the undertaking of mission work elsewhere, and the consequent appointment of sisters in charge. The constitutions were followed by the External Rule which seems to date from about 1879. This was concerned with such matters as rules of prayer and silence, retreats, the regulation of work and the relationships of the sisters with each other and with their families. The internal Rules, which dealt more specifically with the inner life of the sisters, consisted of brief paragraphs on such subjects as purity, poverty, mortification, humility and the use of sacraments; the passages on 'Temptation' and 'After a fault' are nearly identical with those in the rule in use until the 1975 revision, and so are several shorter portions. The section of General Rules governed not only the sisters but all living in the house and was largely concerned with domestic matters. It must have reached its present form by 1885. The Devotional Rule, which was finally adopted in 1889, was discussed in the previous chapter.

The Second Rule represented a considerable advance on earlier efforts, but it was still inadequate. The constitutions were not sufficiently precise and the Internal Rule was very slight. In 1892 the mother was given permission to 'rearrange' the rule and constitutions, and a new version of the constitutions came into force for an experimental period. But the need for more exact formularies was underlined by an unhappy position which arose after Father Herbert's death, when Mother Emma unwisely arranged for the election of a new warden by a *minor* council. The new constitutions expressly stated that the warden should be elected by the council (as the chapter was then called), so it must be presumed that she trusted in the fact that the election was not a matter 'affecting the rule'. It was a foolish thing to do. The subwarden protested, delivered a strong address to the sisters on the duty of rigid obedience to the constitutions, and resigned his office. The community was behind the mother, and the priest chosen by the minor council was unanimously elected, but a dangerous position had arisen, and it is not surprising that the new warden pressed forward with the work of revision.

It was fortunate that Father Cosby White already had considerable experience of sisterhoods. He immediately detected two serious weaknesses in the existing constitutions and insisted on putting them right. So far the Community had never appointed a Visitor, though the new constitutions did mention the office. Father Cosby White insisted on the office being filled, and he was soon able to say that Father Elwin SSJE would undertake the work. He also took care that a clause defining the visitor's powers should be added to the constitutions. It was Father Cosby White too who noticed that the existing formularies made no provision for the removal of a warden from office, and this deficiency was soon remedied. He was also responsible for the change to a vote by ballot at profession elections (1896). The work of revision was steadily carried out during the three years that he was warden. He realised the need for expert assistance in drawing up the new formularies, and was fortunate enough to secure the help of the Cowley Fathers. Thus the new rule and constitutions were largely the work of Father Page and Father Osborne, though there was a certain amount of revision done by Mother Agatha. The sisters had also been invited to give their comments.

It is impossible to discuss the rule and constitutions of 1899 adequately for the simple reason that no copies of them now exist. According to Community tradition the rule was not substantially altered after 1899, and this is supported by the little evidence available. The most important changes were made in 1944 after the merging of the lay and choir sisters. There have been other minor alterations over such matters as silence at meals.

It is possible, however, to say a little about influences on the rule. There is a persistent Community tradition that the rule is based on that of St Augustine. However, a comparison of the Augustinian rule with the present Community rule shows no evidence for such influence. Yet there is some basis for the tradition, for in February 1867 Sister Gertrude was 'requested to reconsider the rule of St Augustine and bring before the Council (chapter) from time to time those rules which she thinks it might be desirable to adopt'. It seems that nothing was immediately done about the matter, but the idea was not abandoned, and the Second Rule does show signs of definite Augustinian influence. The section on humility, and part of the passage about the oratory have been adapted from the rule of St Augustine, and the stress on community of goods is characteristically Augustinian. But it is unprofitable to pursue the subject further, since the Augustinian passages did not find a permanent place in the rule. The only way in which the present rule resembles the rule of St Augustine is in its spirit of moderation and discretion.

The Community's rule was, however, influenced by that of another society, for the rule of 1899 was largely drawn up by two Cowley Fathers, and the Cowley influence, though slight, was pervasive. It is true that portions of the Cowley rule were not incorporated into the Holy Name rule, but there are many similarities of thought and phrase. For instance, the provision for prayer on changing work and the insistence that there should be no sign of haste or annoyance, when speaking to others, are common to both rules. Examples could be multiplied. It says much for the conscientious care of the Cowley Fathers that they could give so much and yet produce a rule so different from their own.

There is little to say about the later history of the constitutions. The constitutions of 1899 were obviously a landmark in the history of the Community. They clearly mark a change of emphasis in the government of the Community. In the earlier years the chapter met irregularly, often quite frequently, and it sometimes decided quite small matters. Now the chapter normally met only twice a year, and it was concerned only with elections, alterations in rule and statutes and really important issues; if the mother wished to consult others on any matters, she referred to a small council. There have been many alterations to the constitutions since 1899. The most important were those of 1932 (due to the taking up of work abroad), 1944 (following the merging of the lay and choir sisters) and 1954 (as a result of the introduction of temporary vows). A further thorough revision which lasted over several years was begun in 1954 in order to bring the constitutions into line with the recommendations of the Advisory Council for Religious Communities.

Before concluding this study of the rules of the first order, something must be said about the distinction between choir and lay sisters which existed until 1944. Such discrimination seems positively unchristian to the modern reader, yet the division of the sisters into two grades was common,[128] and was in accordance with the great educational and social differences existing at that time. Father Herbert is said to have been strongly in favour of two grades. The Community seems to have felt that there were women with a real vocation to the Religious Life who were incapable of the full life of prayer and Office, and that these were called to a life of service. Thus the early name for the lay sisters was 'serving sisters'. They were not confined entirely to domestic work, however, and they took the fourth vow which bound them to mission work. Father Herbert seems to have intended them to be used in simple evangelistic work; for when lay novice Rhoda confided her fears that her lack of education unfitted her for profession his only reply was, 'Education, my child. D'you want education to tell souls about the love of Jesus?' As early as 1877 he proposed that lay sisters should have some time allotted to them for spiritual work. Mother Emma, speaking some years later, said she thought the lay sisters should have almost every day some opportunity of 'philanthropic and charitable work suited to their capacity'. The lay sisters took no part in the government of the Community, however; they had no place in chapter and no vote in the elections of a mother or choir sisters, and they had a longer novitiate. Yet the Community never seems to have been completely happy about the distinction. In 1897 entry to the lay novitiate was closed for a year, mainly for economic reasons. The question of lay sisters was much discussed at the time,

Sisters: Choir, Lay and Associate (1892)

especially because of its bearing on the new constitutions, but in 1898 it was decided to resume the admission of lay novices as before with no restriction on numbers. It was not until 1928 that the actual abolition of the distinction was formally proposed, though it seems that some sisters had been troubled about it for a long time. No change was made, however, and though the matter was discussed again in 1938 it was not until 1944 that the lay sisters were raised to choir rank. By this time the great social, economic and educational changes which had revolutionised English society had made such a step essential.

It is now time to turn to the other orders and grades which at one time existed within the Community. Firstly, something must be said about the associate sisters. It is difficult to describe the exact status of these ladies. They seem to have been half sisters, half associates: one is tempted to call them 'part-time sisters'. They had no novitiate and they were bound to the Community by annual promises only. Their time might be spent 'in the world' or in one of the houses of the sisterhood. When living in the latter they wore a distinctive dress and were addressed by their full name with 'Sister' prefixed to it. Their obligations appear to have varied from time to time. At first they were supposed to keep the sisters' rules when resident in the mission house. Then in 1873 this was changed so that they were only bound by the associates' and general rules, but in 1876 they were brought back under the sisters' rules again. When away from the house they were required to observe only the spirit of their order and to keep the associates' rules. A year or so as an associate sister seems to have been regarded as the equivalent to postulancy. The work they undertook might be quite responsible. For example, Sister Louisa Robson was sister-in-charge of the Community's first mission house at Wolverhampton. No list of associate sisters now survives, but it is unlikely that there were ever many of them. The first associate sister was a Miss Munch who was admitted in 1866, but it is improbable that she stayed more than a year. In 1891 there were three associate sisters and that is probably a representative number. They seem to have died out or been abolished in the 1890s.

For some years the Community also had a second order sister, the Sister Alice Hutchinson whose name figures so mysteriously in the community litany. She was a first order novice who was too delicate for the life and who was therefore transferred to the associate sisters. Subsequently a special rule was drawn up for her and she lived with the Community for the rest of her life, though the second order as such was suppressed in 1894.

The third order, the Servants of the Holy Name, existed for only about five years (1889-1894). Like other Victorian sisterhoods such as Clewer and Ditchingham, the Community found that some of the women who had entered its penitentiary had no desire to return to the world, but wished for a dedicated life themselves. It was to meet their needs that the penitential order was founded. The women who entered as Servants of the Holy Name had the status of lay sisters, and the first order provided their mother and novice mistress. They were intended to be occupied in works of mercy, and when the Parkstone home for incurable women and children was opened they were sent there to work. In all, about eleven women seem to have entered the order, but only four of these had reached simple consecration when the Community decided to suppress the order in 1894. Those who wished to returned to Malvern and seem to have continued their lives in the Community's service. The third order must be reckoned as an experiment that failed.

Although not an order, the associates were originally considered an integral part of the Community. Their help and support were vital during the early years when the sisters were so few in number. Associates could and did stay in the house, and at first they had the use of the Community room, though later a special associates' room was provided for them. Like the sisters, they were under the warden's direction, and thus were likely to develop the same spiritual outlook. All had to undertake some definite work for the house. Since this was not left to personal choice, but was to be 'as directed'; they could be reckoned as being part of the working staff of the Community. Miss Hanbury Jones, for instance, helped Sister Eliza with her school, and Miss Hopgood (Mrs Herbert's sister) worked in the Sunday school. An account of the redoubtable Miss Davenport's work shows that she taught in Sunday school and instituted a library for the children, helped with mothers' meetings and classes and acted as a district visitor. She was interested in missionary work and acted as secretary for the Bloemfontein Association. Much of her time was given to an association for helping young servants, and she also served as a parish guardian. When the sisters extended their work outside Vauxhall, the associates cooperated in the new ventures. The refuge at Worcester was under the care of one associate (Miss Byfield) and the home at Leamington under another. The first three associates were admitted in December 1866[129] and their numbers grew slowly but steadily, so that by 1891 there were thirty-one. The earliest associates were all women, but later men were also received, and by the 1890s there were priest associates. This widening of membership appears to have occurred at about the time associates ceased to be reckoned as a grade within the Community. In the late 1960s the associates numbered nearly 400. They were expected to observe a simple devotional rule.

During the 1870s and perhaps for some time afterwards, the Community also included associate workers. It is difficult to discover much about these women and their work. They were probably of a lower social class than the associates and associate sisters. The Alice Hughes who became an associate worker in 1877 may be the woman who was appointed matron of an orphanage in the parish the same year. Some, if not all, of them lived in the Community house. There were inevitably many difficulties in their position, for though they were not sisters they were subject to many restraints through living in a religious house. For instance, as 'inmates' their dress had not only to be 'neat and simple' but 'to the satisfaction of the superior or sister in charge', which was too much to ask of any woman, however devout. They were expected to attend religious instruction classes given by the mother and to have private interviews with her, and they had to make a public confession of breach of rule. Such rules were too severe for those not bound by religious vows, and it is not surprising that the associate workers did not flourish for long.

It is impossible to end this chapter without mentioning two other groups of people who have been closely associated with the Community. Firstly, something must be said about the companions. The companions came into existence on 6 March 1890 when 21 of them were admitted at a special service. No statement of their *raison d'etre* has been preserved, but it seems likely that they assisted the sisters in their parish work. They died out after a time, but in 1918 it was decided to revive them with a different object. The new companions' rule was designed for those who wished to live a dedicated life, but who had to fulfil their vocation in the world. On 25 March 1919 the first four women made their dedication, after having tested their new rule for a year.

Since 1957 the Community has also had its 'friends'. These are pledged to no rule or specific religious observances, but help the community financially and in other ways.

ENDNOTES - CHAPTER 7

[125]EA Towle, op. cit, p.237.

[126]It is just possible that there may be a reference to the genesis of this rule in a resolution of 6 January 1874 that 'Sisters Emma and Mary draw up rules to be submitted to the mother and sanctioned by the council (chapter) for the privileges of all sisters, associates, and inmates in the new house ... '. But if so, the rules were never sanctioned.

[127]The Second Rule will be discussed here as a unity. It must be remembered, however, that many of its provisions had been adopted at a date earlier than that of the rule itself.

[128]Most communities had two grades. Wantage and Knowle were the obvious exceptions.

[129]They were Mrs Herbert, Miss Louisa Helder (later Sister Faith Louise) and Miss Hanbury Jones.

CHAPTER 8

The Active Work of the Community: England

It is impossible to write the history of a community of mission sisters without including a chapter on mission work. For the mission work is an essential element in their vocation, and if it is not described the picture which emerges is unbalanced and incomplete. It is, however, difficult to produce an adequate account of the active work of the Community of the Holy Name.

Firstly, the material which is necessary for such a study is in short supply. The Community never published reports of its work, it never brought out a magazine, no letters survive, and the sisters were not given to writing their memoirs. Secondly, the Community's work has always been on a small scale. This means that there are few events to chronicle, and no tales of great institutions and grand openings to tell. The third difficulty is a more serious one, which lies in the very nature of mission work. The real essence of such work has always been the helping of individuals in their spiritual lives. About this little can be written, so that any account of the Community's work is bound to be inadequate, since only its more superficial aspects can be discussed. It is essential that this should be remembered in reading the pages which follow.

As this chapter will be concerned with the sisters' active work, it is perhaps necessary to stress at the outset that prayer is an important part of the life in a branch or mission house. These houses have always had their own chapels or oratories. The recitation of the Office and the maintenance of the full rule of prayer are regarded as a vital part of the work of each house, and sometimes (as at Brighton in the 1960s) a priest has wanted the sisters in his parish for the sake of their prayers rather than for any parish work which they could do.

The Community's active work falls naturally into three categories: firstly, parochial mission work; secondly, moral welfare work; and finally, retreat houses and other works. It has been decided, therefore, to avoid a chronological account and to discuss each type of work separately so that its significance may be made more apparent.

Parochial Mission Work

It is not surprising that parochial mission work has always been one of the sisters' main activities, since the Community owed its very existence to the need for mission workers in one poor parish. Father Herbert had never envisaged anything more than a parochial sisterhood, and at first the sisters were so few in number that there can have been no question of undertaking work elsewhere. But a house was opened at Wolverhampton in about 1875-76, and from that date the Community's work was established on a wider basis. The records contain no reference to this important event, which was probably the response to an immediate need rather than the result of deliberate policy.

In 1871 Father Herbert's friend, Charles Bodington, was made Vicar of the parishes of St Andrew and Christ Church, Wolverhampton, and became responsible for two churches which were far apart, badly organised and considerably in debt. To make matters worse, he was surrounded by a hostile faction anxious to take action against him under the Public Worship Regulation Act. Newspaper controversy and heated public meetings followed, and his two churches were 'presented' to the bishop. There was a real danger of prosecution. His opponents hoped to get him committed to Stafford gaol and, though they never succeeded, the years at Wolverhampton were anxious ones. It seems probable that Father Herbert sympathised with his friend in his troubles and sent the sisters to help in his parish, and so the Community began its first work outside Vauxhall.

This first house must have been very small. In July 1876 there were only six sisters and two novices in the whole Community (and one of these, Mother Charlotte, withdrew from community life the next month). Thus the staffing of the new house was almost beyond the strength of the sisterhood, and the first sister-in-charge was an associate sister who had only been admitted recently.

The Wolverhampton house did not last for very long. In 1879 Bodington left Wolverhampton to become Richard Twigg's successor at Wednesbury, and he asked the sisters to transfer their work to his new parish. By November 1879 Sister Louisa and Sister Miriam had arrived and the house was opened. The move to Wednesbury must have delighted Father Herbert. He knew the parish well, several of his close friends had worked there, and it would have seemed fitting that his mission sisters should be established in a place which could claim to be the birthplace of the parochial mission movement. Work was continued at Wednesbury until 1911 when the house had to be closed owing to a shortage of sisters.

The next mission house to be opened was a short-lived venture. In 1883 the Community agreed to send sisters to Emscote, near Warwick, and the house was probably opened in the following year when Sister Louisa Mary became sister-in-charge. A wealthy benefactress, Marianne Philips, had enriched the church and built a mission house, and it might have been expected that the sisters would have settled down in this High Church parish where the Vicar, Dr Dickins, was a pioneer of the Catholic revival and had suffered opposition amounting to persecution for his beliefs. Yet by the end of 1887 they had been withdrawn. The Community had accepted a request to work in Birmingham; numbers were small and one of the existing houses had to be relinquished, and so Emscote was closed only three years after it had been opened.

The Birmingham mission house was in the rough slum parish of St Alban's, a High Church stronghold where the Pollock brothers had endured persecution and mob violence as the result of their successful mission work.[130] The Community can claim no share in their witness, however, for the sisters were not invited to the parish until long after the riots were over. There was a great need for workers in such a parish, and St Alban's become one of the Community's largest mission houses.

These first four mission houses were all begun before Mother Frances Mary's death. They had several characteristics in common. Firstly, they were all located in the Midlands. This is understandable as the needs of the Black Country were well known to Father Herbert, and Mother Frances Mary is said to have had 'a great desire ... to do some work in the Midlands'. Secondly, they were established in unattractive places where the work was hard and difficult. Father Pollock's district was known as Vaughton's Hole. Wolverhampton and Wednesbury were right in the Black Country, which in those days was described as 'a hundred miles of smoke and dirt'. The St James' Church Wednesbury *Bazaar Book* of 1905 gives some idea of the conditions in which the sisters lived and worked. 'It is a parish of tall chimneys and clanging anvils,' said the writer. 'Great factories tower over and shut in the houses of the inhabitants. Underfoot the streets are black with dirt, and above the skies are murky with belching smoke; while at night the roaring flames of the blast furnaces glare overhead.' It is not an inviting picture. Even Emscote was conveniently placed for an attack on the slums of Warwick. Thirdly, the early mission houses were all small ventures. There were probably only two sisters at Wolverhampton; Wednesbury began with two; and Emscote was clearly on a small scale. It is true that there were almost certainly secular workers living in the house too. Thus a Miss Clarkson, 'a lady who has had much experience in nursing the sick,' was expected to join the Wednesbury house. But even so the numbers must always have been small. Finally, all these houses were established in definitely High Church parishes where active and intensive mission work was needed, and where an offensive (not defensive) programme was the order of the day.

The early mission houses have been discussed in some detail since, like all beginnings, they have a special significance. Thereafter, it will suffice to say that other houses were opened up and closed down as the need arose, some of them having very short lives. Until the Second World War work was confined to two areas: the South (with a strong centre in London) and the Midlands (with a heavy concentration on Birmingham where there were several houses). After the war, the mission houses were further dispersed, and over the years have stretched from Newcastle-upon-Tyne in the north to Torquay in the south-west.

A few remarks may perhaps now be made about the mission houses themselves. For one of the first questions to spring to the reader's mind is, 'What were the earlier mission houses like?' The answer, in most cases, is 'perfectly ordinary houses like the rest of those in the street'. For (with the exception of Emscote where there was a specially-built mission house) the sisters have lived in any suitable house which the parish could provide. The mission houses seldom looked ecclesiastical, much less monastic. Even the Vauxhall house, which had been specially built by Father Herbert, was a tall, narrow, inconvenient building of five storeys. It was, in fact, a typical London house of the period, and it looked far less 'religious' than many a Victorian vicarage. In Wednesbury the sisters had a corner house in a small block, and at Balsall Heath (another poor area) their dwelling was made from three small houses knocked together.

In Wimbledon, on the other hand, where they were working in a prosperous middle-class area, they occupied a substantial, many-windowed brick villa, standing in its own grounds. All these mission houses had their own chapels or oratories, and they seem also to have had a parish room or rooms, for the mission house was not only the sisters' home but a centre of parish life.[131] Balsall Heath, for instance, had a gymnasium as well as two rooms for classes and parish business. Moreover, the sisters were not the only people living in the mission houses. In pre-war days there was usually a maid or maids. There might also be one or more ladies who helped with the parish work. For instance, Miss Clarkson at Wednesbury has already been mentioned. The Vauxhall house had as many as three residents and a schoolmistress came in for her dinner too. Miss Parry seconded Sister Joyce in all her works at Wimbledon. Sometimes guests stayed in the mission houses too. The Hove house frequently had lady guests (probably women who needed spiritual help), and a sister can remember that there were sometimes so many that they filled the oratory and the sisters had to go out to the parish church for Communion. It is clear therefore, that mission house life was often far from 'cloistered', for the house might contain quite a variety of people and serve as a centre for numerous activities.

The study of the Community's parish work which follows will be concerned mainly with the years which fell between Sister Gertrude's arrival in Vauxhall (c. 1862) and the First World War. A detailed account of more recent parish work would read like a handbook in pastoralia rather than a history, and the emphasis will therefore be laid on the early period when conditions were so different from those of later times.

It is quite impossible to write exhaustively about the sisters' parish work because it was so varied: it covered anything and everything that needed doing in the parish. An entry in the Wednesbury parish magazine gives a good picture of the variety of tasks performed in an average parish. 'We are already beginning to find out what the sisters have been to the parish,' said the writer. 'Guilds and classes, mothers' meeting, sewing classes, distribution of the *Monthly Record*, mending cassocks and surplices, looking after the altars, visiting the sick and poor, collecting 'trays' for the annual tea party and pence for the pence association – these are only some of the duties they performed.' It was quite true. These were only *some* of the duties they performed, and though many different aspects of parish work will be discussed in the following pages, the account will still be incomplete, for the work of a parish sister was too multifarious to be catalogued.

It may be a surprise that the first aspect of parish work to be discussed will be poor relief. Yet this has been done deliberately. Poor relief was not only an important part of parish work but it also provided the background against which the rest of the work was done. What was accomplished in the guilds, clubs and mothers' meetings cannot be fully appreciated without some realisation of the unpicturesque, unremitting poverty in which so many of their members lived. Since the care of the poor was the concern of the Church, the sisters spent a good deal of time in dealing with the material needs of the people. Sisters recalled the queues which used to wait outside the mission houses. These were composed of people hoping for dispensary notes (which entitled them to free medical attention) and for bread, coal or milk tickets which they could exchange for goods at the local shops. Sisters who took mothers' meetings at Vauxhall received regular payments for the provision of 'tea, food, coal, etc.', and this suggests that needy members were helped. Sometimes coal had to be taken to unheated sickrooms or delicacies carried to those who were too ill to eat the food their families could provide. Convalescents had to be conveyed to the country. Needlework guilds sent bales of clothes for the children, and these had to be distributed fairly. Sometimes rummage sales were organised. These were not intended to be money-making activities, but were a means of providing the poor with respectable clothes at a low price. Sisters and novices made up calico underwear which they sold cheaply to the women who came to their meetings, and when Sister Marion was an old sister she could still remember the screech the calico used to make as Sister Maud tore off length after length to make garments for mothers. The sisters at Birmingham used to collect surplus food from places like the Queen's Hotel, and this was sorted out and taken to needy people, for there were plenty of families who were grateful for the half loaves, the uncooked ends of meat and the soup which were given to them. Old people at Malvern Link can remember how they used to go to the convent when they were children to collect the big jars of dripping that were given away. A sister cook needed to be on her guard too if there was a sister like Sister Patricia around, for she was liable to make off with any food she could find for her poor. The poor were always individuals, not cases, as far as the sisters were concerned, and they identified themselves with them, sometimes somewhat belligerently, as the tale of Sister Patricia and the meat essence shows. At one time the Lambeth guardians used to provide meat essence for the sick and aged poor who lived in their own homes. The essence was supplied by a good firm, but it smelt and tasted horrible. Sister Patricia was inclined to brush aside the complaints she heard about it, but one day she was induced to taste it herself. Her reaction was prompt. Hiding a bowl of the obnoxious stuff up her sleeve, she obtained an interview with the guardians, and once inside the board room she laid it before them so that they should smell and taste it themselves.

The division of Victorian parishes into 'districts', has been mentioned above. The care of these districts was one of the main tasks of parish sisters. For instance, at Vauxhall (1892) sixteen of the thirty-one districts were looked after by eight sisters, while at Wednesbury (1911) four out of five were in their hands; at St Alban's, Birmingham, (1900) five sisters had districts. To be 'out in the district' was a highly-respected occupation to which the sisters devoted much time. In a sense, the district was the sister's hunting ground, for it was here that she found the potential members of her mothers' meetings, guilds, etc.. The people of the district were *her* people, to be cared for and helped in body and soul. It is impossible to discover how effective this district visiting was. In some areas the work must have been very discouraging. Yet something was accomplished, even if all the sisters' high hopes were not realised. When Sister Averil was working in a very bad area in Birmingham, for instance, she was told by a local woman that she must not be discouraged, because the people in her own court had already stopped gambling. Sister Stella's success in visiting the Blockhouse (a very poor part of Worcester) seems to have surprised people, for she had 'a power of stirring in the hearts of many a deeper interest in things eternal, and apparently of compelling an obedient following on the part of some on whom all power of persuasion has hitherto failed.'

Mothers' meetings were always an important part of parish work. Three of the five mothers' meetings at Vauxhall (1892) were taken by sisters. The numbers attending them must have been quite large, for more than 120 attended the Christmas party given for Sister Eugenia's two meetings that year. The weekly meeting at St Alban's, Birmingham, engrossed the attention of four or even five sisters. One gave the address, one played the hymns, one minded the babies, another made the tea and, in the very early days, a fifth was occupied with the penny bank. Some of these meetings were intended for communicants; others were open, and the sisters would invite the women they met in their districts to them. The meetings met the needs of really poor women. This photograph dating from the early 1890s shows a sister with such a group. One is struck by the worn, anxious faces of so many of the

Mothers' Meeting, Vauxhall

mothers. Despite the flowers and ribbons on their hats, it is clear that poverty was a grim reality, and one is glad of the two annual treats, the Christmas party and the summer excursion, which must have been the highlights of the year for some of them. When one remembers the social conditions at the end of the century a party with, 'iced cakes and sweetmeats and crackers and pot flowers', must have seemed like a glimpse of another world. Presumably the 'immense and sumptuous bran pie' with which these parties often ended was the forerunner of the modern bran tub. The sisters obviously gave a good deal of time and care to these entertainments, and it is gratifying to discover that at Malvern Link their parties were often noticed as 'the most magnificent of the Christmas shows'. There are many accounts of the summer excursions, and it is difficult to decide from which to quote. Should one describe the delightful excursion the Wednesbury mothers made to Warwick and Emscote when they enjoyed 'a most bountiful tea' provided by Sister Louisa and returned carrying bunches of flowers? Or should one recount the splendours of the trip to Shrewsbury when, after visiting the castle, museum, churches and quarry, the women had another fine tea (a gift from the sisters) and 'each guest was furnished with a cracker by Miss Burd, a friend of Sister Hope's'?[132]

However, the choice must be made and so it has been decided to quote from the delightful account of the Wednesbury mothers' excursion to Malvern (1894). The contemporary description of the convent is interesting and the writer has distilled the very flavour of the period. The 77 mothers, who were accompanied by the rector, the sisters and several friends, had a very full day. Their journey over, they climbed the hills and visited the town and priory. Then, 'at 4.45 p.m. all assembled for tea, most kindly and generously provided by the sisters in the Link Temperance Hall; and after tea the party proceeded in a body to the Convent of the Holy Name ... Here a hearty welcome was given to us by the sister superior and other sisters in residence, and everyone thoroughly enjoyed the sweetness and quietness of the beautiful gardens. At 6.30 p.m. all assembled in the stately new chapel for the service of Vespers, and very restful and helpful it was to have half an hour taken out of the midst of a busy day to spend in the house of God ... After the service, chairs were brought out on the lawn, and the sisters gave quite a garden party, light refreshments being provided for all. The penitentiary, laundry, ironing room, etc., were then visited and great was the admiration of the mothers at the cleanliness and perfect order which everywhere prevailed, and the only expression of regret was that the whole day had not been spent in the convent amid its peaceful surroundings. Certainly no greater contrast could be imagined than between the bustle and turmoil and smoke of Wednesbury and the calm stillness and pure air of the convent and its environments, and this seemed to strike the mothers very forcibly.' They finally arrived home at 11.30 p.m. !

Younger women and girls were catered for by guilds and clubs. Generally speaking, the guilds were intended for communicants while the clubs stressed the social side, but parish differed from parish, and no hard and fast rule can be drawn. The guilds were another of the sisters' main works. They ran all the six guilds at Vauxhall for women and girls (1893). There were only three guilds at Wednesbury (1889), but they must have been much more difficult to manage because the numbers were so large. Sister Gertrude had 75 members in her guild of St Agnes, Sister Eunice had 96 in St Mary's, and Sister Faith had 104 in St Anne's ward. Usually the guilds had their main meetings once a month, and there were also monthly Communions at which the sisters would lead their members up to the altar. At Balsall Heath, where guilds abounded, there were not only monthly teas but guild breakfasts with boiled sausages. Sister Marion seems to have regarded these as perilously close to bribery. A member of one of the Vauxhall guilds has left a brief description of their proceedings. The girls used to meet at the mission house. First of all the guild office was said in chapel, and if the warden was present an address was given too; tea followed downstairs, and afterwards the guild's 'own' sister would give an address. Girls' clubs seem to have enjoyed their greatest success at a rather later period, though they did exist in the early days. At Vauxhall in the 1890s the Club Girls Bible Class and the Club Girls Tea were held at the sisterhood, and the girls' Band of Hope (a temperance organisation) was run by a sister. The only actual description of a girls' club comes from the 1920s, and though it is slightly later than the period discussed here, it seems to reflect earlier conditions, and is anyway too interesting to be omitted. The club was held in a disused pub on the corner of Vauxhall Street and the ordinary subscription was three pence a week. Its members proudly called themselves the

'Rough Girls'. An old girl recalls: 'Sister Ursula came every evening from eight until ten. She was always the most welcome visitor. The girls however poor and uneducated were always proud to talk to her. We gathered our members by having an open session in the parish hall on Tuesdays where all and sundry were welcome – and even on the hottest nights they would sit round and dance in their coats!! We mainly danced (and) we sat thick all round, about 200 at a time – and dear sister would move gently round the hall speaking to each in turn – Martha Hampson would do likewise and we dispensed tea and cakes. The tea by the way came from the mission house.'

Confirmation classes and Sunday schools also fell to the sisters' lot. They must have taken up quite a lot of time, but they are seldom mentioned. The sisters prepared girls for confirmation, but they were probably not responsible for the adults, for there were plenty of priests available in those days. They taught in Sunday schools, and sometimes acted as superintendents. It is gratifying to note that the appointment of Sister Ruth and her assistants to take charge of the Link Sunday School (1889) led to a 'marked improvement in the discipline and general conduct of the children'. One would like to know more about these Sunday Schools, for many of the sisters were quite untrained and their methods were original and, it seems, effective. Sister Maud, for instance, would ask her class of seven- to eight-year- old boys to assess their own conduct at the children's Eucharist. She would stand in front of them and say, 'Tommy?' and the boy would reply, 'Good,' 'Rather naughty,' 'Very bad,' as he thought right. She said they could always be trusted. Instruction for older girls was provided at Bible classes. These again were too common to get much notice. They seem to have been a first step in the Christian life, and were intended to lead to churchgoing and confirmation. Thus Father Herbert could report (1893) that five members of the sisters' class for factory girls had been confirmed, and that forty of them had also joined the Sunday Bible class.

Although the Community's work lay mainly amongst women and children, a few sisters had a special gift for work with men. Sister Joyce was very successful with boys, and her profession took place in St Peter's church so that the boys might be present. Several of the men's organisations at Vauxhall met at the sisterhood, including their Sunday morning bible class. This must have been the class which Sister Eliza began, and which was so effective that it led to the foundation of the Guild of Apostolic Witness.

In 1891-92 the sisters ran a special winter mission at the mission house, and Father Herbert was able to report that this had resulted in the restoration of seven men to Communion, while seven men, one lad and three women had come forward for confirmation. Another couple also desired confirmation, but they had left the parish. The following year he wrote that the services again resulted in a 'steady increase in the lads brought in touch with the church in connection with the sisterhood. This accounts for the large number of males confirmed.' Not all sisters had the gift for working with men and lads, however, and it is not surprising that a novice who found herself temporarily in charge of the Balsall Heath boys' club remarked rather thankfully when she went to Wimbledon that 'choir boys only used to come to games one evening in the week'.

The sisters also acted as church sacristans or helped with the sacristy work. They prepared for the early service at three of the Wimbledon churches, for instance, and preparation for sick communions was sometimes part of their work. The laundering of altar linen was often in their care (as at Wimbledon, Vauxhall and Balsall Heath).

Two of the sisters' earliest parish works, nursing and teaching, have been left until the end of this section, since they seem to have been practised mainly at Vauxhall. Nursing was Sister Gertrude's[133] special work, and it was not continued on the same scale after her departure. Probably the most the sisters did was to act as custodians for the sickroom requisites which were lent out to the poor. Similarly, at St Alban's, Birmingham, they kept the goods of the Samaritan Society, and at Hove they lent out maternity bags. School teaching, however, has a much longer history. Here again, Sister Gertrude was the pioneer, for soon after her arrival she had established a night school which was open three evenings a week. Sister Eliza's arrival meant that educational work could be increased. The exact date at which she began her 'penny school' is uncertain, but it was well established by August 1865[135] when *The Standard* reported: 'Two sisters of mercy have a penny school in Vauxhall now, in a room lent for the purpose by his Royal Highness the Prince of Wales.' The bulk of this work must have fallen on Sister Eliza herself, though some ladies gave their help. In 1869 the children were transferred to the newly-built St Paul's schools, but the sisters continued to teach in the parish schools for many years afterwards. It is difficult to be sure how many sisters were teaching and which schools they were working in, but it seems tolerably clear that the sisterhoods provided the headmistress of St Peter's girls' school for many years. Sister Elizabeth and Sister Agatha were both headmistresses, and it seems likely that they were succeeded by Sister Eugenia, who did not give up her school work until 1919. Other sisters, such as Sister Agnes, worked as assistants. Apart from Vauxhall, the sisters seem to have done little regular school teaching, and their contacts with schools were only on the religious level. Sister Stella, for instance, was in touch with the young ladies' schools at Hove and helped to prepare the girls for confirmation.

During the latter part of the 19th century, there was little provision made for Moral Welfare work amongst the female population, and, as the authorities became more aware of the scale of the problem, it was an issue which weighed especially upon the consciences of influential Churchmen. Yet only women could properly direct such work; and it was believed that only dedicated women could undertake it successfully. Thus the direction of penitentiaries came to be regarded as the work 'par excellence' of the nineteenth-century sisterhoods.[136] It is not surprising, therefore, that the Community soon added this form of work to its parochial mission work.

The decision to undertake penitentiary work was almost certainly due to Mother Frances Mary. Father Herbert approved of the work; in fact he arbitrarily declared,

'Other works may be done by those not leading consecrated lives.–This cannot.' His wife was actively concerned in penitentiary work; she had her own refuge in London, and later maintained a small maternity home at Malvern. Thus the sisters were likely to receive help and encouragement in their venture. But the impetus came from elsewhere, and it is clear that Mother Frances Mary was the real leader. The chaplain to the Home of the Good Shepherd recognised this when he said, 'The whole work was conceived and established by the love and faith of the late mother superior (Frances Mary Seymour) ... What she did to build up penitentiary work on a sure foundation, to keep it going, and to guide it over the difficulties incident to a new establishment can never be fully told.' It cannot be fully told here either, though a brief sketch of those early years must be attempted.

Penitentiary work seems to have begun in a small way at Vauxhall. Little is known about it now and the only recollection of those early days comes from Sister Grace, who used to tell how she had once been out with one of the so-called penitents and the girl had suddenly taken off her shawl, flung it over sister's head, and run away. Presumably the work at Vauxhall was begun as a preparation for the home which was soon to be established at Malvern.

Early Malvern Penitentiary

The formal decision to undertake penitentiary work was made in 1878, and in the following year (15 May 1879) the Home of the Good Shepherd was opened at Malvern Link in property made over to the Community by Sister Frances Mary for that purpose. Only seven penitents were taken at first as it was considered easier to establish a good discipline and tone with a few girls, though it was intended to raise the numbers gradually. Sister Emma, who had been sent to Clewer for training, was placed in charge of the home. She had the assistance of four voluntary workers (mostly sisters) and a laundry matron, and Mother Frances Mary was often there herself when she could get away from Vauxhall, so the home was well staffed.

The Community began its work at Malvern at a time when the need for penitentiary work was beginning to be realised in the Worcester diocese. Little had been done to meet that need. In 1876 a start had been made in Worcester when the Reverend C J Pilkington and his wife began rescue work in a small house in Chestnut Walk, and in the following year Melrose Cottage was formally opened as a refuge. It seems that even the Worcester Diocesan Church Penitentiary

Association, did not really function until the advent of the sisters. The establishment of the Home of the Good Shepherd gave a great impetus to the work in the diocese. In November 1879 the home was received into union with the Church Penitentiary Association and this gave it status in the ecclesiastical world. In the following year the Bishop of Worcester recognised penitentiary work as a diocesan institution, and he became a subscriber to the work and the visitor of the homes. By this time the Community's commitments had increased considerably, for the sisters had agreed to take charge of the refuge when the Pilkingtons left Worcester in 1880, and in the same year they became responsible for the supervision of the Leamington penitentiary. Thus the sisterhood now had three institutions on its hands. Unfortunately few sisters had the necessary experience for this specialised work, and it is not surprising that the Leamington home had to be relinquished in 1883. It was decided, however, that 'the work had been so marvellously blessed during the tenure of the Vauxhall Sisters that it was clearly right that it should be carried on for the future if possible on the same lines.' This was achieved when the Clewer sisters agreed to take charge of the home. The Community's work thus became concentrated at Worcester and Malvern.

Penitentiary work was built up steadily and solidly under Mother Frances Mary and her death was, humanly speaking, the biggest set-back it had received so far. Yet help came from another source. She had looked to the Reverend G Cosby White of Newland for advice on penitentiary matters, and his interest in the work did not cease with her death. He was chaplain to the Malvern home for a time, and in 1895 he was elected warden of the Community. Thus his help and his generosity were available when they were needed.

The Community had been growing in an unspectacular way, and accommodation at the convent was becoming a problem by the 1890s. The sisters needed the building used by the penitents for their own use. An appeal for a new home met with little response, and the position would have been critical but for Father Cosby White's generosity. He solved the difficulty by building new quarters for the sisters at his own expense (known as the New Wing), and so the girls were able to remain in the original home.

New Wing

There were housing problems at Worcester too. The work of the refuge was expanding and Melrose Cottage was soon too small. Therefore in 1898 a move was made to Field House, a large airy dwelling with a good garden attached. Father Cosby White paid the rent for this house for some years, and in 1910 he managed to acquire the freehold. He conveyed this to the London Church Penitentiary Association who leased the property to the Community at a nominal rent. Father Cosby White also built and fitted up a laundry for the house, and so the girls were provided with employment, and an income was secured from their work.

Such progress was not made without difficulty. Money was always in short supply. The financial support which the sisters had been led to rely on at Leamington proved to be a failure, and this was one reason for their withdrawal from the work, and though the Worcester and Malvern homes were recognised as diocesan institutions, a considerable part of the expenses was born by the Community. Thus in 1882 subscriptions brought in only a quarter of the necessary income and, though they increased, they were still only £260 in 1885 as against the sisters' £412. Moreover, the Community was also providing rent-free accommodation at Malvern and supplying sisters to run the home. As one speaker pointed out, 'The sisters not only gave money but gave themselves – all their life to the work.' A more serious difficulty was the shortage of sisters with the necessary qualities for penitentiary work. This particular problem had been foreseen, and the advice of the superior of a community specialising in penitentiary work had been sought, but she had recommended going forward, as such vocations were rare in her own community and she felt they might as well be found in another. The advice was taken, and the work was continued, but it was always hampered by the lack of suitable sisters, and the Leamington and Worcester homes had to be placed under secular workers. The third difficulty seems a strange and unnecessary one, though it was presumably a real one at the time. It seems that Victorian ideas of propriety and purity were such that sisters undertaking penitentiary work were unaware (or were supposed to be unaware) of the nature of the sin the girls had committed, and that many details of their past lives were withheld from them. Such at least seems to be the meaning of a passage in one of Father Herbert's sermons. 'Who,' he says, 'shall blame the Christian virgin, wholly devoted to the service of the Heavenly Bridegroom, if she draws aside her religious habit from the contamination that she dreads? She has been told that curiosity even about the histories of those she has to tend were sin in her. Ignorance of the mysterious evil increases her shrinking fear ... .' Ignorance did, no doubt, cause fear, and it would have made the work doubly difficult. One suspects, however, that the sisters had often more knowledge than Father Herbert realised.

But facts and figures about institutions, though necessary, have little interest for most people, and so an attempt must now be made to answer the question: 'What was life like in the homes?' Unfortunately a full description of daily routine is impossible, but the details which have been recovered suggest a kind of life, and above all an atmosphere, so different from those prevailing in similar institutions today that the attempt must be made.

Firstly, a good deal is known about the type of girl who entered. Most of the 'penitents' were in their late teens or early twenties, and almost invariably they had 'fallen'. They came from all parts of the country and this may, incidentally, explain the lack of local support for the homes. Most of the girls had been in domestic service, though there was a sprinkling of laundry girls and factory workers, with an occasional actress or circus girl and even the odd organ grinder and tramp. Though a proportion of the girls came from respectable homes, many had had a poor start in life. Some had been positively dragged down by their own parents, like the girl who was had up before the magistrates for begging with her mother, or the young woman who had been settled in service by benefactors but then 'decoyed away by her mother who sold her clothes for drink and then turned her adrift'. One poor girl had been given to tramps by her parents when she was nine. These stories make sad reading.

The Home of the Good Shepherd was run on very definite religious lines. A real break was to be made with the past, and the atmosphere of the home was intended to emphasise this. 'Think,' said Father Herbert, 'of the silent influences of a religious house! The sister's dress – the sign of salvation worn upon her breast – the devotional pictures – the texts upon the walls. All these were intended to have their effect. Quietness, order and obedience seem to have been the points emphasised. Girls as well as sisters had to keep silence times, and, though it is difficult to believe it, Father Herbert declared that they appreciated this. 'They are sad and burdened when they enter,' he said, 'and the quietness and calmness of all around is very agreeable to those in earnest.' Senior girls often asked for a day of silence: 'I want, sister, to think over what I have been taught in class: I want to be *quite* quiet.' The request was sometimes granted and records show that occasionally a quiet day was conducted for the girls who desired it. The stress on obedience was very characteristic of Father Herbert. However, he was probably right when he said that the girls were thankful for discipline and wanted to be saved from themselves. It is no doubt true that they were miserable under a weak or undisciplined lady worker. One can believe that a girl might say to another, 'I am so thankful Miss - is coming home tomorrow for she holds us up all firm like and we never lose marks when she is in charge of us', but one feels a little doubtful about the words attributed to another girl who was received a second time by the refuge matron: 'I could not stay a day at that home,' she said, 'They had no rules there, and we had no peace, we were always noisy and quarrelsome; let me go to a sisters' home, they are strict and loving, I am told, and this is what I feel I want.'

The Good Shepherd Home was planned as an ordered society in which everyone had her exact place or 'grade'. Girls who entered had to promise two years in residence, though actually they could leave at any time. The first six months were probationary and a penitent was not reckoned a member of the home until the end of that time. Girls who stayed on for a third or fourth year were known as 'raised penitents' or 'raised girls'. Two photographs of the girls remain which must have been taken in the early 1890s. These show differences in the girls' dress which evidently reflect their status in the home. The majority wear white waist aprons and close-fitting white caps with bows under the chin, but it seems that the girls in

pale dresses are the juniors and those in the dark frocks the seniors. Five are clad in dark dresses with narrow white neck frills; their aprons have bibs and their towering caps rival the complexity of the Victorian jelly mould. These are clearly the aristocracy of the institution; these must be the raised girls.

HGS Girls

It must be admitted that life in the homes was strict, and not only by modern standards. Father Cosby White welcomed the suggestion that the penitents should do some of the convent housework because it meant they could 'look forward to work in the convent as a certain emancipation from the very strict discipline necessary during their first part of their time in the home.' The danger of strain and unreality in their routine was recognised, however, and there were two or three short recreation periods a day which consisted of 'a good singing of hymns and church songs and of reading aloud'. Thus their day was not quite all 'washing and prayers: prayers and washing'. The girls had 'free access to the mother and sisters at any time for advice and sympathy' and this probably compensated for the strictness of their life. They felt that someone really cared for them and they responded to it.

For the home was successful. It is true that the life they had led made many of the girls unstable. The artist's model 'had a restless longing to return to the theatre' and another girl who had lived in a van 'could not settle after her wandering life'. But if they could survive the first few months, some of these girls did very well. Thus one who came from a 'miserable home', who had been 'wild and bad from 14 years old', and who had lived on a barge (this apparently signified the depths of degradation) ended up 'truly penitent' and was described as a 'very good influence with the others, hard-working and dependable though rough'. Another girl who was declared by a police inspector to be the worst case he had known, 'altered wonderfully during preparation for baptism and (was) very earnest'. Often girls who were not very satisfactory at the home did very well, or at least 'kept straight', after leaving. The majority went into domestic service and one of the problems was to obtain suitable posts for them. They were better trained than the average servant, but comparatively few people would take a girl from a penitentiary, and it was difficult to find mistresses who would trust the girls and make the necessary allowances for their shortcomings and their sometimes difficult temperaments. Some girls were placed in laundries and a few married soon after leaving. Occasionally there was a star pupil like the girl who left to be thoroughly trained as a nurse, or another who 'trained into a very capable cook and went out at £15 wages'. Other successful girls went as matrons to homes. Just once a Cinderella, described as a 'rough but well-meaning girl', was fetched home by her mother to be adopted by a rich American aunt.

A few girls wished to live dedicated lives themselves: these joined the Community's third order (when it existed) or were sent to those attached to other communities. Many girls seem to have had happy and grateful memories of the home. Some returned for holidays or when they were 'between jobs', and others would send little thank offerings from their wages. If they met girls who were in trouble, they recommended them to apply to the home because they had been helped themselves.

The history of the homes must be considered separately in the 20th century, for Field House ceased to be just a refuge and became a training home. The reasons for this change were mainly financial. The home depended largely on laundry work for its support, and it proved impossible to maintain the necessary standards unless some of the girls were more permanent. A few of them were therefore kept for the full training period. According to a report dating from 1884 four girls were retained for the full two years' training, and by 1902 the number had risen to six. This was probably increased again in 1913 when girls were transferred from the Good Shepherd Home which had to reduce its numbers. The house was still used as a refuge, however, and when the Worcester shelter was closed in the early 1920s, its work was transferred to Field House and an 'outside worker' took up residence there. Thus the home seems always to have fulfilled a double function.

With the removal to Field House, the home came more directly under the influence of the Community and, for the first time, some sisters were in residence there. A lady superintendent (Miss Ellis) remained in command of the home, however, until 1903 when Sister Jane, who had begun work in Worcester three years earlier, became Sister-in-charge. She held this office until 1928. Another change which affected the character of the house was made when girls who were in trouble but not 'fallen' were received. This cannot be dated precisely, but it must have taken place by 1920, for the report for that year says that the magistrates were sending girls convicted of theft to the home instead of giving them short prison sentences.

The history of Field House is largely the history of Sister Jane, for Sister Jane **was** Field House. Her complete devotion made her much loved by the townspeople as well as by the girls, and Sister Marion remembered how, 'Everyone in Worcester seemed to know her from the bishop to the shopkeepers who supplied the refuge with necessities, and every face lighted up at the mention of her for years after Field House was closed.' She refused to treat the girls institutionally. They wore no uniform and though other penitentiaries might put their girls in boots and white stockings, she would have none of it. They went out in groups of four or five with a sister or a worker and never in a crocodile. If there were free exhibitions in the town the girls could go, and they had many treats, for the local gentry would invite them to their houses. One of the highlights of the year was their visit to the bishop's house, Hartlebury Castle, with its peacocks on the lawn, a lovely tea and flowers to bring home. Blackberrying was another annual excitement, and there was always a special summer excursion such as a boat trip to Tewkesbury. The home received strong local support. The laundry was well patronised, especially by the local clergy and gentry, and the big sale in the town hall was always loyally supported. The Worcester townspeople were especially generous to the home. In 1921 some of the small tradesmen organised a whist drive which helped to pay for the new recreation room, and three years later electric light was installed thanks to their generosity. A pound day provided enough groceries for two months, 'many contributed by working people who must have denied themselves in order to give.' Working parties made clothes for the girls, and people who had surplus garden produce would send it to the home.

Sister Jane returned to the mother house in 1928 and the work did not long survive her departure. In 1933 the Community withdrew from Field House because it could no longer spare the sisters, and the home continued under other auspices.

Home of the Good Shepherd

The history of the Home of the Good Shepherd was similarly uneventful. The two main problems were accommodation and finance. In 1900, the girls were still living in the building which later became the novitiate wing. However in 1911 Mrs Herbert closed St Monica's, a small maternity home in Ranelagh Road, and the lease was offered to the sisters. The house was close to the laundry and had so many advantages that the Community felt it must become the penitentiary, but it was found that it would only take fourteen girls and so numbers had to be reduced. In 1920 it was possible to purchase the property and as the Community already owned the small house next door, the two were thrown together, thus providing more accommodation. A photograph of the home at this time shows a very plain building. It might be taken for a row of brick cottages, and though a laurel hedge provided a little privacy, it was almost on the road. There were large windows, but otherwise it must have resembled the houses the girls came from, and it certainly had none of the aspect of a great institution. In 1922 sufficient money had been collected to build a new and improved, though still simple, home on the old site, and this was blessed in July 1923. The problem of accommodation had been solved.

Finance was a constant difficulty. Moral welfare work was never well-supported by the diocese, and there was little help from the immediate neighbourhood, HGS depended on its laundry to provide the girls with 'health and active employment' and to cover part of its expenses. Yet laundry work was very badly paid in the neighbourhood and it was not always possible to get enough of it. The Factory Act of 1908, which limited hours of employment, created further difficulties, for the girls were unskilled and work often had to be done twice over before it could be sent out. Plain sewing was undertaken as another means of revenue, but there was only a small demand for this, though the introduction of an annual sale of work was a success.

The character of this home changed considerably over the years. Firstly, the connection with the diocese decreased and was finally dropped. In 1915 the Community relieved the Worcester Diocesan Association of its liability of £100 rent for the penitentiary buildings, but an annual grant seems to have been paid until 1921, when it was withdrawn since none of the girls in the home came from the diocese. The link with the diocese was eventually completely severed, though it has not been possible to date this precisely. The home also ceased to be a penitentiary and began to receive girls who had been through the courts or whose lives needed reshaping. The date of this change is also unknown. In later years girls were sent through the local authorities, who paid for their maintenance. The time spent in the home has been reduced from two years to one. There have been many changes in the daily life of the home. During the 1930s it was decided that the girls who were admitted were younger and less fitted for hard manual work than their predecessors. The working hours were therefore reduced and classes were given in subjects such as nursing, singing, country dancing and needlework. Eventually all outside laundry work was given up, and the girls were only employed in the home and convent.[137]

A further development in moral welfare work was the establishment of St Catherine's House, a hostel for young unmarried mothers (usually under eighteen) who wished to keep their babies. This was opened at the Link in 1945 in what became the guest house, but was transferred to West Malvern in 1955. This proved a most successful move, for the bracing air was excellent for the girls and their children, and the nearby schools and hotels provided plenty of employment. This home was of moderate size and could accommodate twenty girls and their babies. The young mothers usually arrived six weeks after the birth of their children and remained until they had learnt to look after their babies and to earn their own living. If suitable, they were sent to the Malvern College of Further Education for classes in domestic subjects. They were helped to find jobs when they left, and many kept in touch with the home afterwards.

Retreat houses and other works
Mission work can take many forms, and it is not surprising that the Community engaged in several other works in addition to parochial and moral welfare work. Foremost amongst these was retreat work.

The Community had no really suitable accommodation for retreat work in the earliest days, and though ladies may have stayed at Vauxhall for times of prayer, it is improbable that anything organised was provided until after the move to Malvern. Father Herbert took a parochial retreat at the Home of the Good

Shepherd in 1880, but it is unlikely that the house could be used after the number of penitents increased, and it seems clear that the beginning of real retreat work must date from the establishment of the mother house at Malvern. A retreat was being held for associates in 1892 (if not earlier), and when the convent chapel was dedicated it was assumed that it would be used for retreats. However, for some years retreat work could be conducted on only a very limited scale, since there was no proper guest house. When the penitents moved to St Monica's in 1911, however, their old quarters became available, and a proper guest house was established. This could be used for retreats and quiet days and to accommodate ladies who wished to spend some time in a Religious house. Thus one frequently reads of 'a quiet day for ... Sister Gabriel's girls', 'a small retreat for the Guild of the Good Shepherd', 'a retreat for beginners', 'a parish retreat', 'a guild retreat' or 'a quiet afternoon here for workers and other ladies in the Link'.

In addition, there were the legendary ladies' retreats. 'Only 42 ladies in retreat', says one of Mother Vera's letters (September 1916). The organisation of these retreats must have caused many a headache. The guest house was too small to accommodate all the ladies so sisters had to vacate their cells in the New Wing. The retreatants were used to servants and to all the refinements of life, and special efforts had to be made so that convent austerity did not overpower their devotion. Mugs were replaced by glasses; sisters handed the vegetables at table; even wine was provided. Particular efforts were made with the menu. Sister Anne's pretty sweets (which always included castle puddings swimming in raspberry vinegar) were especially noted. Sisters can still remember how the trains for the visitors' gowns swept along the floor as the guests came in to dinner. No wonder Sister Marion said, 'Ladies' retreats were very stylish then.' All this may sound a little strange to modern ears, but it was based on a genuine concern for the guests and was really an expression of the old monastic traditions of courtesy and hospitality. Ladies' retreats are no more: but the convent guest house was used and retreats for associates and small parish groups were held there, until the Community moved from Malvern in 1990.

The Community's contribution to retreat work has increased considerably in recent years. In 1958 the Community took over the Chester Retreat House from the West Ogwell sisters (Community of the Companions of Jesus the Good Shepherd). This house was not a diocesan institution but run by an independent committee. It had always served a wider area than the diocese, and had been especially used by the neighbouring Welsh sees and the Liverpool churches. But there was naturally a special link with the diocese of Chester, for the retreat house was situated in the cathedral close and was the obvious place for ordination retreats and clergy training courses. Retreat work was extended in 1961 when the Community took charge of Diocesan House, St Albans. This was a retreat and conference house, and there were many youth weekends, parish conferences, Christian stewardship training courses, etc., in addition to the actual retreat work. The house was also used as an ACCM selection centre and it is estimated that a sixth of the potential ordinands of this country passed through it. Very few 'open' retreats were arranged for this house. The majority of bookings came from the diocese which, very rightly, had priority, though a proportion of the midweek fixtures were accepted from outside it.

Although the Community has only one guest house nowadays (at the convent), it has had several others in the past. The first of these was at Hartfield. When Sister Stella was at Hove she did a great work amongst educated women and girls, and it was hoped that she might be able to carry on with this when she had to retire from parish work. In 1917 an old country house was rented at Hartfield in Sussex to be a House of Prayer and Quiet, and she was placed in charge of it. The house must have been quite small, for it could only take four guests, but it had its own oratory and a beautiful garden which was looked after by an associate. Guests came to stay for a few weeks at a time. The work prospered, and 10 years later it was moved to larger premises at Mayfield. The Wilderness, as the house was called, was in the midst of beautiful country and there were magnificent views from its windows. It had the unenviable distinction of being built on the spot where the last two men were burnt for heresy in this country. Work continued here until 1940 when it was relinquished, mainly due to Sister Stella's failing health.

Both these houses had a definitely religious character, and in many ways they were akin to retreat houses. Other guest houses had a wider scope. In 1924 the Community acquired St Leonard's from the Herbert family. This was renamed St Catherine's House and was run as a hostel for women and girls. In 1944 the trustees of St Edward's Orphanage, West Malvern, (which was being closed) asked the Community to take over their property. It was decided to transfer the hostel work there and to use the additional accommodation as a holiday home for women and girls. Later, ladies were also received who needed rest and recovery after illness, and some elderly ladies came as permanent residents. But the financing of this home was always difficult, and it was closed in 1955 when the premises were needed for other purposes.

For some years (1947-55) the Community was also responsible for a home for elderly gentlewomen at the Howsells, Malvern Link. This was mainly run by secular workers, but it was controlled by the Community and at first two sisters lived there. It proved difficult to run, however, and in 1955 it was handed over to the local council with the stipulation that the chapel must be maintained; and a sister continued to visit the residents and to take services at the home. The Community has also had various small rest houses such as those at Clevedon, Osmington, Malvern Wells and West Malvern. These were intended mainly for the sisters and not for mission work, and they will not be considered here.

Another work which often involved several sisters was the guild known as the Daughters of the Holy Name. Father Herbert was the son of a rich man, and he could never forget the 'poor rich' who were often no better off spiritually than many a Vauxhall pauper. The Community shared his concern, and therefore the 'Daughters' were founded in 1894. This society was intended for girls of well-to-do families. Its aim was the sanctification of its members. The Daughters were to be living witnesses for Christ in their own homes and in their own station in life. As Father Herbert put it, each member was 'to be a sacrament to society'. The guild was founded with three members and at first the numbers were small, but it grew rapidly at the beginning of this century, and by 1920 it included Daughters who lived as far away as the United States, Canada and Australia, and one who was working at St Katherine's School in Lesotho (then Basutoland). Local branches were formed in Birmingham, Malvern and Wimbledon, in addition to the London branch. The All Saints' meeting in London became a sort of annual reunion. Meetings were mainly devotional, and from 1895 onwards quiet days and retreats were provided. Members used to come to the convent for Palm Sunday weekend, and as at that time each received a palm branch, they must have presented a striking spectacle as they walked to the Link station to return home. Although mission work was not the Daughters' aim, their devotion naturally found expression in good works. At first they attempted social evenings for girls, at which nursing, cooking, etc., were taught. They contributed to charitable causes, and there was the inevitable sale of work. From 1919 to 1925 they were associated with the Community in a larger work, the provision of a hostel for ladies in South Kensington. This served as a headquarters for the Daughters themselves, but it was really intended as a means of helping those who could not be reached by parochial mission work. The Daughters continued in existence until the end of the war years, the last entry in their minute book being that of April 1945.

Two early community works must now be noticed, though they were both short-lived. The first was the Home of the Holy Family at Malvern Link. This was a small orphanage intended for middle-class girls, though it seems that small boys were also taken. Sanction had been given for the adoption of orphans in 1885, but the home was probably not opened immediately. It is known to have been in existence by 1891. In 1897 it was decided to close it. The girls would all have to earn their livings as schoolmistresses, or in similar occupations, when they left, and they needed a higher education than the Community could provide. It was against the children's own interests to continue the work and the orphanage was closed about two years later.

The other early work was the Home of the Holy Name at Parkstone (founded 1890), which was begun to provide suitable work for the Community's third order. Parkstone had been chosen for its sea breezes, its pines and its sandy soil, and Canon Dugmore, an ex-Vauxhall curate, made the sisters welcome there. The home was established in a house previously known as the Castle, and as it was built in that shape it was rather inconvenient and old-fashioned. Sister Vera was placed in charge of the home, which was intended for women and children who were incurably ill. A sister who worked there from 1893-94 says there were nine children and two crippled teenage girls, as well as ladies. When the third order was suppressed in 1894 it was decided to close the home. At Christmas the patients, with three sisters to nurse them, were transferred to Miss Hamilton's home, but there were the inevitable difficulties and in the following year it was decided to abandon the experiment.

Finally, a little must be said about handicrafts. These have never constituted a major activity, for a community devoted to mission work has neither the time nor the personnel to spare for large scale work of this kind. The embroidery room

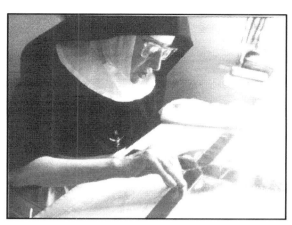

Sister Elaine Completing a Chasuble

seems to have been the first department to be established. Although a little church needlework may have been done earlier, the work was really established by Sister Grace (professed 1881), but though the work expanded under her direction, the convent embroidery room was never a large one.

Printing and book binding were begun under Sister Olivia (professed 1898), and a scriptorium was established by Sister Verena[138] (professed 1901).

[130]For an account of the troubles in this parish see *Father Pollock and His Brother*, Anon., 1911; and J Pollock, *Vaughton's Hole*, 1890.

[131]For instance, a glance at just one number of the Vauxhall parish magazine (June 1892) shows that the mission house was used for meetings of several guilds, three mothers' meetings, a women's Bible class, Band of Hope meetings (girls), a men's Sunday bible class, office of thanksgiving for Holy Communion (men's guild), a working party, the club girls tea and a social evening for the Company of the Holy Name (men).

[132]Presumably the future Sister Beatrice or one of her sisters.

[133]This Sister Gertrude was professed in 1882. She is not the same person as the Sister Gertrude who was the first member of the sisterhood but who left it in 1867.

[134]28 August 1865.

[135]There were 10,000 women on the streets of London alone according to an article by J Armstrong on 'Female Penitentiaries' in the *Quarterly Review*, September 1848.

[136]For instance, the communities at Clewer, Ditchingham and Horbury had been established for this work, and the Wantage Sisters soon adopted it even though Butler was anxious that the school work should be developed.

[137]This home was temporarily closed in 1966.

[138]This sister was subsequently released from her community obligations in order to enter a contemplative community.

CHAPTER 9

The Active Work of the Community: Overseas

Canada

The Community had been established for twenty-five years when it accepted its first call to work overseas. In July 1890 the chapter unanimously accepted a proposal to establish a branch house in the parish of St John the Baptist, St John, New Brunswick, and in the following year a mission house was opened there. It may be assumed that the initiative for this Canadian venture came from the Reverend J M Davenport, a former St Peter's curate and a nephew of Mrs Herbert, who went as a mission priest to St John in 1882. On the 2nd July 1891, Sister Paula, who had been appointed sister-in-charge, set out for Canada. It is disappointing to confess that very little is now known about the history of this house. The sisters were not pioneering in the backwoods. St John had a population of 40,000 and was the largest city of the province; it had many industries in addition to its fisheries, and its harbour, which was ice-free in winter, attracted much traffic. The sisters' work would therefore have been similar to that in an English city, though it must have had a special Canadian flavour of its own. For instance, a sister can remember hearing how the mission house (presumably a timber-frame building) was once moved across the street on tree trunks, and there must have been other interesting incidents. But life in St John had its difficulties too. The sisters were cut off from the Community in England, yet the Canadian house was too small to have had a real life of its own.[139] It is not surprising that it was decided to close the mission house and that in 1901 the sisters were withdrawn.

Liberia

It was 30 years before the Community had an overseas house again. In 1927 the sisters were invited to undertake work at St Kitt's in the West Indies; the offer was tempting but no immediate decision could be made, and in the interval there came an appeal for help from the Holy Cross Mission in Liberia. It was impossible to accept both offers, so Mother Agnes Mary paid a visit to St Kitts to assess the urgency of the work there. She decided that the needs of the Holy Cross Mission were greater, and so in August 1930 the chapter accepted the invitation to go to Liberia.

It was a new and exciting venture which opened up before the sisters, for it involved living and working amongst a primitive people hardly touched by western civilisation. The republic of Liberia had had an unusual history. Unlike most African states it had never been the colony of a foreign power, for it came into existence in the nineteenth century as the result of an American attempt to repatriate freed Negro slaves. Despite great hardships the settlers established themselves along a narrow coastal strip called the Grain Coast, and a republic was set up in 1847. The little state had to weather many troubles, and because of the lack of money and the difficulty of communications, very little control had been exercised by the central government at Monrovia over the indigenous tribes which occupied the interior of the country. Although churches and missions had been founded from the earliest days, they had also been confined to the narrow coastal strip, and the establishment of the Holy Cross Mission in the far hinterland was a real pioneer step.

In 1921 the Order of the Holy Cross (a male Religious order of the Protestant Episcopal Church of America) accepted the invitation of Bishop Overs of Liberia to come and work in his diocese. After a careful exploratory expedition had been made, it was decided to accept Paramount Chief Fofi of Masambalahun's invitation to 'sit down' in his territory, and the bishop assigned to the fathers the evangelisation of the Mende, Bandi, Kisi and Loma peoples. Soon a simple monastery was built at Bolahun, a deserted town site about a mile from Masambalahun. By the time of the sisters' arrival in 1931 the monastery, staff houses and church had been built, and a boys' school and hospital had been established. Tucked away behind the latter was a village of native huts known as Kisitown, which had been constructed for the use of convalescents and relatives of patients at the hospital. Men and boys had asked for baptism, and when Bishop Overs held the first confirmation in 1927 there were forty-eight candidates. However, hardly any women had come forward; few would even enter the church. It was gradually realised that this was due to native custom. Men and women never ate together, never sat together, never walked together in daily life. Moslem women could not enter a mosque, and amongst the heathen, men and women performed distinct sacrifices and prayers. The missionaries were men, and presumably their religion and church were for men too. If the women were to be reached it must be through other women. It was for this reason that the sisters went to Liberia.

Five sisters were chosen for the mission. On 8 April 1931 they sailed from Liverpool on the *Apapa*, and nine days later they reached Freetown in Sierra Leone. The journey was a great adventure to them, but the captain of the ship did not share their enthusiasm. He was deeply worried at the prospect of white women going to the primitive interior, and there was some reason for his alarm since some years earlier there had been serious tribal warfare in the hinterland. He could not persuade the sisters to return home, however, and they were soon setting out on the next stage of their journey.

The journey from Freetown was tiring but fascinating. The sisters sent home a vivid description of their experiences, and though the letter is too long to be quoted in full, some account of their travels must be given, for the first journey to Bolahun sets the scene for the work that followed and gives a far better picture of Liberian society than could be obtained from any dispassionate sociological analysis.

After a weekend spent at Fourah Bay College, the travellers caught the 'Pendembu Express', a leisurely little train which stopped at every halt and took two days to cover 225 miles. A whole coach was reserved for them, and from their camp chairs in an empty wagon they surveyed the landscape. 'You have to picture,' wrote Sister Mary Katherine, 'country untouched by the hand of man, with hills and dales, occasionally broken by a very wide river, sometimes by streams, and always clothed with verdure, either thickly with giant trees, or sparsely and more often with quite average-sized trees and shrubs, presenting a not un-English appearance. Here and there is a clearing either by burning or for a village. We went through many villages and small towns, and at all the stations a quiet crowd of leisurely males pressed up to the carriage windows to see, as Bishop Campbell expressed it, "the circus come to town." The further we got into the interior the more primitive became the huts and the less clad the inhabitants. The children are fascinating, often wearing but a string of beads, and one little scrap we saw with a piece of common string round it. The men and boys were friendly, the females much less approachable and interested. The whole of the way through the bush the only thing we saw in the way of tropical animal life were two varieties of lovely birds, and one monkey. It requires an effort of imagination to realize the hundreds of eyes beholding you through "the Green Wall of Mystery." Palm trees, cotton trees, darkish green; bananas looking like gigantic dock plants are pale reseda; oleanders, frangipani, and all the rest, go to make up a verdure like you get in an English forest in June ... the strong light, and the blue sky make it all very lovely and, of course, here and there, but not to any great extent, you get flaming scarlet and bright orange flowering trees (in the bush) and occasionally some lovely white lilies.' They spent a restless night in the Bo rest house, and then continued their journey to Pendembu, which was reached in the early afternoon. Here they transferred to a terrible old Ford car which needed to be 'prodded and pumped' frequently. The drive to Kailahun along the bright vermilion-coloured roads resembled their train journey, though they were more 'in amongst it all' and saw all kinds of interesting people en route. The sight of the car made Africans dive for the ditch and cling to any stray support while the terror passed; once they caught a glimpse of bush schoolboys with painted faces and mesh tunics trimmed with a sort of fur; another time 'a fine figure of a man, tall, upright, very black, dressed in the least possible, and holding in his hand a bright scimitar', stepped through the green wall of bush to see them pass. Their introduction to the chief of Kailahun was a disappointment, for he was 'a most depressed looking gentleman', but they found the thatched rest house with glassless windows and doors with no fastenings a fascinating place in which to pass the night. After a short drive the next morning they reached Dodo. Here the road ended: and here, they felt, civilisation came to a full stop.

But here also came their first real contact with the mission. As they neared the end of their drive they suddenly saw a host of boys rushing down the road to meet them, waving, shouting and laughing, and so effectually blocking the road that they had to stop and shake hands with the excited throng. They were the first boys from the mission.

At Mrs Moreton's store their carriers were waiting for them, forty to carry the hammocks and twenty to transport the luggage, for from now onwards the only road was a narrow bush trail and the only means of transport was a four-man hammock. There was great excitement as they got into their unfamiliar conveyances. Sister Monica Mary drew a lively picture of their experiences: 'The babel broke out again, and in a few moments I saw little Sister Clare going off gaily with eight huge natives looking as fierce and unclothed as possible. A moment afterwards a man rushed at me saying, "Missus, Missus," and beckoning,

Carriers

and so off I went also! By that time I was thoroughly enjoying the thrill of it all, and it was marvellous to find how absolutely safe and secure one felt alone with these men, of whose language I could not speak a word. I found we had to walk over a "Monkey Bridge", but big black hands came to hold me tight, and I was soon over ... I think my carriers were keen to be in front, as we soon passed Sister Clare and her band, and my men yelled with derision at hers, like children. At first all I could do was just hang on for dear life, as I happened to have a very narrow hammock, and was lying on my back with my feet well above sea-level ... besides all that my bearers were full of energy, and trotted with me, so that I was jolted up and down exactly as one used to be when riding a donkey at the seaside. However, later on I learnt to hoist myself up, and even say my Office as we went, but I was very thankful for a big cushion at my back.' They were carried across rivers and had to negotiate native suspension bridges made of creepers. Sometimes they climbed over huge fallen tree trunks, sometimes the men had to force their way through thick undergrowth. Now and again they came to tiny streams though which their carriers waded, often standing still in the middle like thirsty horses and drinking from a shallow tin which they handed one to another. At other times they were in dense forest and could see nothing but thick green foliage, hanging creepers and great trees whose branches met overhead and shut out the sun.

After a short stop at Masambalshun where they were formally greeted by Chief Fofi, they set off on the last short lap of their journey, which developed into a triumphal progress. As they approached the mission they heard the bell ringing and they were in the church which was filled with a seething excited crowd. A short thanksgiving service followed; then another ten minutes' travelling brought them to the convent which had been newly built for them. Lights shone in every window, a table decorated with flowers and spread for a meal stood in the porch and there were two of the fathers ready to welcome them. Words could not express their feelings at that moment, 'the thankfulness for all the care that had been taken of us on the journey and the big, big joy to find ourselves at last in the Convent of the Holy Name in Africa.'

No major programme of work had been planned for the first year. The sisters had to get acclimatised to tropical conditions. The damp heat of Liberia could be very exhausting, and time had to be allowed for the necessary physical adjustment. As it was, one sister had to be invalided home after a serious illness. They had also to settle themselves into their new convent. They were delighted with the house which the fathers had planned so carefully for them, but the kitchen was not yet built and there were few furnishings and fittings, so much needed to be done. Constant supervision was necessary, for cupboards and shelves had to be made by unskilled carpenters, and the man laying the chapel floor, just did not know how to get the bricks straight. Houseboys who had never ironed in their lives had to be taught to cope with wimples; sisters used to urban conditions had to battle with snakes, rats and insects galore. Fresh meat was almost unobtainable and fruit was bought from a native market with 'irons' as the currency.[140] There was much to learn.

Intensive language study had been planned for the first year. Several native languages were spoken in the mission area, and it was imperative that the sisters should learn some of them. They had been told that Mende was the lingua franca of the countryside and so had begun to learn it in England, but within a few weeks of their arrival they were writing that it was 'rarely understood in Bolahun'. Kisi and Bandi were spoken extensively, however, and soon these were undertaken instead. The task was a difficult one. There was no written literature in either language, there were no dictionaries; there was not even a grammar. All instruction was oral, and the only teachers were untrained schoolboys who could not spell the words they spoke. Various speakers would pronounce the same word somewhat differently, and since the meaning of words was completely altered by the intonation, language study would have been difficult under any conditions. The sisters found it difficult. But they persevered, and in time became quite proficient conversationalists, though languages always remained a problem and preaching was almost invariably done in English though native interpreters.

Acclimatisation and language study had been planned as the programme for the first year. However when Bishop Campbell arrived in May he urged the sisters to get in touch with the neighbouring people at once. The first contact was made on Ascension Day when five native chiefs and their retainers paid a formal call at the convent. At their head was Fofi, the paramount chief of the district, who arrived complete with his state chair and a chicken which he presented to the sisters as a 'dash' (present). This first visit was a big event, but it was somewhat of a strain too, for all conversation had to be through an interpreter. Moreover, the sisters did not know how to entertain their

Chief with Musicians

guests. First the chiefs' photographs were taken. Then someone thought of the gramophone, but as the great men sat in dignified silence it was difficult to tell whether they enjoyed it or not. Then Father Gorham came to the rescue. What the visitors would appreciate above all else was – a cup of tea. So the seven chief personages were each regaled with a cup and a half of this highly-sugared beverage, and after further photography the guests departed.

It was now imperative that visits should be made to the villages. Soon the sisters were walking out to pay afternoon calls. They were accompanied by one or more of their retainers (usually it was Tufa the cook) to lead the way, to help them over such minor obstacles as rivers, and to act as interpreters. Once arrived, the visits followed a stylised pattern. The chief received the sisters in his house, chairs were brought for them and a dense crowd of dark figures gathered round. The stage was set. There was a solemn pause, then the sister did her best to make a polite speech through the interpreter and a 'dash' (probably five shillings) was offered to the chief. Conversation might follow, perhaps about the proposed girls' school, and the chief would give his 'dash' – chicken, rice, oranges, cloth – to the sisters.

Sometimes dancing was offered as an entertainment, and occasionally they were shown round the village. They left escorted by an interested crowd, and the return procession must have been worth seeing: 'Five very hot and dripping sisters, with sleeves rolled up, and frills instead of wimples, then Tufa playing a weird kind of music on a hollow stick he had cut,' and at the rear, 'the small brown boy, in one scanty garment, carrying our roll of cloth balanced on his head, and a loudly protesting chicken in each hand.'

Contacts began to be made at Bolahun itself, and the first steps were taken towards mission work amongst the women and children. Sister Mary Joseph soon had a candidate to prepare for confirmation as Mrs Manley, the headmaster's wife, was already a Christian, and it was hoped that she might receive the sacrament at the bishop's next visitation. The contact with Mrs Manley, an English speaking woman, was an important one, for she was to act as their interpreter and generally introduce them to the other women of the town.

Early one June evening, Sister Mary Joseph, accompanied by Mrs Manley, went down to the village to meet some of the women. 'We started with four,' she said. 'I sat on the mud wall outside one of the native huts and just talked and made friends. They told me they were all afraid of the white sisters, but by the time I had finished there were about nine of the women, and we ended in quite a friendly spirit, and they insisted on walking part of the way home, and begged me to come next week; they said, "We want you to come, and we will not be afraid any more of the white sisters."' Soon a women's meeting was in full swing, for in July they asked for a weekly 'God palaver', and by September it had become so popular that sister was considering holding it in the palaver house as there was hardly any room in the porch of a native hut for herself, Mrs Manley, the women, their children, the snarly dogs and the chickens who all turned up for the meetings. The work of conversion was bound to be slow. Yet there was much that was encouraging, for the next Holy Saturday, after the blessing of the new fire and the paschal candle, a shy little band of women stood up and declared that they wished to be hearers.

In July the first approach was made to the little girls. It was thought that they might be attracted by means of games, but this method had its own difficulties since, according to European ideas, Liberian children did not know how to play. They certainly had no idea of how to play together, and anything in the way of team play was quite beyond them. Nevertheless, one Friday afternoon two sisters appeared armed with one large yellow balloon, one smaller red balloon, a ball, a skipping rope and a picture. The first thing to do was to acquire some children. Here Mrs Manley's help proved invaluable, for she went the round of the huts 'seemingly scolding loudly and generally all around'. But her words made sense to the children, if not to the sisters. She soon gathered up a handful of children and together they made for an open space in front of the palaver house. Fortunately the balloon was soon understood and was bounced about happily in the air, but even balloon games had their snags for the girls were hampered by their little country cloth skirts which kept slipping off, and the mothers wanted to play too, and would have monopolised the game if they had not been prevented. (Even one old granny with a baby on her back tried to join in.) Next they tried a game of ball which went off quite successfully, for they managed to get the children to stand in a circle and throw the ball round in turn. Even a little girl with learning difficulties was able to play after she had been shown many times, and a solid and frightened three-year-old ventured at last into the circle and held up fat hands for the ball. Finally, they all went into the palaver house to look at a picture. Mrs Manley was there to interpret, but it proved too complicated for them, though they listened and seemed to drink it all in. The time had come to say 'Isahu' and 'Malahu' – goodbye and thank you – and to go home.

By the end of the first six months the ground had been well-prepared, and the sisters were ready for more extensive mission work. This can best be discussed under three headings – evangelism, education, and hospital and welfare work.

The beginning of evangelistic work at Bolahun has already been described. The little group of women hearers soon increased to sixteen (1932), and a class for catechumens was added to it. The instruction of these women remained one of the sisters' most important tasks. The description of the preparation of candidates which follows is based on practices current in the 1940s and 1950s; there were some minor differences in the earlier years.

The classes for hearers were very simple, as they were intended for those who were just interested in Christianity and were not committed in any way. In the evening, a sister would sally forth with a lantern, find an interpreter and round up the people. (Since the ordinary Liberians had no clocks, it was difficult for them to be punctual). When everyone was assembled in the palaver house the class began. This usually opened with a hymn in the vernacular, as it helped to draw in the people. Prayers followed, and then came catechism (the mission had drawn up its own Holy Cross Catechism) and a lesson based on the Old Testament. The people listened intently to the teaching, and there was nearly always someone present who could repeat the previous week's lesson almost verbatim.

After two or three years the hearer might become a catechumen. This was a serious decision involving a real break with the past, for it included a renunciation of all 'country medicine' and sacrifices. The catechumens wore a large wooden cross as a sign of their intention to follow Christ, and they were allowed to come to the first part of the Mass. Their classes were held in church, their lessons were based on the New Testament, and they learnt the second part of the mission catechism. The catechumens were potential Christians, and many of them desired baptism. But the obstacles in the way, especially the matrimonial difficulties, were so great that many remained catechumens indefinitely. Thus Sister Mary Katherine could write that only one of her eighteen candidates was in sight of baptism, the obstacle in every case being an improperly-regulated marriage.

Baptism Procession

The baptismal day was a great one. Every effort was taken to emphasise the solemnity of the occasion and the procession of the newly-baptised, clad in white robes and carrying lighted candles, to their places amongst the Christians in front of the altar was especially impressive. In the earlier years the Christians gave a feast for the newly-baptised and Sister Clare described how (1938) the prior gave a goat, the congregation provided rice, oil and pepper, the Christian women cooked the meal, and the headman even produced a basket of oranges for the poor white folk who found native 'chop' too hot with pepper and too rich with oil.

After the first years the work at Bolahun was not confined solely to women. A sister was soon helping with a class for the carriers, and they prepared men for baptism too. Devotional meetings and instruction were also held for the Christians. On Sunday mornings when the Christians were at Church, they held services in the two native palaver houses for all who would come, and when Father Parsell organised a short 'seminary' for the native evangelists Sister Mary Katherine found herself on the staff. In fact they could never be quite sure what would be their next assignment.

The arrival of the sisters gave a considerable impetus to the evangelisation of the surrounding countryside. The fathers had begun 'God palaver' in the nearby villages soon after they had reached the hinterland, but they were few in number (normally only four were stationed in Liberia), and they had had to concentrate their energies on Bolahun. Thus for several years their preaching trips had been sporadic. The arrival of the sisters meant that more places could be reached, and more frequent and regular patrols were begun.

Visits to the instations, as they were later called, were soon started since these villages were in easy reach of the convent. Within a year of their arrival the sisters were giving regular God palaver at Nyoquetahun, Yengbelahun, Tagulahun and Koihimba. Classes were held in the evening when the people had bathed and eaten after the day's work on their farms, so at about six o'clock a sister would set out accompanied by an interpreter carrying a lantern. After a walk of about three-quarters of an hour they would reach the village and say 'Howdo' to the chief. Then the boys would call the people together in the palaver house for a simple talk, prayers and hymns. After classes had been held for some time the idea of baptism was put before the people. Sometimes the response was thrilling. One can feel the excitement in the letter which tells of such an occasion at Koihimba. The sister had gone to her class trying to keep in abeyance the thought that one or two people might come forward for baptism. 'Before I could begin, two girls of 17 or 18 came up and asked to be baptised, then one of our carriers who lives there followed suit. I was prepared to talk about baptism, so I suggested I should start without delay. When I had finished I asked who wanted to give in their names; there was a pause, then one man came forward and gave his name in a way that made me say I wanted his real name - this caused huge mirth. Then he started to question; if he promised to give up what is wrong etc, and after baptism did wrong, would he become unbaptised and cease to belong to our Lord? After explanation and more talk he gave his real name. One after another came forward, and then a pause; at last Mbunde, the chief, jumped up in deep earnestness and called for talk to stop, and cried out: "This is a hard thing to do, very hard, but it is right and I must do it," and he gave me his name, and clung to my hand like a little child wanting sympathy. His son followed, and to my amazement the old, lately broken chief too. I came away with the names of four women, eight men, and a boy; thirteen in all.' Soon afterwards another seven gave in their names too.

If there were Christians or catechumens in the village, these might have a lesson based on the New Testament after the hearers had been dismissed, though sometimes special classes for catechumens only were held. An attractive account of one at Koihima (1934) appeared in the mission journal.[141] Since this little village had no palaver house, the class had to be held in the open air. A straight-looking chair was set up for the sister in a space between the houses and the twenty or so catechumens just gathered round. First the register and attendance cards had to be marked, and this was no easy task as the people crowded round in the dark and the only light was a lantern waved around by a small boy. The interpreter would clear a small space and the catechumens would stand quietly and listen attentively to the teaching.

Sometimes when there were a number of Christians or catechumens in a village they would build themselves a little mud church. At Tagulahun, where the sisters had done much work, there was great rejoicing when this climax to their labours was reached. The blessing of the little building (1941) was chronicled in the convent log book and it is quoted here as it was written, since it conveys so well

Sisters on Trek Crossing Monkey Bridge

the picturesqueness and simplicity of the occasion. 'This afternoon we went at 4 p.m. to Tagulahun for the blessing of the new church. The three sisters and a few girls arrived first and found that arches of green and flowers had been erected. The church was beautifully arrayed and decorated, and seats had been put outside. The church is round with half the wall solid and half only a low wall wide enough to sit on ... At 4.45 p.m. a drum was heard and all the people of the town gathered at the top of the hill and formed two rows, all standing very quiet and reverent. The procession from Bolahun came headed by servers, cross, incense etc. Then Mr Tergusson (a refugee from Vichy-held French Guinea) followed by Fr Bessom vested in cope; and lastly a long line of schoolboys and people and all the schoolgirls in their school dresses and headties. Arriving at the church, Father Bessom blessed it, and then went outside to give a short address to the people, urging them to reverence the church as God's own house and to use it so. It was a most beautiful little ceremony and full of teaching for the people.'

The fathers had begun work in the more distant places before the sisters' arrival and outstations had been opened at Porluma (1926) and Boawohun (1927). Eventually five outstations,[143] complete with school, teacher and evangelist, were founded, and work in many other villages (known as preaching stations) was done from these centres. The fathers and sisters visited these places on monthly treks, and in the interval teaching and prayers were taken by the African evangelists.

The first trek made by the sisters was at the end of 1931, when two of them visited Boawohun. This was an established outstation, but none the less, one of them admitted that she was very scared of going into the wilds alone, for she was a woman, and amongst the Africans women were always given a place below men. But when she reached Boawohun her fears soon vanished, and the sisters really enjoyed the three nights they spent in the town. The object of their visit was to make friends with the people, and a special meeting was arranged for the women and girls who had so far been untouched by the work of the mission. One evening a crier went round the town calling them all to the schoolhouse. However, the women were shy of going in, for their accustomed place was outside. Consequently, the men had to be driven out, and the women led inside; though the men were determined not to miss the proceedings, and they assisted vigorously from outside, joining in the prayers and hymns, more energetically than the women. 'Nothing probably,' wrote a sister, 'will ever be like that first visit – the

had been given, the sister had to hear 'palavers' (disputes), give medicines and injections and finally make a quick inspection of the town.

This chapter has been concerned primarily with the sisters' *work* in Liberia, but before it closes something must be said about their *life* there too. The essentials of that life were of course unaltered. Rule and Office were maintained as in England, though there were adjustments in the timetable. In fact, not only essentials, but many accidentals were unchanged, and it was the 'Englishness' of the sisters which struck the novelist Mr Graham Greene, when he visited the mission in 1935.[146] Yet at the same time the life of the convent was closely linked with that of society around, and this gave it a character of its own.

Firstly, it must be appreciated that during the thirty years of the Community's work in Liberia, society, even in the remote hinterland, was in a constant state of change, and the conditions under which the sisters lived and worked on their arrival in 1931 were very different from those which prevailed thirty years later. After five years in Bolahun, Sister Mary Katherine could already see changes. The appearance of the school compound was different. There were more white man's clothes to be seen, a smartly-dressed boy was riding a bicycle, the women passing by wore more clothing and more English was to be heard everywhere. Unfortunately, clothes and money, which were hardly thought of when the sisters came, were becoming the most desirable things to many of the Christians. On the other hand, there were fewer sacrifices, and less country medicine was to be met with on the trails. Even preaching in the villages was different. Christian law and teaching had got into the people's minds, if not their hearts and lives, and they answered and asked questions intelligently. These changes increased over the years. A few boys from the mission school were sent away to get higher education; others made short trips to the coast. The establishment of the Firestone plantations, the opening of the Bomi Hills mines and the greatly increased demand for strong reliable workmen in other places decreased the number of men in the immediate neighbourhood. Carriers were hard to get. The building of roads and the erection of bridges facilitated contact with the outside world, and the monastery acquired a jeep (1952). The whole countryside was opened up by the coming of air travel, and by the time the sisters left the mission had its own little airstrip. In 1957 a power plant was installed, and the main mission buildings could now be lit with electric light; the introduction of radio, cinema, broadcasting and power tools followed. Street lamps were set up. Even 'civilised' dances in a decorated hall were begun for the young people at the schools. It will be realised that the impact of these changes was uneven and those in the more remote villages were scarcely affected by them. But the fact that society as a whole was changing was significant and meant that adjustments had to be made in the minds and methods of those working there.

Secondly, throughout the sisters' time at Bolahun the work was constantly expanding. In spite of difficulties and setbacks (which seemed very serious at the time) there was a sense of going forward, which is always heartening. Even if relatively few were baptised, there were hundreds who wished to hear the Christian message and made some response. In 1935, for instance, there were so many catechumens (800) that it was difficult to provide for their instruction. Villages begged for teaching. One Christmas (1957) the two Kisi evangelists brought forward as many as 100 people from outlying villages to receive their catechumens' crosses. Sisters on trek would get messages asking them to go to other towns and preach. The Gospel was something new and interesting and audiences were always attentive. Thus the work in Liberia was in many ways more attractive than that in an English industrial town.

Finally, life at Bolahun had a quality all of its own; for Bolahun was a distinctively Christian village, and this quality was emphasised by the fact that it was set in the midst of a non-Christian society. True, traditional ways were respected, even encouraged, and the village had its own native chief, but the ultimate direction of the town lay with the fathers, who saw that it was organised on Christian lines. The whole town would keep a retreat day before a great festival and the major events of the Church's year were celebrated by all the inhabitants. In fact the population of the town was increased at these times, since Christians came in from distant villages and even non-Christians flocked to join in the celebrations. The Christmas feast (when several cows would be slaughtered) was the great social event of the year and the Christmas play, which was acted in the school compound, attracted a huge audience. At the big festivals the church would be packed, not just to the doors, but beyond the doors, for the people crowded the steps and stood outside as well. Boys and girls graduating from the High School kept a day of retreat before the great event and school dances ended with prayer – at the request of the pupils. White people who visited the town were impressed by the welcome they received (everyone brought a gift, however small) and by the sense of a really Christian community.

But the time came when the Community's work in Liberia had to cease. It was becoming increasingly difficult to provide the necessary sisters, especially for the educational work, and a crisis was precipitated by the grave illness of one of the little band. They were officially withdrawn in August 1962, though two remained behind at Bolahun for a short time to help the American sisters of the Order of St Helena who were fortunately able to take over their work.

The Community's decision to withdraw from Liberia did not mean that the connection with Africa would be broken, however. Indeed, the first steps had already been taken towards the acceptance of new responsibilities in Basutoland (Lesotho). In August 1959 the Bishop of Basutoland visited Malvern in order to ask the help of CHN for his diocese. At the time of his visit Basutoland was still a British protectorate, though it has since become an independent state as Lesotho.

The country owed its existence to the great Chief Moshesh, who had established himself and his following at the natural mountain fortress of Thaba Bosiu at the time of the Lifaquane Wars. He had soon consolidated the remnants of the unorganised and semi-independent tribes who were fleeing before the ravages of the Zulu warrior, Chaka, and within six years he had become the most considerable chief amongst his people. Horses and muskets were acquired and the Basuto became a mounted people, but his position was still precarious, for in

1836 the Great Trek started and the country around Basutoland began to be settled by the Boer farmers. There was endless conflict between the settlers and the Basuto; the British at the Cape were also drawn in, and in 1868 the country was recognised as British territory at the request of Moshesh. It became one of the High Commission territories and, as a result of gradual political development, was granted independence in 1966.

Christianity reached Basutoland in 1833 when Moshesh invited the missionaries of the Paris Evangelical Missionary Society to settle amongst his people. They established themselves at Morija and had soon trained teacher-evangelists who conducted small churches and schools over a wide area. In 1862 the Roman Catholics arrived and Moshesh, who decided that churches were like doctors and it was best to consult more than one, allowed them to settle in his country. Their numbers were few at first, but in this century they greatly increased to the point that the Roman Catholic Church became the largest Christian body in the country, and since 1915 the paramount chief has been a Roman Catholic. Not until 1876 did the Anglican Church make a modest beginning at Leribe, but its numbers gradually grew until it became the third largest Church in the country, and in 1950 the diocese of Basutoland was established.

The bishop's aim in visiting Malvern in 1959 was to put before the community the needs of the Society of St Mary at the Cross, a small community for African women which was established in his diocese. The society had been founded at the request of certain Basuto girls who had come in 1923 to visit Sister Marion at the house which the Community of St Michael and All Angels had opened in Leribe. They had a question to ask. 'Is the Religious Life only for white lady? Can we be sisters too? Can there be African sisters?' Sister Marion had said, 'yes'; and so in 1924 the Society of St Mary at the Cross began.

The society provided a simple form of the Religious Life which was suited to the needs of Basuto women at that time. The sisters lived in rondavels, the traditional thatched huts of their people, and as far as possible Basuto ways of living were preserved. Father Parsell OHC, who visited Leribe in 1940, described the society as 'like Bethlehem' in its poverty and simplicity. The direction of the little society remained with the Community of St Michael and all Angels, and Sister Marion, whom the girls had approached in 1923, was given to them as their superior. The sisters ran a hostel for children attending the Church school at Leribe, took Sunday school, and gave classes in the parish; a small branch house was also maintained at Teyateyaneng. Numbers always remained small; and though in more recent years two Zulus entered the society, the majority of its members were Basuto.

However Africa was in the midst of a period of rapid development, and great changes were taking place throughout the continent. The growth of education and the rise of nationalism affected the climate of opinion even in rural Basutoland, and the apartheid policy of the South African government made people conscious of differences of race and colour. It no longer seemed right that communities of African and European sisters should live next to each other under different material conditions. The time had come for a multi-racial community. The Community of St Michael and All Angels, which had so generously cared for the African sisters in the past, could not meet the new need, for their mother house was in Bloemfontein in the Union, and owing to the Group Act they could never receive Africans to live with them there. It was for this reason that Bishop Maund approached the Community of the Holy Name, which agreed to explore the venture, and, if it were God's will, to take the initial step in faith. It seemed it *was* God's will, and the Community began to make plans to open a new branch house in Leribe.

ENDNOTES – CHAPTER 9

[139]A photograph taken in 1899 shows two sisters and a postulant at a Sunday School treat. It is quite possible that this represents the whole strength of the house.

[140]These were thin strips of iron, about 12 inches long, which were worth just over halfpenny each.

[141]*Hinterland*, August 1934, p.3.

[142]Quoted from RE Campbell, *Within the Green Well*, n.d., pp.201-202.

[143]These were Vezala, Foya Dundu, Vahun, Goldolahun and Pandemai. Porluma and Boawohun were closed.

[144]*Hinterland*, April 1932, p.2.

[145]The Reverend A E Russell, chaplain general of the Community from 1958.

[146]'It was Sunday in Bolahun, unmistakably Sunday. A herder drove out his goats among absurdly Biblical rocks, a bell went for early service, and I saw the five nuns going down in single file to the village through the banana plantations in veils and white sun helmets carrying prayer books. They were English; tea with them (a large fruit cake and home-made marmalade and chocolate biscuits wilting in the heat and delicious indigestible bread made with palm wine instead of yeast) was very like tea in an English cathedral town; it was an English corner one could feel pride in: it was gentle, devout, childlike and unselfish, it didn't even know that it was courageous. One couldn't help comparing the manner of these nuns living quite outside the limits of European protection with that of the English in Freetown who had electric light and refrigerators and frequent leave, who despised the natives and pitied themselves.'
Journey Without Maps, 1948, p.76.

CHAPTER 10

The Later Mothers Superior

So far little has been said about the superiors who succeeded Mother Frances Mary. This has been inevitable since the community's history has been discussed under aspects instead of chronologically, but the deficiency must now be met, for this book would be incomplete without some account of those who have guided its life and work. Although the main emphasis will be laid on the characters and personalities of the superiors, a brief summary of the main events of their terms of office will also be included, for in this way the various threads which made up the community's life can be drawn together, and the necessary chronological sequence provided.

The two superiors who followed Mother Frances Mary are rather shadowy figures. Mother Emma (Emma Mackintosh Goodearl), who came into office in October 1888, was one of the earliest members of the Community. She was born in Highgate in 1839, but her family probably moved to Vauxhall later since she was an early member of the Society of the Holy Name. She was a young woman in her late twenties when she joined the sisterhood, and it is to her credit that she stood firm throughout the difficult time when she and Mother Charlotte were the only sisters. Although she had entered as a lay postulant she was professed for the choir (1870), perhaps because of the outstanding natural gifts she possessed. Father Herbert and Mother Frances Mary both thought highly of her, and she held many offices in the community. In 1876 she was made superior of the Wolverhampton house and three years later she became the first sister-in-charge of the Home of the Good Shepherd. She also served two terms as novice mistress. The most important event during her period of office (1888-1897) was the building of the chapel, and the New Wing was also added to the convent at this time. The preliminary work on the revised rule and constitutions was also due to her initiative. Many new works were begun but, strangely enough, none of them really flourished. The second and third orders which she founded were soon given up, and neither the home at Parkstone nor the Malvern orphanage lasted very long. The mission house at St Paul's, Walden, was closed after three years, and though the Canadian house remained open longer, it was always on a small scale. It is probably that her dreams were too grandiose to be realised. If the draft constitutions reflect her influence (as is likely), she had visions of a great hierarchical order under a mother general with daughter houses with their own superiors and novitiates – a concept which bore no relation to the actual strength and resources of the community. Not surprisingly, she found life in the Church of England increasingly unsatisfactory, and in 1899 she joined the Church of Rome. She speedily regretted her decision, however, and after a period of probation in New Brunswick was restored to full community.

One can but pity Mother Emma. She was an emotional woman from a narrow background, and she can have had few educational advantages. Her outlook was rigidly Anglo-Catholic; the notes for her novices classes might have been (and probably were) taken direct from some Roman manual. Such a woman was bound to find life difficult in the Church of England, especially if she was placed in a position of authority, and it is understandable that she eventually found her home elsewhere.

In 1897 Mother Agatha (Martha Gregory) came into office. She was born at Bisley, Gloucestershire, in 1844 and was about thirty-five when she entered the Community. She was a teacher, trained at Wantage, where she struck up a close friendship with the future Sister Bessy, who later became a noted educationalist. Butler had wanted her for his own community and could not believe that she would join the amateurish little sisterhood at Vauxhall, but she could not be deflected from her original purpose. She was professed in 1882, and probably spent most of her earlier community life teaching, though she was assistant novice mistress (not an onerous post) from 1891-1894.

Mother Agatha

Mother Agatha was a large woman, Rather awe-inspiring in later life; but her appearance belied her character, for her kindness and 'big loving heart' are what were really remembered. She believed in and loved her daughters, though she had no illusions about their imperfections, and it is said her courtesy was such that she spoke to her youngest postulant in the same way as she addressed Lady Grosvenor. She had a special affection for the young, and when at the convent would always slip out at 12 o'clock to see the children coming away from school. Her understanding of their minds was profound. According to one story, she once put the worst boy in charge when she had to leave a class. It worked admirably, for when she came back she found them all toeing a chalk line and the words 'hall bad' scrawled in chalk upon the floor!

Her religion was very simple and Christ-centred. 'There are some who looked at our very holy nuns,' she once remarked, 'but I think it is better just to look at Our Lord.' A sister describing her simply said, 'She lives hand in hand with Our Lord.'

No important developments took place during her term of office, though there was a steady expansion on former lines. The number of mission houses was increased, for ten new houses were opened as against five closed, and although the Canadian house was amongst those relinquished, the community was able to help the Church overseas by training the first members of the Community of the Sacred Passion. Moral welfare work showed steady progress. The move from Melrose Cottage to Field House allowed for further expansion, and although numbers had to be reduced at the Good Shepherd Home, when the girls were transferred to a house apart from the convent, both they and the sisters benefited by it. The completion of the revised rule and constitutions (1899), which was a landmark in the Community's history, also belongs to her term of office.

Mother Agatha was in poor health and suffered from insomnia during her last years as superior, so that she had to rely largely on her assistant, Sister Angela, for day-to-day administration. It was clear that the burden was too great for her and in 1915 when she came out of office, she went to live at Malvern Wells where she was in charge of a small rest house. The remainder of her life was spent there and at a small house at Clevedon where she died in 1928.

It is a sorrow to have to write so inadequately about the next superior, for the simple and humble Mother Vera (Ellen Cable Lake) was one of the holiest sisters the Community has produced. 'Your Community has at least one saint and that is your present sister-in-charge,' said Father Denny when she was superior at Vauxhall, and all who really knew her would endorse his verdict.

She had been one of Mother Frances Mary's novices, and her entry was linked with the Community's short tenure of the Leamington penitentiary, for her family, who lived in the town, knew Mother Frances Mary well and she was able to reconcile the dismayed parents to their daughter's vocation. Sister Vera's life had not been limited to the Midlands, however, for she was educated at Margate and later trained as a nurse at the Westminster hospital. She was professed in 1886 and probably worked at the Home of the Good Shepherd during the next few years, but when the Parkstone home was opened in 1890 someone with nursing training was needed and she became head of the home and mother of the third order sisters. When this work was closed down she was made superior of the Vauxhall house, and held this post for nearly twenty years.

She was an ardent mission sister. It is said that she always went for the lowest and never minded what conditions her work took her into. Although her love of poverty taught her great compassion for the very poor, her sympathies were not limited by type or class, and she did much spiritual work amongst the large contingent of ladies who acted as district visitors at Vauxhall. Her love and concern for people were sustained and lasting. For instance, she kept in touch with Lilian, one of her invalid children at Parkstone, for the rest of her life, enabled her to learn a trade, and got together a sum of money so that she always had a reserve on which she could fall back. There was little time for parish work at Vauxhall where she was responsible for a large household of sisters and workers, but she knew many of the people, and sometimes took the boys' Band of Hope or a Sunday school class. She was sweet with children and loved to slip in to help with their guild meeting at the mission house. It was typical of her that she should write at Christmas after the First World War: 'I think, in all our houses, we should try to make it a marked and very bright one for any children we have to do with.'

She was elected superior in 1915 and held office for ten years. It was not easy to succeed Mother Agatha. Many of the sisters were devoted to her. Moreover the observances of the rule had become somewhat relaxed, as her illness prevented her giving adequate attention to community affairs, and discipline needed to be tightened up. Mother Vera was further handicapped by coming to her office straight from a mission house; she had filled no post at the convent and did not know many of the sisters well, while her natural shyness and reserve made it impossible for her to force herself on others. Physically she was a frail woman (she had only one lung), and she had two operations during her time in office.

It is surprising to hear that she was a ruler, yet this was so. Community observance was tightened up and much more attention was paid to the rule of silence; yet everything was done in an unobtrusive way, for Mother Vera fitted herself round other people, so that she might be said to rule from below rather than from above. At the same time she never hesitated to reprove if it was necessary. When a sister spoke angrily at a Vauxhall mothers' meeting about an irregular and unreasonable demand on the penny bank, Sister Vera pulled her up sharply there and then, and years later she reproved her before the whole Community when she spoke about a sister from another community in a critical and unwelcoming spirit. Yet it was this same sister who said that Mother Vera found fault-finding very difficult because the sisters' failings were such a grief to her.

She was a very gentle person. 'The wimples are too stiff. We aren't meant to be stiff, we must be soft and yielding,' said she to a sister newly in charge of the laundry. At Vauxhall she had been good with 'difficult' sisters, who loved her, and when she became Mother her concern for others was shown in a multitude of ways. She studied her sisters from every angle, summed up all their needs, physical, mental and spiritual, and did her utmost to meet them. Even flat feet were noticed, and she always began her interviews by enquiring about the sister's family. Her sensitivity made her very conscious of the feelings of others, and there is a charming story of her taking the novices out to pick violets on the day a new mistress was to come into office; she knew how they must be dreading the change.

At the same time she was very practical. 'My dear, are you teaching the novices how to treat their brooms?' said the Reverend Mother to the sacristan', and it was she who started the choir novices doing some of the housework. Nothing escaped her – she even noticed that a handrail was needed on the back staircase. She used her sisters so as to get the best out of them, and she took care that novices should gain experience of different kinds of work. 'Can you cook dear?' said she to a novice. 'No.' 'Then what would you do on a desert island?' – and she was despatched to the kitchen to learn. Another novice who was working there was removed after a week; her apple puddings were so good that there was no need for her to learn. Mother Vera's practical outlook was shown in her attitude to time, for she hated wasting it and invariably knitted when she talked – the knitting was always the same, a matinee coat, because she needed no pattern for it.

Mother Vera had two natural enthusiasms, nature and books. Her interest in nature was not that of a scientist, it was a love of living things. She could never understand Mother Stuart's[147] devotion to hunting; but it must be admitted that despite her fondness for animals she was terrified of cows, not an unnatural weakness in a townswoman. The flowers in her room had always to be picked from the hedgerows, for it was the wild ones that she loved. Her Sunday walks with Sister Marion were one of the highlights of the week; they would start out together at 10.30 a.m. and sometimes it was quite difficult to get her back in time for Sext. Perhaps it was to be expected that a great nature lover, Wordsworth, should be her favourite poet.

Sister Marion said she had never known anyone so keen about books as Mother Vera, except her own sister, Miss Amy Lake. One of the first things she did when she was elected mother (probably that very afternoon) was to take Sister Marion into the rose garden and tell her that they must have a library and that she was to be librarian. A room was allocated, and the two collected all the suitable bookcases they could find, and gathered together the books which were scattered in various places in the convent. Once a sister remonstrated when Mother Vera was found struggling up the cellar steps carrying a very dirty bookcase. Her reply was characteristic: 'I can't think why, as soon as one is mother, people think one cannot carry anything.'

Her great devotion was to St Francis. She had a tiny picture of him in her cell, and on his feast day she would invite half a dozen or so of the more junior sisters to a little festival. There were readings from *The Little Flowers* and some talk, and a bar of chocolate was shared around. On one of these occasions there was great enthusiasm over the spirit and life of Francis, and the sisters declared their ardent desire to be his followers. But one remained silent, wondering how this life would fit in with the Community of the Holy Name. And the mother, without looking up, but with exquisite sensitivity, stroking the pages of the book in a characteristic way, said, 'You know, I think it is so wonderful how one saint is for one person and another for another, but only Our Lord is for us all.'

Her affection for St Francis reflected her own deep love of poverty. It is possible that she was drawn further than the Community in this direction, but she did not try to force her ideas on others, as the story just quoted shows. Her own feelings came out in many little ways; her clothes were greatly patched, for instance, and she was always anxious to avoid expense. The embroidery room sisters were faced with a difficult task when she determined that a new set of vestments should not cost more than £5, but by joining bits of material together they managed to make them for the price. The bare dining tables at the convent were due to her too. Yet the poverty she loved was not just a poverty of material things. It was a deep poverty of the spirit, and an observant sister said that although she knew so many people and was always working for them, her inner life was a solitary one. She depended solely upon God.

Humility was one of her strongest characteristics. She once said, 'Some of us seem to think that when we are professed we have a status, but a religious has no status', and she certainly never assumed one herself. As one sister remarked, there was no self about her. Though she loved poverty, she would give up a patched wimple because a sister told her it was unfit for a mother superior, and it was typical of her to insist on washing up the tea things on Christmas Day.

There was nothing outwardly notable about her term of office. No new mission houses were opened and three existing ones were shut. But the scope of the community's work was widened when the Hartfield guest house was opened, and in 1924 another guest house was established at St Catherine's, Malvern. Hostel work was begun in London, but this did not prosper and had to be relinquished after six years. She had a special affection for the girls in the Community's homes, and as a result of her concern, the Home of the Good Shepherd was rebuilt on more modern lines.

In 1925 she resigned her office. She was made infirmarian, a post which she loved, as her whole desire was to serve her sisters, but she was not strong enough for the work and soon had to give it up. Three years later (1928) she died after a long and terribly painful illness. She lay in her bed looking utterly peaceful, content to suffer as God willed, a pattern of simplicity and patience. The sisters were always greeted with a bright smile if she was conscious and she enjoyed a little joke. 'Tell mother,' she whispered when near to death, 'I have not always chosen the hardest part.'

Mother Vera was succeeded in 1925 by Mother Agnes Mary, who had previously been her assistant. The two were very different in character, and therefore worked admirably together since they complemented each other.

Mother Agnes Mary (Charlotte Agnes Parker) was only nineteen when she entered the Community in 1893. Little is known about her family, but she is believed to have been born in the Midlands and she must have come from a comfortable, prosperous home. Her father was a builder, presumably in a big way of business, since he was able to send her to Germany to study music. She said that she had given herself completely to God when she was very young, and the

Agnes Mary as a Novice

spiritual side of her nature must have been very apparent, for when her sister went to Father Suckling of St Alban's, Holborn, to ask why he advised her entering a convent when she was so young and looked so miserable about it, he only replied, 'I have never seen so marked a vocation.'

Almost the whole of her long life was spent at the mother house. As a novice she worked at the orphanage and acted as sub-sacristan. Her 'six months' were spent at St Alban's, Birmingham, and she went to Vauxhall for a short time after her profession, but she soon returned to Malvern as choir mistress, a post which she held again later in conjunction with other offices. Her experience of mission houses therefore was very limited, though when

156

she became mother she visited them conscientiously and tried to understand mission house life.

She became novice mistress before she was thirty and filled this office for seven years. Her novices were very devoted to her, and she had their complete confidence. Strict over essentials, she did not fuss over trifles, and a novice caught in the act of vaulting over a novitiate table was only asked, 'Novice X, how did you do it?' And she had to show her. (The novice in question was an ex-gymnastics teacher.) When her term of office ended she became guest mistress and during the next few years she established a vast correspondence with people outside the community who depended upon her for spiritual help. This made her conscious of the needs of women who were not strong enough to follow the Religious Life, and so eventually the companions were founded. (Many of them were her ex-novices.) As assistant superior (1915-25), she came to know most of the sisters well, for she made a point of seeing all those from mission houses when they came home for retreat. Thus she was well placed for her work when she became mother.

A sister, when asked about Mother Agnes Mary, remarked on her simplicity and 'all-of-one-piecedness'. It was a shrewd comment and it explains the difficulty one finds in trying to write about her. Where should one begin?

'Mother Agnes Mary gave us prayer,' said Mother Elfrieda when summarising the work of her predecessors, and it is true that prayerfulness was her dominant characteristic. She had almost a contemplative vocation herself. Hours were spent in chapel in addition to the time required by the rule, and sisters grew used to the sight of the little figure kneeling upright on the blue carpet of the sanctuary step. Every afternoon she was in chapel for three quarters of an hour, and she was often there after supper too. She might be found at prayer in her sitting room, and a sister going in to see her would notice that her lips were moving. The sister who slept above her said she often rose in the night to pray and that she would get up before the rising bell in order to have extra time in chapel. Novices on the top floor declared that she prayed aloud during the night. She always said the priest's prayers as well as the congregation's part at Mass, and if she was absent she said the whole service through. The regularity of her prayer was quite extraordinary; no one dared interrupt her during her fixed times – whatever the reason. She once told a sister how she had noticed that the plants were withering and needed watering. But it was time to pray. Should she water them? No. She must go and pray and the plants must wait until later on.

She was probably responsible for putting worship, especially the Office, so much to the front of the Community's life. The Office really was the 'work of God' for her. Her own recitation was clear and emphatic, no hurrying, but also no woolliness or slowness, and there was a strong sense of rhythm and purpose in it, typical of her attitude in all things. When she became choir mistress she was able to make use of her previous musical training, and she taught the sisters very thoroughly, laying great stress on pronunciation and an impersonal delivery. Plainchant was a real means of spiritual expression to her; it was music supernaturalised, purified of everything extraneous, of all emotion and all personal interpretation. She could not stand an organ accompaniment. 'Accompanied plainsong is like putting a lark in a cage,' she said. At the same time she expected the chant to be intensely alive, and there is a lovely story of her as an old sister trying to tell a young choir mistress what was lacking in her chanting. Ordinary expression got her nowhere. Then, accompanying her words with a vigorous gesture: 'It wants Oomph,' said she. She was interested in anything to do with the liturgy. Only the best was good enough for chapel; vestments had to be made of rich materials, and a little heated greenhouse was built in which plants could be grown for the sanctuary. A copy of Zundel's *Splendour of the Liturgy* was kept permanently in her cell because she loved it so, and she was keenly alive to the Liturgical Movement in the Roman Catholic Church.

The growing emphasis on the more contemplative side of the community's life may have been due to her, though it is possible to over-emphasise this, for Sister Verena, who succeeded her as novice mistress, also influenced the Community in this direction, and it is said that there was once a small group of sisters at the convent who were studying the contemplative life with the idea of bringing the Community into that ethos. Be that as it may, there does seem to have been a shift of emphasis, probably very gradual, during the next period in the Community's life, and although this need not have been solely due to Mother Agnes Mary, she undoubtedly led the sisters that way, by both example and precept. Since she was a decided character they were bound to have their effect.

She held her office from God and for God. Her main work as mother, as she saw it, was to train the Community, to teach the sisters how to fulfil their vocation and to uphold them by her prayers. 'I will try to be good and help you,' she said at her first conference, and she kept her word. Her love for the sisters who had been her children for twenty years was very great, and she showed tremendous care for each individual. She watched over newly professed sisters very carefully. One sister says that she saw her daily for the first fortnight after her profession. Any mistakes in behaviour were looked into – not only from the senior sister's point of view but from the culprit's too. She interviewed every sister when she came home for retreat, and notes were sent to sisters when they moved from one house to another. Sisters in Liberia received individual letters by every mail. She remembered each sister's profession day, writing out a little quotation on a tiny card. Her letters and notes always contained a spiritual message arising from her understanding of the needs of those to whom she wrote. Often her daily walk was taken with one of the younger sisters so that she might talk to her, probably about spiritual things. A sister said that one never came away from her without a beautiful or spiritual thought.

Mother Agnes Mary had a tremendous respect for and appreciation of other people, and always wanted them to be themselves. In a sense, all her geese were swans, and she helped to make them so. Her charitable approach made her treat others living in a much lower plane as being much better than they knew themselves to be, and when they left her presence, though they did not feel themselves less sinners, they were filled with hope. At the same time she was clear-sighted and not easily deceived, and a novice who once lied to her (implying she had read a recent book) realised that she had spotted it immediately and was grieved. She had a very deep understanding of a few people, and was able to help a great many more, but everyone could not respond to the type of guidance she could give, though she was always ready to give herself out to seemingly unrewarding people.

There was nothing remarkable about her spiritual teaching. She had no gifts of words, or of exposition, as a study of her class notes shows. A sister who owed much to her says that what mattered was not so much what she said as the way she said it. It was not that she spoke, she was spoken through. Her teaching might be said to flow naturally from her own experience, and to reflect her temperament. As might be expected her whole emphasis was on the interior life. 'We steep ourselves in prayer,' she wrote to one aspirant, 'so that we may bring others to Our Lord.' 'We want to be so full of Him that we just breathe Him forth and take His peace to those we visit,' she said to a sister. It was her emphasis on 'giving peace' to people which made her insist that the sisters should never show an appearance of haste. She stressed the necessity of just 'being' and 'being still'. She hated people talking in chapel. Several sisters have described her as a personification of the rule. When she was old and deaf she would come right up to the table with her ear trumpet when the rule was read aloud at conference and listen to it as if for the first time. This symbolised her whole attitude. Perfection was the goal she put before the sisters, and she looked on the rule as the means of attaining it. She was especially anxious that the rule of silence should be carefully kept, and she is said never to have broken it herself.

Mother Agnes Mary was a natural ruler. A picture of her as a young novice shows a girl with an unusually resolute expression. Being a very decided person, she always acted with complete conviction, and others followed her instinctively. According to one sister, it was quite an ordeal to take her about in London, for she just walked straight across a busy London street, supremely confident that the traffic would stop for her. Some people were rather in awe of her. One American priest wickedly christened her 'The Empress' (for she was very dignified) and curates quailed before her. Now and again a natural imperiousness did flash out, but it was only momentary, for she had real humility and realised that she was nothing without God.

Her breadth of outlook was surprising in one who had entered a convent so young. She loved to know what was going on, whether in the Community or in the world, and she was tremendously aware of everything that was happening. She is said to have read *The Times* through every day, and a friend noticed that contemporary events nearly always formed the basis of their conversation. She read widely and intelligently on many subjects and was keen to see the latest books. Even in her last illness she was reading the *New English Bible* (which had just come out) and was pointing out the interesting new lights it showed on St John's Epistles. Her capacity for taking in new ideas was, in fact, quite remarkable, and she realised long before many younger sisters that the time had come for the Office to be shortened.

Enthusiasm was one of the strongest traits in her character. Every moment was lived vividly. She was thrilled to send sisters to the hinterland of Liberia where white women had never been seen before. A friend remembered 'the lovely child-like delight' with which she described her first experience of an escalator; it was 'like a fairy staircase,' she said. This enthusiasm used to bubble out of her so that her whole personality sparkled. Her very walk was full of decision and liveliness, and people could tell that it was her coming from a long way off.

Anything beautiful attracted her, and there is a charming story of her dancing round the room as a young novice, lifting her skirts and crying, 'Just look at my lovely blue petticoat.' She was a natural aristocrat and had a genuine taste for quality. It gave her real pleasure to see pretty china when she went for her rest, and she loved the fine fabrics to be found in the embroidery room. The work of the scriptorium fascinated her, and the very day before her death the sister responsible for it was allowed to take her a card she had planned herself which had been accepted by SPCK. Many of her rests were spent in Devon, and she loved the moors, where she would search for fine mosses. Astronomy was another interest; she would sometimes draw a sister out after Vespers to look at the stars, while those working in Liberia would get letters telling them what constellations they should look out for. Music was, of course, her great love. She sometimes used to play her violin to the sisters, but as her deafness increased she had to give this up, and so one day 'Brother Raphael' was sold. This cost her a great deal for she felt she was losing a friend.

Her term of office might be described as one of consolidation. During the time she was mother the Community suffered from financial difficulties, the novitiate was small and, towards the end, there were further problems caused by the Second World War; thus one would hardly expect to find a spate of new works. Three mission houses were opened, but five were closed, and Field House and Mayfield (which had replaced the Hartfield guest house) were also given up. The decision to open St Catherine's House as a hostel for mothers and babies was made at this time, however, though it had to be implemented by her successor. Undoubtedly the biggest development in the community's active work was its extension overseas, and to the Liberian convent she gave her full support, encouragement and enthusiasm. Yet the real importance of her term of office did not lie in active works but in the more domestic and interior side of the Community's life. The abolition of the distinction between choir and lay sisters meant that the Community could develop on a more united basis. Many improvements were made to the chapel, and a tradition of dignified worship was established. Most important of all, the interior life of the sisters themselves was deepened and built up.

In 1945 her term of office expired and, at her own request, she was not re-elected. She was now almost 71, her health had never been strong, and she knew it was time to give up. Yet there were still more than sixteen long years of waiting ahead of her, for she did not die until 1962. Many sisters have said that these latter years were marked with the cross. Changes had to be made in Community ways, and though necessary, these were bound to be painful to one who had known the past.

Furthermore, she had spent almost all her Community life in positions of authority, and it was difficult for one who was used to being at the centre of things to stand aside.

She received the news of her last illness, when she knew it to be incurable, with joy. 'Have you heard? I have got my ticket home,' she said to the chaplain. A letter to a friend expressed her feelings more fully: 'This is to be given a real share in the cross,' she said, '... to learn to be utterly dependent on others, in some most humiliating ways. I feel it is for me to strive to leave myself completely in the blessed hands of God, and strive to look straight through Him in all ... It is a lovely way home, isn't it?' A letter received from her a couple of months before she died was full of joy. She spoke of the wonderful orderings of divine providence – 'quite breath-taking at times.' 'He is all love always.'

When Sister Elfrieda became mother in 1945 a gust of fresh air swept through the community. It is difficult to exaggerate the different atmosphere she brought with her. All her predecessors could look back to the early days of the Community, and even Mother Agnes Mary had been Clothed by the founder. Mother Elfrieda, although born in Victoria's reign, had entered the Community late in life; she knew the troubled Britain of the inter-war years and came from the world of emancipated women. It was only to be expected that she should differ from her predecessors.

Irene Huleatt (for that was her family name) was born in 1882, the youngest child of a family of ten. Her father was an Anglican priest of Irish stock, a hunting man and rich, so she grew up in very comfortable circumstances. She was educated at an excellent English boarding school and at a famous finishing establishment at Lausanne, and then settled down at home to enjoy the pleasant social life which fell to the lot of a girl of her class. It must have been a cultivated household, for one hears of Shakespeare readings at home. The family knew many interesting people, and when Irene was a child she received a weekly letter from Lewis Carroll. Her father was a much-travelled man[147], and obviously a good deal of care was taken over the daughters' language study, for their mother used to take a house on the continent for the summer holidays when they were young.

The outbreak of war in 1914 did not make a great difference to her life at first, but she became a VAD and in 1917 was posted as an ambulance driver to the Etaples convoy in France. The work was hard, for the hours were long and members drove by night or day in all weathers, and since the cars had no windscreens the drivers had little protection from the weather. The convoy was especially distinguished for its work in evacuating the wounded during an air raid when an ammunition dump was hit and continued to explode, making the rescue of the men particularly perilous. Miss Mountbatten, who organised the evacuation, became her great friend. During the last push towards the end of 1918 the girls had to work for three days and three nights without any rest, driving all the time, their eyes glued up with sleep, rocking with fatigue when stood on their feet. Yet Irene's sense of duty was so strong that she insisted that the ambulances must be cleaned and ready for instant use before the drivers went off duty. In December 1918 she was mentioned in despatches. At the same time she was ready for any fun that was going. A girl in her section tells how she would go off to dinner at Paris Plage or Le Touquet, and how she would hire wonderful cars to drive in off-duty time, striking terror into the hearts of the French country people by her driving. The same writer describes how she had seen her come into the huts on an icy evening with bottles under her arm, and the girls, who were all called in to share, sat round on the floor drinking priceless champagne out of tin mugs.

When the war was over, she joined Sarah Mountbatten in London; and the two worked together to help the Forces for a while. They then decided to set up house together in the country. They settled at Upcerne Manor, a lovely Elizabethan house in Dorset which belonged to Sarah's brother. The little village church was built in the grounds and Irene became one of its churchwardens. Later (1934) the friends moved to Madams Mead, a house specially built for them in Wyke Regis, overlooking Portland Harbour.

The Future Mother Elfrieda

A sister who knew her in those days described her as a thorough countrywoman, rather buxom, usually dressed in very well-cut tweeds with a beret. She said she walked 'with a manly stride', which sounds very much in character, for she was a great sportswoman. As a young woman she had been a keen (some say an international) hockey player, but her great interest was golf, and she was captain of her local club and of her country, and president of the Ladies Golf Union of all England. One year she went to France as non-playing captain for England. When the two friends moved to Wyke they had their own boat built, and they were also fond of sailing on the Norfolk Broads, and though Irene did not inherit her father's passion for riding, she took a lively interest in racing. She was also a keen motorist and had one of the first cars to be seen in that part of the country. These early models were somewhat unreliable and liable to break down at inconvenient times, so that she sometimes arrived back in the small hours of the morning, to be received with maternal scoldings by her housekeeper.

When she was a child she had been a great reader. According to one story she once read all the books her father had bought as Sunday school prizes in one day. Learning was certainly no effort to her. Yet one could not call her a bookish woman; probably it would be better to describe her as 'well informed'. She had travelled widely since she was young, and this contributed to her great breadth of outlook. Her relations were scattered all over the world, so a trip to India or the

Far East to see them seemed quite natural. She knew some parts of Africa too, especially Egypt, and on one trip she and Sarah ventured further into the desert on camel-back than any white woman had ever been before.

Superficially her life was a purely social one. A Dorset friend tells how she once thought Irene's only interests were travelling, golf, bridge, etc.. But when she remarked flippantly to a party of mutual friends that her friend's life was one round of pleasure, she was told in no uncertain terms that Irene Huleatt's little finger was worth more than all the rest of them put together. She was always 'quietly, very quietly, helping people'. It seems that she hated people to 'show off' or push themselves forward, even when it was only the case of a game of golf, and this probably explains why she avoided committees and obvious forms of public work. Her good works were invariably hidden ones.

As a young girl she had thought she had a religious vocation, but her mother needed her and so she had put it on one side. Years later the call returned to her. She probably first came into touch with the Community in 1930-31, when two of the sisters spent a winter at Cerne; and in 1935 she became a companion. This could cause problems. She was a keen bridge player. Did her new dedication permit her to play for money? Every summer she spent a month at the convent and, dressed in a three-quarter-length white coat, an immaculate tea towel on her arm, like the perfect butler, she carried out the duties of the pantry worker. But it was not enough. She found she must go further, and in 1938 she was received as a postulant. It cannot have been an easy decision to make, for she was a sophisticated woman with a wide experience of the world, and she was bound to find the restrictions and limited outlook of the novitiate frustrating. Moreover she was completely undomesticated, and though she might have managed the convent pantry work, she had no idea of how to make a bed or darn a stocking. (A fellow novice remembers seeing her going out for the day with friends, dangling a small, neat paper parcel on her little finger. The said parcel contained stockings – for them to mend for her!) As it was, her natural instincts sometimes got the better of the 'religious' decorum expected of a novice, and there is a famous story of the day she walked over the golf links and saw a beginner muffing his strokes. Suddenly she could bear it no longer, and striding over to the embryo golfer she took the club from him, saying: 'You've got your stance all wrong! Let me show you'. There and then she gave a demonstration, watching over him afterwards to see that he did it correctly. The poor man was overwhelmed with surprise to find himself suddenly taken over by a large nun, and the horror-stricken novice returned to the mistress to confess the enormity of her behaviour. But in spite of difficulties she persevered and in 1941 was professed.

A short period in a mission house followed, but in May 1944 she was recalled to become novice mistress. Little more than a year later (August 1945) she was elected mother. Thus she was soon faced with heavy responsibilities. She declared that she was probably the first novice mistress who could say that she had been in the novitiate with her novices, and one sister who had a very long novitiate knew her as a fellow novice, novice mistress and mother. No one who had known her intimately as a novice or newly-professed sister ever took advantage of this relationship when she became mother, but her position was not an easy one, since she had only a short experience of the life in which she had to lead others. This caused her many difficulties, especially during the first few years. Moreover her humility made her feel that she had nothing to give her contemporaries – they knew so much more; and she sometimes deferred too much to the judgement of those whose experience was greater than her own.

She was not always the conventional Reverend Mother. This was a great joy to younger sisters but could distress those used to former ways. An aspirant who was once driving her to Tymawr remembers vividly how they stopped in Great Malvern and she went into a shop, emerging with a bottle of ginger beer. 'I'm tired of coffee,' she said. On another occasion she took a newly-professed sister for a walk and, seeing an ice-cream van on the common, purchased two ices. As they strolled along, ices in hand, she frankly admitted, 'I do hope we shan't meet the assistant superior suddenly.' It was disconcerting to some to find that their superior thought nothing of buying a Sunday paper and reading it on a bus, and that she was not above 'thumbing a lift' into Worcester when late for an important committee. One cannot believe that either of her predecessors could have been described as 'the life and soul of the bus queue', as she was on one occasion.

Her chief characteristic was joy. One sister described her as 'bouncing with fun', 'and she chuckled and shook when she laughed. The very sight of her face made people smile. She often chided the sisters for being so ready to observe fasts and so reluctant to keep festivals. There was always a merry twinkle in her eye, and her keen sense of humour made her spot the funny side of the simplest incidents. For instance, when she was a companion she occasionally drove Mother Agnes Mary out, and a sister remembers the amused expression on her face as she watched the mother and sisters tucking into one of her delicious luncheon baskets (specially ordered from an hotel) while someone solemnly read aloud from a pious book.

She was full of common sense and very practical. One of her first actions on encountering the heat of West Africa was to roll up her sleeves and say that the sisters *must* have short-sleeved habits in future. Another time a frightened novice rushed to her room: 'The kitchen is on fire,' she cried. 'Then put it out,' replied the mother firmly; but she followed her downstairs and applied the fire extinguisher herself. She would sometimes appear in the pantry, remove a sister's apron from her, try to tie it round her waist (it was almost certainly too small) and wade into the washing up herself, and if the convent was short-staffed she might well seize a knife box and help lay the tables. She would send sisters out on to the hills 'to blow the cobwebs away', and someone worried or depressed was likely to be issued with a detective story.

Wherever she travelled she picked up friends - she never went on a railway journey without doing so - and the Community's gardeners and odd-job men loved her. She used to see all guests who came to stay at the convent, and her relationship with associates and friends was a very close one. Her judgement of character was very shrewd. 'And don't think you'll get through the novitiate without shedding buckets of tears,' she said to one aspirant, and she was quite right. Another guest (who had long desired the Religious Life, but who had been held back by family responsibilities and then personal illness, and who thought she would never be accepted by a community) went to see her toying with the idea of becoming a companion. 'Come and look at the hills,' said Mother Elfrieda, drawing her to the window. Twenty minutes later the dazed visitor found herself on her way to chapel with a list of postulant's requirements in her hand and the date of her admission in her head. Mother Elfrieda had summed up the situation only too accurately. It was to the very old and the very young in community life that she most revealed herself. How the old sisters loved her – and the novices; she felt she had something to give to both groups, and give she did. She was especially good at understanding the difficulties an older woman had to face in the novitiate and she knew the right remedies to apply in the circumstances. She sensed when she was needed and a novice who went to her feeling she could carry on no longer inevitably left her laughing and with new courage. With her own generation she had not, in some cases, the same affinity, she had grown up in a rapidly-changing world and they in the cloister.

Rather strangely, there is little to be said about her spirituality. This is probably because it was so deep and simple. One sister described her as just 'consecrated naturalness'. Her attitude was one of complete trust and she had a great sense of God's providence ruling over her life. She was always upward-looking: 'I will lift up my eyes unto the hills' was her theme for a profession retreat. She regarded a Religious vocation as both a joy and a great privilege, and an aspirant who remarked casually, 'I feel quite at home. I think I'd like to stay,' was told promptly, 'You can't come in on that basis.' She expected that sisters would give themselves completely, do anything, spend themselves utterly. Her talks when the novice mistress was away contained depths of experience packed into a very few sentences. Gethsemane and Calvary were subjects on which she had obviously meditated deeply, and all she wanted when she was dying was to be able to see the crucifix on the wall.

She was mother for only eight years, but her term of office was an important one, for it occurred at a time when changes had to be made, and she had the courage to make them. One of the most painful decisions concerned the future of the Vauxhall mission house. The history of the Community and the parish were so closely intertwined that a break seemed impossible, yet a dozen sisters could no longer be spared to work in one parish, and the large house was expensive and quite impractical to keep up. The drain on the Community's resources was proving far too heavy, and so in 1950 it was regretfully relinquished. Since new work was immediately taken up at St Saviour's, Pimlico, however, a London house was still maintained. The other changes in the Community's works were smaller ones. New houses were opened at Coventry and Wellingborough, and Mother Agnes Mary's decision to open a mother and baby home was implemented. A home for elderly ladies (The Howsells) was also opened. Mother Elfrieda was much interested in the Liberian mission and made two trips to inspect the work on the spot, but there were no spectacular developments overseas during her time.

Her practical approach was shown by the improvements she made to the convent buildings. One of her first moves was to put in more bathrooms and cloakrooms; the refectory, scullery and larder were enlarged and cold air storage installed. As Community numbers grew during the post-war period, the wisdom of this policy became apparent.

She was called to bridge the gap between the old world and the new, and to bring a more modern approach to community ways. Rigid customs and practices were broken through. This was painful to some who had grown accustomed to the old ways, but it was necessary if the Community was to go forward, and it led to renewed vitality. Her own spirituality was very 'Anglican' and she saw the Community as part of the whole Church, not as an isolated unit. She once said, 'It's all very well for CHN to be "hidden" but we mustn't be invisible.' The convent was brought back into closer contact with the diocese and sisters undertook more outside work, such as parochial missions, instead of just working within the parishes where the mission houses were situated. Since she had many friends and outside contacts the Community was brought into touch with other communities and the outside world. She liked events to take place at the convent. For instance, a moral welfare conference for Anglican sisters was held at Malvern, and the annual retreat for mothers superior was planned to take place there the summer she died. It was rightly said, 'Mother Agnes Mary deepened our life, but Mother Elfrieda widened it.'

She had always been a strong woman, but towards the end of 1952 her health began to give way, probably due to a great deal of worry and distress which came to her at this time. She was sent to St Thomas's Hospital for investigation early in 1953 and a major operation followed. She was allowed to go to her friend Miss Mountbatten for her convalescence, but her strength gradually decreased, and when she returned to the convent at the end of May it was clear that the end was very near. Yet weak and ill though she was, her power of attracting others remained. Even the ambulance men who brought her home sensed it. They had been given tea in the guest house, but afterwards the sister found them strangely reluctant to leave. Then the truth came out: 'Would it be possible to see mother once more before we go?' The answer had to be 'no', for she had already been taken to the infirmary wing. 'Well, will you give her our kind remembrances – she is so wonderful.' Even in her great weakness her spiritual power had got through, and (as they said) she had helped them.

Mother Elfrieda died on 30 May 1953. A special chapter had already been called for 11 June at which Sister Audrey Mary was elected her successor.

Mother Audrey Mary

ENDNOTES – CHAPTER 10

[147]A famous mother general of the Society of the Sacred Heart.

[148]Mr Huleatt served as an army chaplain for many years. This had taken him as far afield as China. He was chaplain to Lord Raglan at the time of the Crimean War and knew Florence Nightingale. After he left the army he often visited Canada, though his great love was for the East. He was a great horseman, and once in the Crimea when the troops were cut off and there was dire need for medicine which was at the port, he was pointed out by a scout as the only man who *might* get through without being spotted by the enemy. He could and did.

CHAPTER 11

The Community and the Church

So far, the Community has been discussed as an isolated entity, an independent organism, existing in its own right and living its own life. It has never been considered in a setting wider than the parishes in which the sisters worked, or seen in relation to the life of the Church as a whole. It is important, therefore, to consider the Community against this broader background, with regard to its relation to other Religious communities and its concern for the worldwide Church as expressed by its participation in the ecumenical movement.

Firstly, as far as its place within the Church of England is concerned, it can be said that the Community began its life with an episcopal blessing.[149] Like all Victorian sisterhoods, it was very much a private enterprise, and continued to be so, but it did not originate without the knowledge and consent of the diocesan bishop. When Sister Gertrude came to Vauxhall, the Bishop of Winchester was Richard Sumner, a much-respected Evangelical leader. He was not, however, opposed to the formation of sisterhoods as such. As early as 1845 he had been prepared to consider the formation of a sisterhood within his diocese (it never materialised), and according to Father Nugee, he had visited his little community at Wymering, 'extreme' though it must have been; in fact it is said that, 'He gave them his benediction in the most fatherly manner, and expressed himself delighted with the working of the institution.'[150] This being so it is not surprising that he gave his sanction to Sister Gertrude's profession during the dedication festival of 1865. His letter of 23 June 1865 giving his consent was still extant in 1893, though unfortunately it was subsequently lost. Since he was unable to be present himself, he gave permission for one of the bishops preaching during the festival octave to admit the novice to profession. Thus it was Bishop Morrell, the coadjutor Bishop of Edinburgh, who received the vows of the first sister.

Episcopal sanction does not seem to have been asked for subsequent professions, and it appears that Bishop Sumner's consent, once given, was considered to confer sufficient recognition on the community. In the years which followed the sisters' lives and thoughts were almost exclusively devoted to the parishes in which they worked or to the institutions which were under their care, and they took little part in the wider life of the church. It is only in recent years that they have taken a more active part in diocesan life.

It is pleasant to record that the Community's centenary celebrations in 1965, though deliberately unostentatious, included a visit from the Archbishop of Canterbury, who addressed the sisters in chapel and visited the West Malvern home, and a celebration of the Eucharist in Worcester Cathedral when the Community was invited by the bishop and dean to sing the service on Michaelmas Day.

During the nineteenth century the Community seems to have been unconcerned by the divisions within the worldwide Church. Engrossed in the day-to-day work of their parishes, the sisters had little time or thought for the Churches of the continent, and they would have regarded the English Nonconformist chapels around them as sectarian and schismatic and their ministers as interlopers. This was Father Herbert's own point of view. He does not seem to have shared the concern for church unity which was so characteristic of the Wednesbury clergy, though a book of prayers shows that the subject was not completely absent from his thoughts. Mother Frances Mary's great interest in non-Anglican Churches seems to have been exceptional.

Thus it was not until about the 1920s that the Community began to be involved in work for unity. The first sign of interest in ecumenical matters occurs in 1925, when Mother Vera's letter shows that the Holy Name was one of the forty-two Anglican communities which had agreed to give their Mass intentions on Mondays and Wednesdays in Lent 'for an awakening of an earnest desire for Unity in all Christians and blessing on the Conversations at Malines'. The Community also decided to use a special memory after Terce for the same object and this continued to be used daily after Lent had ended. In 1932 the community observed a week of prayer in which the pope had invited all Christian people to join, and by 1936 (if not earlier) it was keeping the novena for the reunion of Christendom.[151] Mother Agnes Mary was one of the superiors who signed the declaration on reunion which appeared in the Church Times early in the following year, and it was then that the Saturday Mass and Office were first observed with a special intention for reunion.[152] Sometime before 1939 the Church Unity Octave began to be kept and was observed with a night watch. Thus by 1940 the Community's concern for reunion was established.

At this time there were few actual contacts with those belonging to other Churches. As early as 1925 a Russian nun, Sister Margaret of the Community of the Mother of Unhoped-for Joy, had spent three weeks at the convent when she was in England seeking advice for her community in its work of building up colonies of Russian refugees in France. Another pleasant incident (1938) was a gift of sweets from the foundress of a Roman Catholic nursing congregation (Sister Beatrice's sister) so that the Community might share the anniversary of their founding. But it was not until the post-war years that any real contacts were made. In 1946 a Dutch deaconess came to stay at the convent, and from then onwards there were many contacts with foreign Churches and communities, especially with the deaconesses of the Swedish Church and with the Grandchamp community. Several Grandchamp novices were sent to Malvern for short periods of training during the years which followed the formal constitution of the community, and Mother Genevieve visited the convent several times. Since the 1950s the sisters have taken part in ecumenical pilgrimages and conferences, and the Community's centenary year saw the beginning of a close friendship with the Benedictine nuns of Stanbrook Abbey.

There were few close contacts with other Anglican communities during the early years. The one exception was the Society of St Margaret. This was a well-established and thriving community when the Vauxhall sisterhood began, and it gave its help generously to the new venture. It was to East Grinstead that Sister

Ellen was sent to be trained for her work as assistant superior, and it was in the St Margaret's novitiate that Mother Frances Mary received her religious formation. This meant that the Community's debt to East Grinstead was a big one, for its future development depended very largely upon her. There was probably much help and advice given in the years which followed, and a book of meditations on *Esther* still remains which was sent by the East Grinstead novice mistress to Sister Emma (her Malvern counterpart) to 'spare you a little trouble and thought in preparing instructions for your children'.

The Community was entirely dependent on secular priests for spiritual help during its early years. The revival of the Religious Life for women preceded that for men, and the first stable male community, the Society of St John the Evangelist, was not founded until 1865, and it had to establish its own life before it could help others. Father Benson and the other Cowley Fathers often preached at St Peter's, but there is no evidence of a close connection with the Community until the 1890s. By this date Cowley Fathers were taking Community retreats, and they also provided the preachers for the important services which were held at this time. Father Black gave the sermon at the festival Evensong which followed the laying of the foundation stone of the chapel, Father Hollings was the preacher when it was dedicated two years later, and Father Page gave the address at Sister Joyce's profession. Their help was especially important after Father Herbert's death, for it was to Cowley that Father Cosby White turned for assistance in reviewing the rule and constitutions, and it was Cowley which provided the Community with its first two Visitors. Father Page resigned from this office in 1908, but the Community continued to look to Cowley for advice and spiritual help, and when it was decided to appoint a confessor extraordinary (1939) a Cowley Father was asked to undertake the office. Members of the society also gave great help to the Community by taking its retreats, though in later years it was equally indebted to the Community of the Resurrection and (since 1954) to the Society of St Francis.

For the first forty years or so, the Community was fully occupied in trying to establish its own life, and until this was done it was in no position to help other communities. However, when in 1908 the bishop-designate of Zanzibar, Frank Weston, asked for help in training the novices of the new community he was about to found in Africa, the Community was able to agree to his request. He admitted the first postulant on 4 July and she was clothed four days later; two more postulants arrived in September, and in May 1910 the first five novices of the Community of the Sacred Passion sailed for Africa. They were accompanied by a sister from the Community of St Margaret of Scotland, Aberdeen, who was to act as their superior, for the Community of the Holy Name had no sister with experience of overseas missionary work who could help them over the difficult first few years. Novices continued to be trained at Malvern until about 1915 and, in all, nineteen entered the novitiate and thirteen sailed for Africa. Sisters who were on furlough stayed at Malvern for rest and retreats until they had an English house of their own.

A sister was also lent for a year to help the newly formed Community of the Sisters of the Love of God (founded 1906-07).

There was a close relationship with the Community of St Clare in its early years. After the first novices of this community had been trained at Tymawr, they were established in the former retreat house at Freeland. For the first six months the mother superior of Tymawr came over periodically and continued to direct the new community, but this could not go on indefinitely. The Society of St Francis therefore asked CHN for help and in 1951 a sister was sent to act as superior until one of the Freeland sisters was ready to hold office.

In recent years the Community has been privileged to help two other communities which, in the changed circumstances of the modern world, were no longer attracting sufficient vocations to ensure their own life. In 1956 the sisters of the Society of the Holy and Undivided Trinity[153] came to live at Malvern, and the community provided a sister to act as their superior. A few years later (1963) sisters were sent to Saltley to assist the Society of the Incarnation of the Eternal Son,[154] a small community, Franciscan in spirit, which had done great work with orphan boys.

The Community has also had especially friendly contacts with the Australian community of the same dedication – the Community of the Holy Name, Melbourne. Sisters visiting England have usually stayed at Malvern, and the insertion of the Australian community's name in the English community's litany in 1948 symbolised this friendship.

There remains the difficult task of trying to assess the Community's place amongst others. The nineteenth century saw the birth of a host of women's communities. Peter Anson describes forty of these in The Call of the Cloister, and another twenty are briefly noticed as small communities.[155] Even a cursory study of the Victorian Church reveals other small or short-lived ventures which are not named by him. Thus the Community of the Holy Name was only one of many sisterhoods, all founded in the brief space of fifty-five years, part of a great upsurge of new life characterised by the call to a life of dedication and devotion and a desire for more 'catholic' worship. These early sisterhoods had much in common, apart from attempts to live the Benedictine life, and, except for Mother Lydia Sellon's enclosed Sisters at Ascot Priory, all these communities led the mixed or active life. Moreover, they undertook the same types of work. Specialisation was rare, and a mixture of teaching, nursing, penitentiary, parish and orphanage work was common to almost all. The Mission Sisters of the Holy Name seem, therefore, to differ little from their contemporaries. Even their dedication to the Holy Name was not unshared, for 'The Name of Jesus' was taken as its title by a community founded in Essex in 1881.[156] Yet as the early history of the Community is studied against the background of contemporary sisterhoods, its distinctive characteristics become clear.

Firstly, the Community was distinguished by a great simplicity. At first this was due to circumstances, but it continued after it had begun to grow and prosper. This simplicity is an elusive quality to describe and it is probably more successfully conveyed by example than argument, for the Community's buildings demonstrate this aspect of its spirit quite conclusively. Most nineteenth-century sisterhoods felt an urge to establish themselves in conventual buildings which *looked* both monastic and medieval.[157] These great edifices were probably designed to convince the world and the sisters themselves that they really *were* nuns. Yet, strangely enough, the Sisters of

Chapel and Cloister

the Holy Name seem never to have so much as contemplated the erection of what might be called a 'real convent'. The mission house at Vauxhall, which Father Herbert built specially for the sisterhood, looked a perfectly ordinary London house, and when a new wing was added to the mother house at Malvern it was an unpretentious structure without one ecclesiastical feature. Only the cloister which connected the chapel with the two main buildings had doors and windows of ecclesiastical pattern. Thus the Gothic revival had little influence on the spirit of the Community, and there are few signs of romanticism amongst its early members. The sisters were content to be rather than to appear.

This simplicity may have been due to the community's second characteristic – its Catholic Evangelical spirit. A study of the early sisterhoods shows that the priests responsible for their foundation and subsequent direction were almost invariably Tractarians or 'Ritualists', protagonists of the advanced High Church party, and their members were ladies who had been influenced by their teaching.[158] But the founders of the Community of the Holy Name had a somewhat different background. 'High Church' and 'Ritualist' Father Herbert might be, yet he belonged to the small group of clergy who had come under Robert Aitken's converting power, and Mother Charlotte and Mother Frances Mary shared this spiritual background. This inevitably had its effect upon the Community. It is hard to describe the difference this made to the spirit of the community, but a difference there was: a greater freedom of spirit, perhaps, a greater stress on personal experience, a greater devotion to the *person* of Jesus, certainly a great stress on reality in religion. The dedicated lives of the early sisters were simply the result, the logical outcome, of a personal commitment to Jesus Himself, and Mother Frances Mary's notes show that the sisters were pointed towards a direct intimate relationship with Him through the powers of the Holy Spirit, rather than directed along a carefully mapped out path towards religious proficiency. This Evangelical spirit was also sometimes shown by a fear of undue reliance upon forms and institutions which could become ends in themselves. This is best illustrated by Mother Charlotte's words to a parish worker who was rashly urging the advantages of guilds as a help in the spiritual life without giving, as the mother thought, due prominence to the necessity of spiritual life in the soul before becoming a member of such an association: 'If you tie them up in a guild,' she said, 'without grace or liberty in their souls, you are only binding them in bundles to burn them.'[159]

The third characteristic of the Community was its strong mission spirit, though it is not easy to define the difference that this made. The works in which it was engaged were similar to those undertaken by other communities, and sisters of mercy and sisters of charity were concerned with the souls as well as the bodies of those to whom they ministered. The answer seems to be that it was a matter of emphasis. The fact that the sisters had from the first included the word 'mission' in their official title is significant, and it is possible that they were the first sisterhood to do so.[160] But whether this was so or not, the stress on mission was deeply impressed upon the formularies of the early sisterhood, and was from the first a distinguishing mark of the Community.

ENDNOTES – CHAPTER 11

[149]AR Ashwell, *Life of Samuel Wilberforce*, vol. I, pp.290-293.

[150]*First Report of the Royal Commission on Ritual*, 1867, p.51.

[151]It is probably that the Ascensiontide novena of prayer (begun in 1897 by Leo XIII) is meant by both these references.

[152]This intention is now made on Thursdays.

[153]Founded 1849 by Marion Rebecca Hughes, who is believed to have been the first woman to take religious vows since the Reformation.

[154]Founded 1894 by Gertrude Bromby.

[155]1964, pp.220-478, 528-530, 603.

[156]PF Anson, op. cit., p.528.

[157]Wantage is the obvious exception.

[158]The Community of the Epiphany, Truro, founded by Father Herbert's friend, Bishop G H Wilkinson, is an exception. It belongs to the same Catholic Evangelical background as the Community of the Holy Name.

[159]L. Herbert, *op. cit.*, p.18.

[160]The Wymering sisterhood seems to have been sometimes called a mission sisterhood (*Kalendar of the English Church*, 1871), but the sisters were also known as sisters of charity and sisters of mercy (ibid., and P F Anson, op. cit., p.375) so they can perhaps hardly claim the title. The Community of the Holy Cross (founded 1857) considered itself a mission sisterhood (Alan Russell, *The Community of the Holy Cross*, 1957, p.32.)

Part Two

CHAPTER 12

Mission Work – England

As was the case in many other communities, Moral Welfare work had always had a place in the Community's mission and outreach and, for many years, provision had been made in two traditional residential homes: the Home of the Good Shepherd and St Catherine's Mother and Baby Home. However, as the Welfare State continued to develop its own provision of services, there was no longer any call for houses such as HGS; and it closed in 1966.

St Catherine's, which had opened in 1944, moved from the convent into the former St Edward's Orphanage buildings in West Malvern in 1955. The girls, who came through Local Authorities and Voluntary Organisations all over the country, were only eligible for a place at the home if they intended to keep their babies. They stayed for two to three years and took part in physical education, needlework and cookery classes. They shared the housework, did their laundry and prepared feeds for the babies, but they also worked half-time at a factory, in service, or in schools. Before they left for work, bottles and other necessities had to be left ready for their babies, so that the other girls could look after them while they were out. For their final six months they stayed at home full-time in preparation for making an independent life for themselves and their child when they moved to their own flat.

As the years passed the Local Authority regulations became more stringent: they covered issues ranging from the size of rooms and other household provision to the proximity to local amenities. Directives instructing staff on how to manage the home also increased exponentially. Local Authorities policy changed, and small flats were provided for unmarried mothers and their babies, in preference to seeking a place in homes such as St Catherine's. Consequently, in 1969, CHN's involvement in the work came to an end and the home was closed.

Party for CSCS Children

The house itself was offered to the Commonwealth Students' Children's Society.[162] The children's mothers were studying in England, the majority training as nurses, before returning to their own countries in order to improve the healthcare provision there. Previously the children had been cared for in foster homes, which often proved unable to provide for their particular needs, or had attended day nurseries. There was a desperate need for proper residential care. CHN provided a sister, who had the help of two trained nursery nurses and two volunteers from the Community Service;[163] in addition three resident parents, and other volunteers helped at the weekends. The children were aged from a few months to seven years, and in 1970 the centre housed twenty children from Nigeria and the former Biafra.[164]

In 1974, sisters being needed elsewhere, CHN had to withdraw from this work.

Changes also took place in the Community's work with guests. In 1955 the Howsells, a home for elderly ladies, was handed over to the Local Council, and the West Malvern Guest House (which had gradually evolved into a second home for elderly ladies) was also closed.

From 1963 onwards, guests and visiting Associates or Companions, who had previously occupied a wing of the convent itself, were accommodated in St Saviour's, the large villa opposite the convent, the former St Catherine's. This provided guests with much-improved accommodation, for they now had their own chapel, refectory and garden. Although, at first, many regretted not being in the convent itself, the advantages of the new arrangements soon became apparent.

St Saviour's Guest House

The Community continued to be involved in retreat work. The demand for places of retreat, the provision of space and silence, often within the context of the daily worship of a Community, increased tremendously during the 1960s and 1970s and CHN was able to respond to this need when they accepted invitations to take over the running of Diocesan Retreat Houses. From 1961-1974 sisters worked at St Alban's, and from 1969-1978 they were also at St Teilo's Retreat Centre in Cardiff.

At first, sisters were fully occupied with the work generated by the day-to-day running of these houses and in the extending of hospitality to guests and retreatants, who arrived with many different needs. In January 1969, however, that pattern began to change when it was agreed that a further two sisters should go to St Albans, to enable the sisters there to do mission work in the diocese in addition to looking after the house.

In 1958, CHN agreed to take over the running of Chester Retreat House and, as sisters were to remain there for the next forty years, it is possible trace some of the developments in the nature of their work over that time.

Chester Retreat House

The house had initially occupied a single property in the corner of Abbey Square, on the doorstep of the cathedral. However, the growth in the popularity of retreats led, in 1965, to the adjacent house being incorporated into the Retreat House, in order to provide the extra accommodation needed. Some modernisation of its rather spartan conditions was also necessary, and so during this period both fabric and facilities underwent a major transformation, but one which sought to retain a basic simplicity.

During the 1980s, weekends were predominantly booked for parish group retreats, whereas bookings during the week included clergy retreats and selection conferences both for those hoping to train as ordained ministers in the Church of England, and for those hoping to do so in the Church of Wales. Around this time, a deliberate move was made away from sisters spending the majority of their time in domestic duties, by arranging for secular staff to be employed in the kitchen and the house.

With a household of six, sisters were then free to respond to invitations to speak to groups further afield, and to lead quiet days and meditations. The sisters ran an occasional retreat, which was open to all and they responded to a growing number of requests from those who wished to have an IGR.[165]
They were also involved in the ministry of spiritual direction at the house and, increasingly, in parish and chaplaincy work outside it.

CHN maintained its work in a number of different parish mission houses and branch houses and, during the 1950s, continued to withdraw from its larger mission houses, in order to begin work in smaller houses, which could be staffed more effectively. In addition to the original mission house in Vauxhall, the houses at Wellingborough, Staveley, Birmingham and Stepney[166] were also relinquished. New, smaller houses were opened at Brighton, Torquay and Newcastle-upon-Tyne.

Involvement in Sunday schools, mothers and toddlers' meetings, confirmation classes and parish visiting still formed the backbone of sisters' work, but the growth of the Welfare State meant that there was no longer the same extent of serious poverty to relieve. Consequently, sisters no longer needed to organise vast parochial teas, and the former blanket house-to-house visiting was replaced by selected visits: for a pastoral or a funeral visit, to give Communion to the housebound, for a pre-baptism discussion or marriage preparation. Methods had become more informal too: guilds[167] being replaced by home-groups, and mixed-sex groups being prepared together for confirmation.

Teaching in Sunday School

New forms of parish work had also appeared; the visiting of Care Homes for the elderly, the involvement in hospital and university chaplaincies, work in schools and with newly-arrived immigrants.

CHN's first Newcastle house opened in 1961 in Elswick, a district where professional people, such as doctors and lawyers etc. had lived in the grand houses, three or four storeys high and containing large basements. When their owners moved further out of the city into smaller, modern-built houses, the older properties were converted into tenements and eventually a very extensive district became a 'slum area'.

The local parish of St Matthew's was destined to be united with the adjacent parish and the property in all the streets surrounding it had been condemned to demolition. New blocks of flats were to be built and the whole area reconstructed, and it was hoped that sisters would prove a stable presence at this time of upheaval and dislocation, and provide the local people with moral support and a listening ear.

Within the first few years of being in Elswick, some of the condemned streets were demolished and blocks of flats built in their place. A number of these flats were for the elderly and the sisters soon found that many suffered a great deal of loneliness and isolation in their new homes. One elderly lady, who had been moved from her small condemned house which she had kept very neat and attractive, showed a sister around her new flat with all its modern gadgets. She was very proud of it, with its glass doors and cupboards. Later on the same sister called again. At first there was no reply to her ring but, after a short time, the old lady came to the door, looking miserable and shaken. Moving into the kitchen, she put her head down and sobbed. At length she said, 'Sister, I can't bear it. I am so lonely. When I was in my old house I could open my door and call across to a neighbour or slip in next door to my friend. Here, I open my door and there is nothing but this bare empty passage with all its closed doors. The lift frightens me and I don't know anyone who lives in this building. My friend, who lived next door and I asked to be moved together, but the authorities took no notice. She's in another block altogether.' Fortunately in this case, when the sisters contacted the authorities they were able to make an arrangement for the two friends to be housed together in the same block, but the problems caused by relocation were vast and complicated.

Once the sisters were established in the area, they were able to gather together a group of women for a weekly afternoon meeting, which offered friendship, gospel teaching and simple worship. However, by 1969, the extent of the clearances in Elswick made it necessary for the sisters to move house, and they continued their work in St George's parish, Jesmond.

Bible Study in Walker

Early contacts with the hospital paved the way for the incorporation of a sister into the chaplaincy team and, in 1973 another sister took on a similar role at the university. The chaplaincy centre provided an office for chaplains of the three main denominations: Anglican, Methodist and Roman Catholic. It also housed a students' sitting room and dining hall. Twice a week, sisters would attend the early Eucharist and join in the communal breakfast which followed. They also visited the halls of residence, and shared supper with the students who lived there one evening a week. Various Christian organisations met at the centre: the Anglican Society, the Roman Catholic Newman Society and the Christian Union (which was ecumenical). Sisters attended some of their meetings, and found ways to engage with the students. Certain individuals would indicate that they had found it helpful to talk, and arrange to meet with the sister, every week or fortnight, either in the chaplaincy office or at their homes. The sisters also held regular Sunday afternoon teas, informal occasions which enabled them to get to know those living in the student flats.

In 1980, at the request of the recently-appointed vicar, the Community moved house again into the tough Walker district, and were to remain there until 1993.

During the 1960s and 1970s, the number of sisters in Community continued to fall, so that even the houses which needed only five or six sisters soon came under pressure. Reluctantly, the decision was taken to close the houses in Coventry, Brighton and Torquay in order that sisters might be available to respond new invitations.

Consequently, by 1973, the Community was in a position to open a new branch house in Basingstoke,[168] where sisters would work with the newly-formed team ministry, which covered the town centre and several 1970s new council house estates. There, the team of clergy, together with the hospital chaplains, met with the sisters each week in order to plan together the pastoral work in the parishes.

Although originally invited to be a 'house of prayer', the expectation soon developed, that the sisters would have a very active role, and be able to build up their network of contacts and develop relationships in many different settings.

On the Popley estate, a house celebration of the Eucharist was held in four different areas, so that the clergy and sisters could rotate and meet different groups of people. Neighbours, who felt comfortable dropping in for a small, informal, weekday Eucharist in the sisters' house, would never have dreamed of attending worship in the Parish Church on a Sunday. On the Brighton Hill estate, meanwhile, a mothers and toddlers group began to hold a simple service at their weekly meeting.

After a period of several years, the sisters moved into a small council house on the Oakridge estate which, having previously been the local police house, had a room which was ideal for meetings between vulnerable people and their social workers, or those from the education and health services.

Parish Visiting

In order to enable such new patterns of mission and outreach to evolve according to the changing needs of society and of the church, CHN decided to withdraw from St Alban's Retreat House in 1977 and St Teilo's, Cardiff in 1978. It was then in a position to open a small house in the new town of Basildon, later that year.

Basildon was a large new town[169] and the three sisters were able to share in their neighbours' experience of settling into an area where all were recent arrivals. They had a wide brief and, though supported by the parish financially, were not committed to sacristy work, but free to discern where they might best be involved. The parish had a team ministry with four clergy, including a hospital chaplain. Sisters were able to help with pastoral needs identified by the ministry team, including those at the hospital, but also to become involved with local needs, where they felt best able to help.

One of the sisters, who had been a teacher before entering community, went into the local comprehensive school to introduce herself, and found herself taking an RE class for an 'A' level group! She was also involved at a local primary school.

In responding to the needs, both of the local churches and also to those of their neighbours, among whom they lived and prayed, the pioneering work of the sisters in the Basingstoke and Basildon houses enabled a different pattern of branch house work to evolve – one which would be developed in other houses in the future. The Basildon house closed in1985 and the house in Basingstoke in 1989, as sisters were asked to work in other areas of the country.

The diocese of Zululand is linked with the diocese of Carlisle, and on a visit to the country, the Bishop of Carlisle had met some of the CHN sisters there, and had been greatly impressed by their life and work. As there was no Religious community in his diocese, when a new vicarage was built for St John's parish in Keswick, he took the opportunity to invite sisters from the English province to establish a branch house in the old vicarage.

The sisters were asked to establish a 'house of prayer and hospitality', and to be a spiritual resource for the diocese. In addition to making the vicarage - renamed Holy Name House - a place of welcome for all, they were soon in demand to give addresses, and lead prayer workshops, quiet days and retreats in parishes situated in many different parts of the diocese. They also designated one sister to be the Parish Sister for St John's church.

In the early 1990s, the diocesan work was relinquished, but the Community's life of prayer and hospitality continued at Holy Name House until the final group of sisters withdrew in 2009.

At the 1984 Chapter, when the Community agreed to go to Keswick, it also responded to an invitation to open a house with three sisters in Radford, an inner city area of Nottingham - one sister to work at each of the three local churches. In 1992, after discussion with the Diocese of Southwell, in which Radford is situated, CHN negotiated a change to the remit of the house. It was to remain a house of prayer and to be open to respond to local needs, but no longer to provide a sister to work in each of the churches.

It was necessary to make a break with the previous pattern, so the sisters decided that they would no longer attend staff meetings or church committees etc., for the first three to four months at least. When they attended the Eucharist, they would be there as ordinary members of the congregation, and not in any ecclesiastical role. They did go visiting and engage in pastoral care, but were no longer Parish Sisters in the traditional sense.

As they lived their particular lifestyle among their neighbours, joining in with neighbourhood events, shopping locally, walking the local areas, people around began to drop in, and relationships were gradually built up. Sisters often found themselves on the margins – for instance, there was a Mental Health Project for those who were finding it hard to be in the community, and sisters spent time there, sitting around and generally and loitering, so that they could network and gradually become drawn in to Local Associations and Community Groups.

Lunchtime Eucharist in Radford House

The Eucharist, held at the house each Friday, was followed by a simple bread and cheese lunch, and on average fifteen people each week squashed into the tiny chapel, and ate together afterwards. As far as individual ministry was concerned, the sisters needed to find out where they could serve the area best; eg. one sister attended a local surgery, giving time to listen to patients, whose ten-minute appointment with their doctor could only begin to scratch the surface of their complex needs. On several occasions one of the sisters gave the 'Thought for the Day' on Radio Nottingham and several of the local people acknowledged this, owning it as a contribution from 'their neighbourhood'. In common with many other households, the small community cared for two elderly sisters, enabling them to make their own contribution. The house itself was well used by people seeking quiet or a listening ear, and it was also able to provide a room where a local retired priest and psychotherapist could see clients, many of whom would not have been able to afford counselling otherwise.

By being in the neighbourhood, living alongside the people (but with their own distinctive lifestyle), sisters were sharing the things that mattered to their neighbours: going to the same shops, having the same hassles with dustmen, living with the disruptive behaviour in the alleyways, noise at night etc. In 2006, the Nottingham household moved to a smaller house within the area and remained there until 2009, when CHN withdrew from the work in Radford.

ENDNOTES - CHAPTER 12

[161]Approved Schools were introduced as a result of the Children and Young Persons Act 1933. They were residential institutions to which young people could be sent by a court, either for committing offences or because they were beyond parental control. They were mostly run by voluntary bodies, but subject to regular visits from Home Office inspectors.

[162] The Commonwealth Student's Children's Society (CSCS) was an organisation responsible for the welfare of the children of students from commonwealth countries.

[163] Community Service Volunteers, founded in 1962 by Mora and Alec Dickson, is the UK's largest volunteering and training charity.

[164] Biafra, officially the Republic of Biafra, was a secessionist state in south-eastern Nigeria that existed from 30 May 1967 to 15 January 1970.

[165] An Individually Guided Retreat (IGR) is usually based on the Ignatian Spiritual Exercises. The Spiritual Exercises are a compilation of meditations, prayers, and contemplative practices developed by St Ignatius Loyola to help people deepen their relationship with God. In an IGR the retreatant is given a series of bible passages with which to pray, during a silent retreat, and meets daily with a retreat guide, who will help them to reflect on each day's prayer and offer guidelines and resources for the next day.

[166] This house had replaced the house at Pimlico in 1955.

[167] A guild was a society for a particular group of lay people within a parish, eg. altar servers, mothers, men etc.

[168] Basingstoke, an old market town was developed rapidly in the 1960s as a London overspill estate.

[169] The New Towns were built as a result of the New Towns Act 1946. They were usually developed around the historic core of a small town, and were designed to deal with the housing shortage in London after the devastation of the Second World War. Basildon was designated a New Town on 4th January 1949.

CHAPTER 13

At the Convent

The wholesale changes for Roman Catholic Communities, resulting from the Second Vatican Council (1962-65), also had an impact on Religious within the Anglican Church and a number of meetings and conferences, arranged to explore issues of common importance regarding the purpose and ordering of the Religious Life, were attended by CHN sisters.

The first 'Conference for Religious' took place in Oxford in July 1964 and reported that, 'a lot of rather sweeping changes are taking place in the work and purpose of Religious communities as a whole.' Further conferences were held in 1967 and 1974, in Oxford and York respectively. In 1974 the Communities Consultative Council was set up to be a representative body of Anglican Religious and the following year CCC Area Meetings were held, including one at Malvern.

During the years of the mid-20th century, many requests were received for a pair of sisters to assist on 'a Mission'. The Mission Team was generally led by priests who were members of men's Religious communities and 'the Mission' usually lasted between ten days and a fortnight.

Mission Team

There was a great demand for sisters to do this work - during 1954, the Community was asked by the Reverend Mother to pray for pairs of sisters helping on nine such missions.[170] A sister who was part of a team on many missions, records that her first mission in May 1955, was led by one of the priests of the Society of St Francis and covered one Welsh-speaking and two English-speaking churches. Another SSF brother led the meeting for the junior children after school and the two CHN Sisters took charge of that for the seniors. They met in a church and had at least sixty senior children, who one of the sisters put through a rigorous knee-drill! One day a boy let off a cracker, thinking this would throw this little sister, but she didn't bat an eyelid and responded in her usual soft voice, (she had been a Norland Nanny!) 'Oh no, dear, we don't do *that* in God's house' - end of trouble!

Although requests to assist on traditional parish missions continued to be received, the number decreased over the 1960s and 1970s and other requests for sisters reflected a gradual change in the church's approach to mission and ministry. Sisters were still invited to preach, to give traditional addresses and to

189

say formal Offices when leading retreats and quiet days; but also to lead discussions and run Advent and Lent Courses with group participation; to lead prayer workshops on different ways of prayer, which included times of informal prayer, to lead school assemblies and help at children's clubs and to participate in Youth Work initiatives. Youth Work became important in the 1970s, as society began to recognise the emergence of the concept of 'teenagers', who had their own culture and needs. Churches set up Youth Clubs and sought to involve the young people in worship with the introduction of music groups with guitars and drums and the singing of new choruses alongside or in place of the traditional hymns. Christian Youth Weeks and Pilgrimages grew in popularity, including to the ecumenical community of Taize.[171] CHN soon received requests for a sister to teach and help at youth weeks, held both in England and abroad, and several have accompanied groups on pilgrimage to Taize.

During the 1970s, CHN sisters, living at the convent, began to develop more contacts in the local area. Roman Catholic sisters from the nearby Stanbrook Abbey invited CHN sisters to visit them during the week of prayer for Christian Unity.[172] Links were also made with Malvern Priory and other nearby churches, including some of the more evangelical churches.

This was the time when the Charismatic Renewal Movement[173] was beginning to influence developments in both the Anglican and the Roman Catholic Church and it also had considerable influence within the life of Religious communities, CHN included. In August 1973, the Community studied a paper on 'Life in the Spirit' and the following year during the Easter Day Mass, there was the opportunity to receive 'Anointing and the Laying on of Hands'. Sisters attended a 'Celebration Conference for Religious' which studied 'the place of music, movement and drama in the formation of the human personality and its application to renewal in the Religious Life' and there were also opportunities for them to take part in courses on the development of the Healing Ministry and on 'Pastoral and Prayer Counselling'. In July 1978, Mother Penelope attended an Anglican Leaders' Conference for Spiritual Renewal' and in 1979, sisters attended an Anglo-Catholic Renewal Conference. In August 1982, Sister Margaret Magdalene of the Community of St Mary the Virgin, Wantage, was invited to the Malvern convent to give a series of addresses on 'New Ways of Expressing Worship'.

In 1977, two sisters took part in a television programme about the Religious Life and, in August 1983, others took part in the BBC Religious Affairs Programme 'This is the Day'. Sisters were also interviewed for local radio programmes and made regular contributions to their 'Thought for the Day' slots. On a lighter note, a team of sisters took part in the TV quiz show 'Busman's Holiday'![174]

Some of the requests received by the Community in the late 1970s and thereafter, led to situations in which some sisters would develop various individual ministries.

Working with Deaf Children

In 1979, after previous short visits to Roedean School, it was agreed that Sister Renate should serve there as chaplain for a year. CHN sent a sister to be part of the chaplaincy team at Bangor University for a term, and another spent a term at Lincoln Theological College. For three months in the summer of 1982, Sister Jennifer Mary was attached to the Lee Abbey Community.[175] Sister Carol was later to become one of the Lee Abbey's lay chaplains, for a period of several years.

Meanwhile, within the Worcester Diocese, Sister Lilias began a ministry among the Deaf.

The events, in which sisters took part, were quite varied: in July 1980, Sister Carol attended her first meeting of the General Synod of the Church of England, having been elected to represent Anglican Religious, whilst some of Sister Jane Cecily's songs were recorded and others took part in prayer marches and other protests.

In order that the Community could keep abridge of developments in issues of social concern, various speakers were invited to the convent to talk about their field of knowledge. One of the items covered was the new Nationality Bill,[177] which was due to be introduced at that time.

Prayer March

ENDNOTES - CHAPTER 13

[170] General Letter 7 January 1954.

[171] The ecumenical Taizé Community, in <u>France</u>, whose brethren originate from over thirty different countries, was founded in 1940 by <u>Brother Roger Schutz</u>. Each year over 100,000 young people make a pilgrimage there to experience its prayer for peace and reconciliation, its liturgy – a blend of silence and simple meditative chants, and simple communal lifestyle.

[172] The Week of Prayer for Christian Unity, usually held from 18-25 January, is an ecumenical event, involving Christian communities across the world.

[173] The Charismatic Renewal Movement began in American Protestant churches in the early 20th century. Charismatic Christians believe that the gifts of the Holy Spirit, as described in the New Testament, are available to contemporary Christians through the infilling or baptism of the Holy Spirit, often accompanied by the laying on of hands. These spiritual gifts are believed to result in: speaking in tongues (the language of the spirit – consisting of connected speech-like syllables), the interpretation of that language, the hearing of prophecies, healing, and discernment of spirits (the supernatural power to detect the realm of the spirits and their activities and discern whether or not they are of God.

[174] Busman's Holiday was a British television game show, in which each team of three contestants shared the same career. They were dressed in their regular work clothes and the rounds of the quiz included one on their own profession.

[175] Lee Abbey is a nationwide ecumenical Christian organisation which has a vision of "sharing Christ through relationships". Its 280-acre site near Lynton, North Devon has a house which functions as a conference, retreat and holiday centre, whilst providing a home to the members of the community who runs it. This community is made up of young people, from many different countries, who say a daily Office together and work, either in the house, or on the estate. They are usually members of the community for a few years, before moving on to other employment.

[176] CND - the Campaign for Nuclear Disarmament was founded to advocate unilateral nuclear disarmament by the UK and opposed the building of nuclear power stations. It also lobbied for international nuclear disarmament and for tighter international arms regulation. At Easter 1958, it supported a well-attended 52-mile march from London to the Atomic Weapons Research Establishment at Aldermaston and, thereafter, organised annual marches.

[177] The British Nationality Act 1981 reclassified British citizenship into three categories: British citizenship, British Dependent Territories citizenship and British Overseas citizenship.

It provided that British citizenship - held by those with a close connection with the United Kingdom, Isle of Man and Channel Islands - would *automatically* carry a right of abode in the UK. The other categories of British nationality would not automatically hold such status. It thus removed the automatic right to citizenship by birth in the UK, and was therefore a subject of considerable controversy.

CHAPTER 14

Mission Work Overseas: Lesotho

In August 1959, following a visit by Bishop John Maund of Basutoland, CHN had agreed to open to open a branch house in Leribe and to work towards the incorporation of the Community of St Mary at the Cross (SMMS) into the Community of the Holy Name.

After Bishop John had discussed the proposition with the sisters of both the Community of St Michael and All Angels in Bloemfontein and SMMS in Leribe and obtained their approval, the next step was for Sisters Alphonsina, Hilda, Adelaide and Gertrude to spend two years at the convent in Malvern, learning the traditions and customs of CHN with the other new English novices. After two years of training, they were admitted to full and equal membership of CHN and, in 1962, returned to Basutoland, in company with a group of English sisters, to work together to establish a multi-racial convent, where the other African sisters of SMMS would be trained in the ways of CHN, whilst maintaining their own culture and customs.

Though the Community in Malvern had tried to prepare in advance for their arrival, there were bound to be some misconceptions. Bishop John had mentioned that most Basotho had porridge for breakfast, so the kitchen staff duly prepared porridge, just for the novices' table. Several CHN novices enjoyed this extra treat, but not the Africans. They took one taste and avoided it. What had not been explained was that the South African porridge is made of mealie flour, from ground, dried maize or from kaffir corn[178] and is therefore a totally different consistency!

Over the next two years, whilst the African sisters learned to adapt to the ways of CHN and the English sisters chosen to be the pioneers in Lesotho attempted to learn Sesotho, the local language, the lengthy process of obtaining visas was completed, passages were booked well in advance and trunks and packing cases were filled with all the requisite equipment.

In October 1962 on the return journey, after two weeks on board the *Athlone Castle*, the four African Sisters, accompanied by Sisters Mary Francis (appointed Sister Superior), Felicity and Marjorie Jean, (who had both worked in Liberia), Rachel Christine, Jean Mary and Mother Audrey Mary (who was to stay for the first three months), docked at Cape Town.

Certain items, peculiar to the Community, had been taken out from England and these included a trunk which was full of grey material so that new CHN habits could be made for all the SMMS sisters in Leribe as soon as possible after arrival and a tea-chest containing shoes for them to wear. Unfortunately, this caused havoc when Sister Rachel Christine, who had signed the paperwork, was totally flummoxed by the questioning of the Customs' officials - they wanted to be sure there was no plan to sell it all!

The 'Athone Castle'

Bishop John met the group on the quay in Cape Town and had made arrangements for hospitality there for the day, as the train going north wasn't due to leave until 9 p.m. St Monica's Mother and Baby Home, whose matron was a school-friend of Mother Audrey Mary, had agreed to look after the group and the first thing they were introduced to on eventually arriving there at about 10.00 a.m., having survived the complications of customs and immigration, was 'morning tea'. This was no simple cup of coffee and a biscuit affair, but a table laden with scones, sandwiches, cakes and biscuits. After refreshment, the staff had organised a car trip round the bay to see some of the sights of Cape Town and the beauties of the coastline. They had had experience travelling on South Africa's railways, and were very generous in equipping the sisters for their 42-hour journey up to Ficksburg. Food and drink were supplied for all, and blankets and pillows for the African sisters.

At the time when the sisters travelled through South Africa to Basutoland, the Nationalist Government in South Africa had been in power for fourteen years and their policy of apartheid[179] was well established. It had been enforced with authority and brutality. A group of Acts had been passed which made almost any form of association between the people of different races in the country illegal. These included the Group Areas Act, delineating where different racial groups could live, the Mixed Marriages Act, forbidding sexual relationships between the racial groups and several Segregation Acts. The train journey gave the English sisters their first experience of living under apartheid conditions, as the African sisters had to be in a separate section of the train set apart for the Bantu,[180] and sleeping berths were not provided for them (hence the kind provision of blankets at St Monica's. 'Nie Blankes' ('Whites Only') was a notice seen in all public places at that time and the sisters had to get used to seeing them and obeying them! As they approached Leribe, their feeling of excitement grew, though it was tempered by a degree of apprehension, as they waited to meet the other members of SMMS.

Once in Leribe, a right turn from the main street revealed the solid, stone church of St Saviour's and the small, iron, gate, which led to the convent directly behind it. On the other side of this gate, the sisters of SMMS were waiting. They too had been preparing for this adventure and the changes it would mean to their community life. As sisters of the two communities waited to greet each other, there was both excitement and trepidation about the immediate future.

196

The African sisters were anxious that the practical preparations they had made would not be suitable. They had put fresh grass in some of the mattresses, so that CHN could have fresh ones when they arrived, anticipating that they would sleep in the house where the CSM&AA sisters had slept. But what would happen if CHN wanted to sleep in the same accommodation as SMMS immediately? Different diets and ways of working would be two other areas of particular concern. Sister Lucia was able to explain why her sisters were so diffident about coming to eat with the English Sisters, despite having had instruction from one of the sisters of CSM&AA in the correct way to lay the tables and use knives and forks! They had only ever been into the house previously, to do manual work for the CSM&AA sisters, and so to eat together in that house would be a culture-shock, to which they would need time to adjust.

For the three returning African sisters (Sister Adelaide had decided that she was not called to the Religious Life and been taken home during the course of the journey) it was a great homecoming and they were awaited with expectancy and excitement. But they had lived with white people and eaten white people's food for more than two years; would they have forgotten how to be Basotho? They came back wearing a different religious habit; would they still be at home with their African sisters?

The English sisters had tried to learn a little Sesotho. They were open to understand Basotho customs and way of life, but *they* too had anxieties. Would the two groups be able to understand and trust each other? Would they be able to survive on each other's food? Would it be possible to apportion work, other than on racial lines, so that there would be very little inequality?

However, all these questions were put to one side as they were met by Sister Calista, who was sitting at her spinning wheel. She leapt up enthusiastically with a greeting and was soon joined by other sisters who rushed to form a welcoming party. The English sisters were very grateful that rooms had been prepared for them, for all the preparations that had been made for them to have a bedroom each in the main house that first night, and more than ready for their first night's sleep at the new Basutoland branch house.

At Vespers on the following day, Bishop John officiated at a short formal admission ceremony during which the SMMS sisters who had not been to England, became novices in CHN, dressed in their new habits and wimples. The whole group now faced the task of getting to know each other and the English sisters began the task of learning their way round.

Originally, the main house, built towards the end of the 19th century, had been the rectory of the first Rector of Leribe, Canon John Widdicombe. Substantially built of burnt brick, it contained nine rooms. The stoep[181] ran the length of the house and provided a cool place to sit during the heat of the day. This was the house which had been occupied by the CSM&AA sisters and, in addition to bedrooms, dining room and sitting room, at the far end of the central corridor, two large rooms had been added, for use as classrooms. These were soon to be converted into the refectory and kitchen.

The grounds belonging to the house were extensive and, as mission work and community life had developed, the buildings had expanded. Nearly all the other buildings were of built of mud, with thatched roofs, in the traditional Basotho style. They had been built at different times, as need dictated and were either long low buildings, or traditional rondavels.[182]

Some of the long buildings were used as dormitories for the hostel children – each with one end curtained off to form sleeping quarters for the sister on duty. The rondavels were used as offices for those in charge of the hostels and one of the larger ones was used as the sisters' refectory, while the children had a small, separate dining room near to the kitchen. All these buildings were very simply furnished and most of the food was cooked in large three-legged pots, over an outside fire.

Leribe Chapel

One good-sized brick building, situated at the opposite end of the compound to the main house, was used as the sisters' chapel. It had been built with the help of funds from English communities when the African community was fairly new. The sisters had decorated its interior walls with geometric designs, similar to those on their own homes, and although it was close to the hostel buildings, the noise from the children was too little to be disruptive.

As the sisters began to live together, one of the main unifying elements was the common prayer of the whole community; they met seven times a day for corporate prayer (Offices). All the Offices were in English, but fortunately the majority of the Basotho sisters had a considerable amount of English, as it was taught from the first year in school and from the fourth year upwards all lessons were given in English. However, though *the Offices* were in English, *the daily Eucharist* was in Sesotho and, as the English sisters were already familiar with its form and content, it provided a golden opportunity for them to hear the language spoken, and to become more familiar with its rhythms and cadences. By joining in with the responses they were able to gain confidence in speaking Sesotho themselves and to improve the standard of their pronunciation.

On Sundays they attended the Eucharist at the parish church, where hymns were in Sesotho, but often set to familiar English tunes, which enabled the sisters to concentrate on the language. Certain words and phrases were repeated so often in the liturgy, that they became an integral part of their mental furniture. However, learning a new language in this way was not altogether satisfactory, as the vocabulary and phraseology of the liturgy were not the most appropriate for communication in the kitchen and the garden, or in general conversation!

It was appropriate that some areas of the Community's work be continued by the African sisters alone. Sister Calista and one lay helper taught a small number of young Basotho women at the Weaving School, and St Mary's Hostel cared for approximately forty school children, aged from 6-11, who were resident there in order to be able to attend schools nearby.

The English sisters could, initially, be of most use in the 'domestic' work of the convent. It required a willingness to work sensitively alongside the Africans, learning how they managed with the limited resources available, eg on Mondays, which was wash-day, work started at dawn, when an enormous tank outside the laundry was filled up with water and the wood fire underneath it was lit and kept fed, whilst the Community was in chapel. By 8.00 a.m., the water was boiling and every zinc bath was commandeered and filled with clothes for soaking. From that time onwards, sisters worked together: scrubbing, rubbing and rinsing. By dinnertime all the washing was on the line and, before the end of the afternoon, it was ready to bring in. Tuesday was ironing day, when all the flat irons were heated up on primus stoves for, until 1973, the only establishments in Leribe with electricity were those which provided their own generators.

Feeding the Hens

Two other areas, in which sisters of both races could work together, were the kitchen and the garden. The only kitchen available at that time was small, and was tucked away at the back of the main house. It was equipped with a domestic size wood burning stove named 'The Modern Mistress', whose three-gallon water tank ensured a constant supply of hot water. The five-hundred gallon tank outside the kitchen was attached to the main supply of water in Leribe and filled from that during the hours in which the mains opened their taps; in that first dry October that would have been for only four or five hours daily. In spite of these limited catering facilities, it was felt essential that all the sisters should begin to eat together as soon as possible.

While it would take some time to be fully integrated, so that all were eating and sleeping the same building, with a Common Room that really was a 'common' room, the first step was taken when everyone began to meet in the refectory for mid-afternoon tea and general conversation. It was at one of those occasions that the English sisters experienced the African gift for mimicry, as Sister Anastasia began to take off first one and then another of the English sisters. Through bursts of tears and laughter, the others egged her on with shouts of, 'do Mother Audrey Mary', or, 'do Sister Mary Francis'. Simply by walking across the room with one hand in a particular position, she had captured the idiosyncrasies of one or the other. As a bank of such shared experiences was gradually built up, everyone became more at ease with one another, and their initial fears and anxieties began to melt away.

As the next step was to eat together, a great deal of consideration had to go into the production of a suitable menu. The staple food in Basutoland is 'papa', ie. porridge - made from ground maize or kaffir corn-flour which has been cooked to a stiff paste with water. It is eaten with sour milk, with vegetables or, on the rare occasions when the family can afford it, with meat and gravy. 'Papa' is to the Basotho what potatoes are to the English. It was therefore essential to use dishes from both cultures to ensure that none felt deprived, while all had a balanced diet.

Sister Marjorie Jean's main task was to develop the garden and to make the convent as self-sufficient as possible in fruit and vegetables. The land in front of the main house was dark with: overgrown wisteria, laurel, dusty cypresses and rose bushes - some reaching to a height of twelve feet. Between them were hard laterite[183] paths, and the bare red earth was obstructed at intervals by trees, simply left where they had fallen, victims of lightning.

A group of local prisoners was engaged to clear the land of overgrown bushes and trees, taking the wood in exchange for their labour, and a patch of the cleared land was earmarked for development as a vegetable patch. It was hard land, needing pickaxes to break it up, and the digging in of a great deal of compost and manure to bring it back to life.

All available water was needed for domestic purposes – there was none to spare for use in the garden. However, by digging trenches to make use of the convent's rubbish and waste water to feed and water the soil, and then recovering them once filled, a sizeable plot of fertile soil was created where beans, radishes, lettuces and various other types of vegetables and salads were planted. For every bush and tree removed, fruit trees were planted, including plums, peaches, apricots and figs.

Later, a lawn, flower beds, and a rose bed were planted in order to enhance the approach to the convent, as well as climbing plants which could hide the giant water tanks.

Bulk supplies of food and other items had to be fetched from Ficksburg on the bus. These were privately owned, the majority of owners having just one or two vehicles, which they drove themselves, and they varied considerably in road worthiness - few would have passed an English MOT test! They lined up at the bus stop in the market place and touted for custom; only when the buses were completely full, every available seat taken, and people standing or crouching on every square inch of floor space, would the bus set off. The return journey could be even more hazardous as everyone was returning, laden with shopping; Sister Marjorie Jean recalls making such a journey, lugging rolls of chicken wire, sacks of fertilizer, garden stakes and wood, all for use in the garden. Large items were loaded on to the roof and firmly tied down, but the rest had to be crammed inside with the passengers.

Petronella the Cow

As the shops did not import milk from South Africa, milk powder had to be used in its place. Although several households in the town kept a cow, they produced only enough milk for that family's needs. The Assistant District Commissioner, however, had a surplus, which he was willing to sell to the sisters, and he suggested that they look after his cow while he was away on leave, to see if they would be able to manage a cow of their own. Herding cows and milking them was not something any of the sisters had done before. Although Basutoland had always been an agricultural country, and most people counted their wealth in cattle, their care had traditionally been a male preserve. A few of the sisters were game to learn and have memories of dark cold mornings, on which they would take out a stool and bucket and pray that the cow would be co-operative. On the whole, that proved to be the case, and the Community decided to invest in a cow of their own. The first was named Petronella and she was soon joined by a second, Anna; both gifts from parishes in England who wanted to assist the Community in a practical way.

At the start of 1963, Mother Audrey Mary returned to England accompanied by Sisters Calista, Francina and Frangeni. Of the ten SMMS sisters who had greeted the newcomers, Sister Anastasia was the senior and, had she been unwilling to take part in the task of uniting the two communities, then the experiment might have failed. She knew very little English and worked hard at helping all the new sisters to speak Sesotho more fluently.

Two of the other elderly senior sisters were Sister Anna Pabatso and Sister Mary Magdalene. The former was no longer very active, but spent many hours crocheting dozens of white girdles for sale to the clergy. Her particular contribution to the Community was to clean everyone's shoes on Saturday mornings, in preparation for the Sunday Mass. She would find each sister and demand, with powerful gestures, that they remove their shoes. Then, as they continued to work barefoot, she sat on the lawn surrounded by a motley assortment of shoes and sandals. Polish was very liberally applied, and she would continue to brush and polish, until the shine reached her exacting standards.

Sister Mary Magdalene was disabled, having had polio in her younger days. She wore calipers and walked with a stick. She was a very gifted needlewoman and could often be seen, outside under the trees, passing on her skills to a small class of girls or young women who had dropped out of primary school, in all probability because their parents could not afford the fees. The acquisition of simple sewing techniques would help boost their employment prospects.

Sister Maria looked after the wafer bakery, Sister Veronica Mary, originally from Zululand, taught in the primary school and Sister Elizabetha was in charge of one of the hostels. The final member of the group was Sister Lucia, who had joined SMMS only a year before CHN sisters arrived.

Basutoland is a small country in southern Africa, similar in size to Wales and in the early 1970s the population was around one million. The lowlands are five thousand feet above sea level, which gives the air clarity and purity and from almost anywhere in the country there are views of the mountains, snow-capped in winter. The majority of the population live in the small villages and depend on the land and their cattle to survive. Good rains produce a good harvest; but poor rains, often mean no food. It is, therefore, no surprise that Basutoland's motto is 'khotso, pula, nala' (peace, rain, plenty).

Basutoland Landscape

Education is seen as a way out of poverty and families work hard to scrape together the school fees. Girls often go to school earlier than the boys, as it is traditional that the eldest boy should do the herding, until the next one in the family is old enough to take over. However, in the 1970s few children completed primary school, and fewer still went on to secondary education, so it was rare for adults to gain secondary or professional qualifications at that time.

Basutoland could not provide jobs that would bring in a living wage and by the mid-20th century, two thirds of Basutoland's male population was working in the gold and diamond mines across the border in South Africa – the only job available to them. They would go for nine months at a time and were housed in single-sex hostels on the mine compound. None of this was good for the development of family life in Basutoland, nor for the cultivation of the land, but it *did* bring in an income. The women worked in the fields, looked after any livestock and brought up the children.

One of the main works of the Community was the care of primary school children, separated into two groups according to their age, in the two hostels. Thanks to those hostels, it was possible for children from the mountains and from isolated villages to get a primary education, for there were no schools in their own neighbourhoods. Hostels were popular with parents who could afford to pay and there were definite advantages for the children: they had a well-lit space in which to do their homework, regular meals, and only a short walk to school. There was always a long waiting list. In common with all school boarding hostels, the children were responsible for many of the daily chores and, for half an hour before school, they all had their scheduled tasks. On Saturday mornings the major manual work was done: all the furniture was taken outside so that the floors and walls could be washed, and the windows cleaned. By mid-morning all was spick and span, and the workers had their break, with a cup of juice and bread spread with peanut butter. They then prepared to go into town for their weekly shopping trip.

Another way in which the Community raised an income was through the work of the Weaving School. In 1911, the first sisters of CSM&AA had gathered together a group of girls and taught them how to spin, weave and dye, using the mohair from Basutoland's sheep and goats. By 1962, the school was well established and was receiving government support in the form of the teachers' salaries. Its aim was to provide young women with a skill, which would enable them to earn their own living. The sisters who taught there drew a salary and, in addition, other sisters who were proficient weavers had their own weaving room next door where they produced goods for sale.

Wafer Bakery

A further Community enterprise was the Communion wafer bakery, a department which had been run for many years by Sister Maria. Unfortunately, when she had encountered a problem with the consistency of the wafers, she had had no-one to whom to turn for advice, and had consequently lost some of her customers. It was arranged, therefore, that Sister Jean Mary should spend a week at the bakery of another community, situated in Pietermaritzburg, in order to learn from them, and, hopefully, find a solution to the problem. This bakery was much bigger than the one at Leribe and, as they had their own electric supply, they could use efficient electrical equipment, which allowed them to increase their production rate considerably. The sisters in Leribe, having no electricity, were dependent on using primus stoves for several more years to come. Although most of the tips Sister Jean Mary was able to pick up had to be stored until such time as the CHN wafer room could be enlarged, she *was* able to bring home an immediate solution to the problem in hand.

The income from all these activities, together with Sister Veronica's teaching salary enabled the sisters to be self-financing, though it left no surplus for major capital expenditure, eg. to update the buildings.

However, as the hostel had increased their intake, it was essential to provide an extra dormitory for the girls. As the best solution was for the sisters to vacate their dormitory, it was decided to build an extension on to the main house, where all the sisters would be accommodated. There was a convenient site to the west of the house and finance was provided by the 'Africa Fund' in England. A simple rectangular, double-storey building, containing twenty-four single bedrooms, was built, and it was named 'Jerusalem'. Each room had a bed, a chair, a painted orange box to serve as a bedside table, a small cupboard and chest of drawers, a paraffin lamp and hooks on which to hang habits.

Only once the move was in process, and the sisters struggled to manoeuvre the essential furniture into the rooms, did anyone realize there had been a minor error in the initial measurements. Rooms that should have measured eight foot square, turned out to be much narrower than expected. Father Dove and Sister Mary Francis had done the calculations together and, in passing on those figures to the builder, had forgotten to add the extra inches needed for the thickness of the walls! However, as everyone was more than grateful for the extra space available, in comparison with their previous accommodation, and so relieved to have a room to themselves, it was all accepted with good humour!

This move made other changes possible, and the outhouse, where Sister Marjorie Jean used to sleep, was converted into a more spacious wafer bakery. Some of the simple equipment seen on the trip to the Pietermaritzburg bakery could now be purchased and this, combined with the improved techniques, made it possible to improve the quality of the wafers, advertise more widely, and thus build up a larger customer base.

The Church Sewing department was also developed. The only other source of supply for priests and catechists was in South Africa, sometimes as far away as Bloemfontein, a ninety-mile journey from Leribe. As most of the churches wanted their servers in cassocks, there was quite a lucrative market. If there was a large order to be completed quickly, then anyone who could hold a needle and sew straight would be press-ganged into helping. It would not have been unusual to see groups of sisters, almost hidden by the voluminous red material, seated outside in various parts of the garden, either making buttonholes or hemming, in order to get an order finished on time. The sisters were constantly involved in a delicate balancing act between making enough profit to keep the Community viable, and providing a service which the Basotho clergy could afford.

So far this history has focussed on the Community's work within the convent; but both CHN and SMMS were called to mission work, and sisters have engaged

Sewing Department

in pastoral and evangelistic work wherever they have lived. CSM&AA sisters were very well-known in the parish, and not only within the confines of Leribe camp or village. Sister Marion had been known to spend many hours out on trek, on horseback, visiting some of the outlying villages, and ministering to the people there. The population of Basutoland was so scattered, that a parish might cover 20 – 25 square miles, divided up into several smaller centres known as outstations. Many of them were only accessible on horseback, which meant that for a missionary priest going to Basutoland, the ability to ride was almost a prerequisite. He would go on trek to visit his outstations, once or twice a year, spending two to three weeks there at a time.

For the rest of the year, they were generally cared for by catechists, who were usually men or women whom the people trusted. Such catechists might be teachers, or farmers, or housewives and members of the Mother's Union. They led worship on Sundays, prepared candidates for baptism and confirmation and looked after the sick or those who were bereaved; they also conducted funerals.

When SMMS was founded, the sisters were also trained for pastoral work. They were sent to visit some of the villages, or outstations - those within a walking distance of a couple of hours each way. Several sisters were each responsible for one particular village which they visited at least once a week. Leribe village, visited weekly by Sister Anna Pabatso, was perched on the side of a mountain, a six- to eight-mile ascent from the mission station in Leribe town. All land belonged to the Paramount Chief[184] and could not be sold. It was allocated by the local chiefs and, as long as the plot was used, either for building or cultivating, it remained in the possession of that family but, once it ceased to be used, it reverted to the Chief. Many of the houses were built of stone, it being readily available on the mountain-side, and many families started with two rooms and added more piecemeal, as needs dictated and funds allowed. In the 1950s, the congregation of Leribe village had built their own church, a firm stone building with a zinc roof, and later added a primary school, thus making it typical of the outstations of the parish.

The only strip of tarmac road in Lesotho was the two-mile strip in Maseru, the capital, built for a visit by the Royal Family in 1947. It was still in fairly good condition in the 1970s, and gave the capital some kudos. All other roads were at the mercy of the weather: when it was wet, loose stones, ruts - which turned into rivers, and potholes, could all prove hazardous, and under dry conditions, the dust made driving conditions almost as difficult. However, as it had become increasingly difficult, without transport, to provide supplies for the greater number of children in the hostels, a VW Kombi[185] was purchased. At that point none of the sisters had a driving licence, which meant someone had to learn to drive fairly quickly. The local garage sent one of their drivers to spend the week in Leribe and in order to give a couple of the sisters an intensive course of driving lessons. That one week became two. When the sisters asked if they could have the driver/instructor for a further week, the manager of the garage raised his eyebrows and said, 'You mean you haven't learnt to drive in a week?' Sheepishly they said 'No,' and a further week was granted. At the end of that time one of the English sisters passed her driving test and later other sisters, including the Basotho, gained their licence too.

Communication with England and with the rest of South Africa had its difficulties in the 1960. The postal service was slow and unreliable and, as the convent had no telephone - partly because Lesotho's telecommunications system was so antiquated, the best option, when the message was urgent or important, was to prevail on the hotel down the road for the use of theirs.

SMMS had been continuing to attract vocations right up to the year prior to CHN's arrival and, between 1962 and 1964, three more postulants were received. The father of one of them, Angelina, had come to the convent on two separate occasions, intending to take her home - a father still had considerable authority over his daughters according to Basotho custom. However, the fact that Angelina was over twenty-one and therefore legally entitled to make her own decision, meant that he left without her.

In August 1964, having completed the statutory two-year novitiate in CHN, ten  former SMMS sisters were elected to Life profession as full members of CHN, the formal ceremony being held on 6th October 1964. In the December of that year, when the three sisters returned from England, there were two further Life professions and one profession in First Vows, and all were well

Profession in Life Vows 1964

supported by the people of the parish who had shared in the growth and development of the Community.

That brought the total of African sisters in CHN up to seventeen, sixteen of whom were in Life Vows and the other in First Vows; there were also four novices.

It had always been part of CHN's plan, once SMMS had been incorporated into CHN, to open a small house where the sisters would be more fully involved in the pastoral and evangelistic work of the diocese, and while discussions on the subject were taking place, it became known that the Principal of St Catherine's College, Maseru, was preparing to leave once her replacement had been appointed. St Catherine's was a Teacher Training College, preparing young women who had completed their own primary school education to teach at lower primary, or infant school level. Running an institution like the College would be a new venture for CHN, but it would also be a work in which sisters of both races could be involved together. Although at that stage there were no black sisters qualified as teachers up to college level, it was envisaged that this would soon cease to be the case. However, the black sisters *did* have plenty of experience and expertise in running boarding accommodation for schools. Mother Audrey Mary and Sister Mary Francis made a preliminary visit to the college, which resulted in the proposal that it should be the site of the first African Branch House. Passed by chapter in January 1965, it marked the first occasion on which both African and English sisters could take part in the discussions and vote on the proposal. With a view to opening the house in January 1966, at the start of the new school year, it was announced that Sister Ruth Ellen would take on the principal's job and that Sister Mary Ruth would be the sister-in-charge of the branch house.

St Catherine's College

At the beginning of term, the majority of the students being boarders, they arrived the day before classes were due to begin: on foot, by car or taxi - more like a minibus, and the transport of the poor. Some of them carried their trunks on their heads, while others carted large items of luggage between them. All arrived, clutching their school fees, often to be paid in cash, and the principal sat in her office during the afternoon and evening, to receive the fees and issue a receipt. The positions of school secretary or bursar did not exist in the 1970s; the principal and her deputy were expected to manage all the administration in addition to their teaching responsibilities.

Like other colleges of its kind, St Catherine's was small, the total school roll being about eighty students, so by the end of the day, Sister Ruth Ellen had had the opportunity to meet each of the students individually, and to hear, from their own lips, the correct pronunciation of their names.

About a third of them were new entrants, and all had completed eight years of primary school. However, the fact that they had all started at different ages, or had had to have a gap in their schooling when money ran short meant that they started at St Catherine's between the ages of 15-22, and left aged between 18-25. Some of them were already married and had children of their own, who were left with relatives; others had already gained experience as unqualified teachers, and had saved their salary in order to further their studies and become qualified. The teaching staff was mainly Basotho and Sister Ruth Ellen was relieved to have the support of Miss Peck, the former principal, who had offered to stay on for a year and guide the 'new girl' through the intricacies of Basutoland's teacher training system, and to introduce her to its education department.

The group of sisters in the house were all involved in the work of the college. Sister Gertrude Jabulisiwe looked after the hostels, being responsible for the catering, and for the maintaining of discipline in the dormitories, and Sister Mary Ruth, a former nurse, dealt with all ailments and accidents.

In company with all secondary establishments in Basutoland, St Catherine's had a rule that only English should be spoken during the week, both in class and in free time. The Basotho were very proud of their own language and heritage, but also practical about the need to learn English, as any contact with the world outside South Africa had to conducted in that language. However, Sesotho flourished at weekends, when the compound buzzed and rang with music and songs, as students did their Saturday morning chores, before dressing in their freshly- ironed uniforms to go into town for their weekly shopping trip.

The college continued to grow and develop, influenced by all the changes brought to Basutoland by Independence. The new government of the independent Lesotho had the freedom to seek financial help from other nations, in order to develop their country's potential and improve her infrastructure and welfare services. Until this point, most of the schools, hospitals and clinics were established and run by the missionary societies and the churches. At the time Lesotho became independent, America and many European countries were more than willing to provide aid, as they saw this small, landlocked country as bastion of freedom in the face of the apartheid policies of the South African authorities. The Community benefitted from this generosity, being able to access funds from several agencies, in order to improve their work in the fields of education and childcare.

Sadly, just after Easter 1966, CHN suffered a devastating blow with the sudden death of Mother Mary Francis. On the way back from Maseru to Leribe, the car in which she was travelling had blown a tyre and overturned, leaving her seriously injured, and she had died on the way to the hospital. The local community had no inhibitions about coming to express its sympathy and its own grief, and a constant procession of people, from all walks of life, arrived at the convent, to tell of their appreciation of Mother Mary Frances and to offer their support.

The funeral was very well attended, and the men of the congregation shared the task of carrying the coffin to the graveyard; the whole congregation processing with her to her final resting place. They stayed, according to their custom, singing hymns while the grave was filled in, another task in which all the men played their part.

Sister Marjorie Jean was appointed as the next sister superior; the sisters gave her their full support, and together they continued the process of integrating the two cultures as fully as possible. After full consultation, more of the offices were conducted in Sesotho, and a greater number of African sisters were drawn into positions of responsibility within the Community.

Around this time the Community was discussing the next round of building work; little-used areas were converted into a viable sewing room and a cooler, more spacious wafer room. The main house was also in need of some upgrading: ceilings were lowered and the walls stripped of their mud surface and re-plastered with cement. There was a constant struggle to maintain the right balance between such development and the Community's commitment to simplicity of lifestyle and its vow of poverty. This balance was even more difficult in a country where, for so many, poverty was grinding and life-destroying. However, the work the sisters were engaged in was serving the church in Lesotho and beyond. It was also providing employment in a country where so many were desperate for work. In building for the future the Community was at one with the spirit of the country at that time of Independence.

Sister Marjorie Jean continued as sister superior for just over a year, at which point Sister Christian arrived from England to succeed her; both sisters were to remain in Africa for many years. In 1967, Sister Christian was appointed as regional superior - a first step towards the creation, in December 1969, of a separate Southern African Province of CHN. The following June, she was appointed superior of the new province.

During the 1970s, the Community continued to grow, and to increase the scope of its work. In 1972 mains electricity finally arrived in Leribe, and was installed at the convent, enabling the wafer bakery to upgrade its equipment at last! In July 1973 the new Leribe Craft Centre was opened, in order to take an increased number of students into the Weaving School and St Mary's Home Economics School which, together with the Training Workshops Salesroom, occupied its three units.

As well as practical training, the centre also provided a basic curriculum of English, maths and science. The Home Economics School became residential in 1976, and St Mary's Hostel stopped taking in other boarders, and was set aside to accommodate its students.

Later a sheltered workshop was set up for the disabled; this was a non-profit-making charity (any profit which *was* made was used to supply accommodation for disabled schemes in other parts of Lesotho).

Leribe Craft Centre

In 1973 St Catherine's introduced a new Junior Secondary Course leading to the Junior Certificate,[186] which was now essential for all who wished to enter for their Teaching Certificate course. In 1975, when all Teacher Training was transferred to the government-run National Teacher Training College, St Catherine's continued to provide secondary education. A sister continued as principal and other sisters taught in the school until, in 1983, sisters being needed elsewhere, the management of the College was handed over to a secular principal.

In 1974, instead of opening another branch house, it was decided that a mobile unit of three or four sisters should be made available to engage in the work of pastoral care and evangelism; this unit would to go to one centre for a month or

St James Hospital, Mantsonyane

two and then to move on to another. At Mohale's Hoek, however, this initial period was extended for a year, and at the end of that year it was decided that this was the right place to open a second branch house, and a new house was built for the sisters, to replace the temporary accommodation in which they had been living during the trial period. The house opened in 1975.

By 1976, sisters had taken part in many training courses, studying mainly theology and evangelism and their contribution to the work of the diocese was increasing as they were invited to sit on Diocesan Boards and Committees, including Ordination Panels.

In 1977 a small houses was opened at Mantsonyane for three years in order for sisters to work at St James Hospital.

As the sisters continued in the Religious Life, they were invited to help other new communities, in their early years. In 1978 four sisters stayed for a month to help the newly-established Community of St Paul's at Maputo, Mozambique, and continued to make regular visits over the next few years in order to give advice and support.

The process of creating an independent province of CHN in Lesotho was a gradual one. Firstly sisters had been encouraged to gain experience in governance by serving on the South African provincial council, and then, in December 1979, a deputy superior was appointed, to work alongside Sister Christian. Two years later, elections were held for the office, and Sister Frangeni became the first African provincial superior.

Over the next three decades, there has continued to be a regular exchange of sisters between the Lesotho and English provinces, and of correspondence between the superiors. General letters to the whole community also keep sisters of both provinces up to date with each other's news and prayer concerns.

6 October 2012 marked the 50th Anniversary of CHN's arrival in Leribe, and the day was celebrated with a thanksgiving Eucharist and feast. The occasion drew together sisters from all three provinces of CHN, some of whom had also been present on that first day. It was a joyful occasion, the service being followed by a programme of speeches, songs and dances. One of these was a warrior's dance, performed by prisoners from the local prison - the same prison from which the working party had been sent in the early days to clear the ground around the convent. A great feast rounded off the day, and the brass band, which had led the procession and accompanied the hymns, played gently in the background until people had eaten their fill; then the tempo and decibel level increased and the celebratory dancing began, all joining in as they felt moved.

In 2014, there are twenty sisters in the Lesotho Province. The majority are based at the Convent in Leribe, while two others are at the branch house in Mohale's Hoek, 140 miles south of Leribe. Among the other work there, the sisters continue to support a crèche for pre-school children aged between eighteen months and five years.

One sister remains in Namibia, where she is engaged in pastoral and evangelistic work. During her first year there, three girls arrived asking to test their vocation to the Religious Life. After spending three months with CHN in Zululand, they moved with Sister Gertrude to the Onekwaya West Mission Station to start a five-year postulancy. In 2007, they established a kindergarten for the local children. In 2014 they made their profession, and the new Community was recognised by the church authorities.

The Craft Centre, though now privately run, is still supported by CHN; and a sister is still responsible for the hostel where girls stay during term time. The church sewing department continues to be patronised by clergy from Lesotho and South Africa, and another department now makes uniforms for various church organisations and schools. The sisters are also looking at ways to develop the work of the wafer room.

Professions in Namibia

Visiting the Villages

The Community remains very committed to pastoral and evangelistic work and has developed a particular ministry to those families affected by HIV/AIDS - 30% of the population are HIV positive. A project, known as the 'Volunteers of Love', has been initiated to help victims of the disease, by tending to them in their homes.

Sisters continue to receive various forms of education, and Sister Malefu has a post as an environmental nurse at the local hospital.

ENDNOTES - CHAPTER 14

[178] Kaffir corn is another name for the grain sorghum, a species of grass native to tropical and sub-tropical areas.

[179] Apartheid was a system of racial segregation enforced by the National Party governments of South Africa, who ruled from 1948 to 1994. The Group Areas Act, delineated the areas in which different racial groups could live, the Mixed Marriages Act forbade sexual relationships between members of different groups and several Segregation Acts segregated education, medical care, beaches, and other public services, and provided black people with inferior services.

[180] The term 'Bantu' was used derogatorily to refer to the bantu-speaking people of South African by the supporters of apartheid. 'African' was the term used by those opposed to apartheid.

[181] A stoep is a verandah.

[182] A rondavel is a round-shaped thatched hut, whose walls are usually constructed from stones found locally bound by mortar of sand, soil and cow dung.

[183] Laterite soil consists of earth, soil and small stones; it is used to build dirt roads.

[184] The Paramount Chief is the highest level political leader in the area.

[185] A VW Kombi was a van with side windows, like a minibus.

[186] In South Africa, high school begins at grade 8. After the first three years students take their Junior Certificate - equivalent to GCSEs, and at the end of the next two years they take what is known as the Matriculation (matric) - equivalent to A levels.

CHAPTER 15

Mission Work Overseas: Zululand

Bishop Alpheus Zulu of the Diocese of Zululand and Swaziland had, for several years, been asking CHN to set up a new branch in *his* diocese, as there was no Religious community in that country. In 1946, together with the Archdeacon, Philip Mbatha, he had founded Iviyo Lofakazi Bakakristu – A Movement for Christ's Witnesses. This was a parish organisation, based on the Rule of the SSF tertiaries,[187] which bound its members to live under a rule of life, seeking to put the claims of God first: in worship, in prayer, in almsgiving , and in church attendance. The organisation took off and grew exponentially and its two founders realised that some of its female members might be called to the Religious Life. However, as there was no Religious community in the diocese, he had on several previous occasions approached Sister Christian in Lesotho to see whether CHN could open a new branch house there.

By August 1967, the Community was in a position to give him the response he longed for, and it was arranged that a meeting to discuss the matter at further length would take place in November, when Mother Audrey Mary would be there on one of her regular visits from England.

On 28 November 1967, Mother Audrey Mary and Sister Christian set off to drive from Lesotho to Zululand. This involved crossing borders and passing through the Orange Free State in the Republic of South Africa, requiring them to stop for passport inspections. Nevertheless, they made good progress, having time, whilst passing over the tail of the Drakensberg Mountains, to admire the wonderful panoramic view. The landscape to the right was composed of miles of hills, wooded, for the most part, and with very steep grassy valleys in between. The valleys provided grazing for cows, whilst the almost precipitous hillside down from the road became a playground for the many rock rabbits. The journey continued with a descent to the gentler landscape of Natal, where they drove on to Nqutu, and the Charles Johnson Hospital, where they enjoyed the hospitality of Doctors Anthony and Maggie Barker, the medical superintendent and his wife.

After supper that evening, a small group consisting of: Bishop Alpheus Zulu, the Archdeacon Philip Mbatha, a local priest, Mother Audrey Mary, Sister Christian and Sister Veronica Mary, who had returned from England, after completing her two-year teacher training course at Newcastle University, met to discuss the position.

Just before the meeting had started, the Bishop had introduced three girls, who felt that they had a vocation to the Religious Life. Once the meeting began, it was soon agreed that it was right for CHN to open a house in Zululand. The Bishop pointed out that, as there were two CHN Zulu sisters already professed, so that there were potential leaders available, the new venture should begin 'at once'! The sisters he had in mind, were, at that time, committed to other work, and he was soon made aware of the many other issues, which would need to be resolved, before his dream could be realised. Committing the matter to prayer overnight, the meeting was adjourned until the next morning. When the group reconvened, it became clear that it would be necessary for the girls to return to their homes, until CHN could set up a branch house there. Consequently they needed a house in which to live together for a period, whilst all the necessary arrangements and preparations were being made. Archdeacon Philip generously offered them the use of an empty clergy house, close to his own in Maphaphoma. It was important that they should have a recognisable identity and, therefore, it was decided that they should be known as the 'Daughters of the Holy Name'.

At this second meeting, it was agreed that the sisters would be responsible for helping to furnish the house, clothe the girls and provide money for their upkeep, whilst they were under the care of the Archdeacon. CHN would also produce the translation into Zulu of: a simplified form of the Divine Office, a very simple rule of life, and a short admission service, which would be held in Church.

The Archdeacon's role would be to prepare the house which he had offered, to ensure the welfare of the Daughters, both physical and spiritual, and to liaise with both CHN and the Bishop. He would also supervise the Daughters' timetable and suggest ways in which they could help in the parish, visiting the sick and preaching to the unconverted.

At the end of November, two new girls, previously unknown to Archdeacon Mbatha, had written asking to join his group. Meanwhile, the Community and the Archdeacon got on with their preparations. Sister Christian had a series of Saturday afternoon meetings to work on the Zulu translations with Sisters Veronica Mary and Gertrude Jabulisiwe, and plain blue pinafore dresses, to be worn over white shirt or pullover, and white veils were made to fit each of the girls. Furniture and bedding, essential kitchen equipment and crockery, and an initial supply of food were all collected together, ready for the move.

It had been agreed that the Archdeacon would let Sister Christian know when the house was ready, so that she could return for a further meeting with the Daughters, and see them settled into their new home.

By January 1968, when the move took place, two more girls had arrived, and they were joined by Sisters Veronica Mary and Gertrude Jabulisiwe, and also Sister Elizabetha, from Lesotho, to help and encourage them as they began to test their vocation to the Religious Life.

The occasion coincided with a meeting for clergy of the deanery, and they were delighted to incorporate the Daughters admission' service into their own pattern of worship.

The names of the first seven Daughters were: Kate, Eunice, Olpha, Almitta, Thembikile, Doris and Audrey. Kate, who was an older woman and appointed their leader, was fluent in English and thus able to interpret for the group. The group of girls was officially named the 'Daughters of the Holy Name', and, during the admission ceremony, promised to live under a Rule of Life which included: regular times for prayer and bible reading, attendance at church, manual work, and parish visiting and evangelism, under the guidance of the local priest, and with teaching by Bishop Alphaeus and other clergy. The five girls, who had been expected, were clothed in their new uniform and given their Zulu translations of the Divine Office.

During the course of the year, Sister Christian visited the Daughters, when it was possible to obtain a permit to do so, and they also spent time in Leribe, having a retreat. They gained a good understanding of the Religious Life, and proved themselves well-suited to pastoral and mission work. Further aspirants continued to appear, and it soon became clear that more accommodation would be needed in the near future.

Daughters of the Holy Name

Isandlwana Convent

After taking Sisters Christian and Veronica to see a few other sites, Bishop Alphaeus took them to Isandlwana, where St Vincent's Church had been built to commemorate the officers who had died in the battle there, during the war between the British and the Zulus. The valley itself was barren and dotted with white mounds where the bodies lay buried near where they had fallen.

Close to the rectory, was an empty property which had previously housed the assistant priest. Bar the creation of a kitchen, little needed doing to the property and there were also three good-sized rondavels, one of which was suitable for conversion into a chapel. The property was situated about two miles off the road, but there was a post office and store about half a mile below the hill.

The decision to apply for use of the buildings was made, and plans were put in hand by the Bishop, who obtained the necessary permission and engaged the services of a reputable Afrikans builder from the Transvaal, who had been working in the area. He was well-known and able to begin the work almost immediately.

On Christmas Eve 1968, a telegram was received from the builder, asking that the opening of the house might be postponed as, 'the kitchen stove has not arrived, and the building is not quite ready'.[188] When an advance party of sisters arrived a few days later, in order to prepare for the opening of the house in January, they soon discovered that this had been a masterpiece of understatement!

Not a single section of the house was finished. Where there *were* any doors, they were found to be locked. Nonetheless, easy access was still available, as none of the windows had yet been glazed! The only rooms to have both a roof *and* a floor were piled high with furniture and building materials and, although the sisters managed to locate the new cooker, as the kitchen itself did not yet exist, its presence was of no immediate use. As there was no obvious place to sleep, and the party had no tent, there was no option for them, but to create a space for their beds by hauling around all sorts of building materials and sweeping up the worst of the debris. The builder finally arrived to find that he had met his match in the sisters, and suffice it to say, progress was rapid from that time forth!

On 8th January 1969, having arrived from Mapaphoma the previous day, the Daughters were admitted by Bishop Alphaeus in St Vincent's Church, as postulants in CHN; Sister Veronica Mary taking office as their superior. Three more girls were admitted as postulants in February, and the original seven were clothed as novices in April. Three of the seven then accompanied Mother Audrey Mary on her return flight to England, in order to spend their novitiate there. A pattern of interchange of sisters between Isandlwana and Leribe was also established, as all were determined that CHN should be, and *should be seen to be*, one multi-racial community.

The small community soon settled into its new home, creating a vegetable garden, rearing about two dozen chickens and milking the six cows they had inherited, 'not very good ones but alright to practise on!', in Sister Gertrude Jabulisiwe's opinion.

The chapel, created from a large rondavel, with a thatched roof and stone walls, was dedicated by the Bishop, with all due ceremonial, on 11th December and, of special note, was the design of the altar, which was quite unique. The top was of local red wood, and it had a carved and burnt design along the edges, comprising mostly crosses - though at one end there was a jubilant choirboy throwing out his arms and praising the

Saying the Daily Office

Lord with gusto! Meanwhile, the base was a trelliswork of white poplar, constructed in a balanced, yet unsymmetrical, design. The altar was moveable and reversible and had a different design on each side. Altogether, the whole effect of the chapel was simple, yet devotional; blending traditional African designs with those of a later period.

In common with the Community in England and in Lesotho, CHN sisters at Isandlwana also sought to be as self-sufficient as possible. In 1970 a workroom was set up for the production of cassocks and church vestments, and grass mats and beadwork, to be sold locally, were made by the novices. The original plan to turn the old clinic into a guest-house had had to be abandoned, as the government was tightening up on all visitors' permits and did not encourage them to stay in the reserves at all. It also proved almost impossible, at this time, to obtain permits for Mesotho sisters to stay at Isandlwana, although those from Zululand were still able to go to Lesotho.

The first group of professions under First Vows, and then, three years later, the taking of their Life Vows, were both occasions of major celebration, not only for the CHN, but also for all the people of the neighbourhood and surrounding districts, who continued to support them and make the Community its own.

One such celebration took place on 24th August 1971, when the first Zulu novices were professed under First Vows. All the clergy of the archdeaconry, having attended a meeting at Isandlwana the day before, were to camp in the rectory overnight and processions of women could be seen converging from the surrounding hills with bedsteads, blankets, crockery and food carried on their heads, to help out the rector's wife. It had been agreed that the Community should give everyone a meal of sorts after the Profession, but no-one had any idea of how many to cater for. In the morning a steady stream of cars, trucks and motorbikes on the approach road gave anxiety over whether the supplies of food and drink could possibly hold out! However, as proved to be the case on this, and all subsequent, occasions, due to the generosity of local folk, who arrived bearing all manner of contributions to the feast, there was no cause for concern.

The service was held, not in the convent chapel, but in the church, due to the large numbers involved. The Bishop in full regalia, two archdeacons, five priests, a small boat boy, two girl servers and thirty-two catechists were all packed into the sanctuary and the rest of the church bulged at the seams with the crowd. Three years later, on 24th August 1974, another great celebration was held when these same sisters went on to take their Life Vows.

The development of the pastoral and evangelistic work of the sisters began when they started to visit the kraals[189] in the area round the convent, but they soon began to move further afield. For instance, during Lent 1971, three novices stayed for a few weeks' intensive visiting in the parish of Etaleneni, about thirty miles away.

St Vincent's Parish Church at Isandlwana began to take on new life as the new rector, Father Edmund Xulu, and the sisters made friends with the people of the neighbourhood, resulting in a number asking for instruction in the faith. The sisters helped with these classes and, in the afternoons in church, held prayer groups, which were soon quite well-attended.

An increasing amount of evangelistic work was taking place in other nearby parishes too and, in order that they may be better equipped for the task, sisters embarked upon a variety of different types of training. In 1971, two sisters took a course at the Lutheran Bible School and Sister Gertrude Jabulisiwe took a six months' Church Workers Course at the Methodist Lay Training Centre in the Transkei.

It was also made a priority that sisters, where appropriate, should further their school education and, eventually, train for the teaching and nursing professions. In 1971, the first two sisters attended St Augustine's High School near Isandlwana on a three-year course leading to their Junior Certificate and found themselves doing quite a bit of mission work on the side with staff and students, and, in 1974, two other sisters went to complete their Primary Education at a school in Hlazakazi, about eight miles away from Isandlwana. A small house was built there, in which they lived during the week, returning to the convent at weekends.

In 1973, the first branch house opened in Maphophoma. The Community had been given an excellent site, close to their old home beside the church and plans had been drawn up for a small house for four sisters. In addition, an outside room had to be built as, under the laws of apartheid, Sister Christian was not allowed to sleep under the same roof as the African Sisters. (Until then, when she visited, she had been compelled to drive thirteen miles along a bad road, night and morning, in order to sleep in a 'white area'.)

Though the sisters' main work in Zululand was mission and pastoral work, and many people came to them for prayer and help at both CHN houses, they were also invited to become more involved in Diocesan Work, teaching on theological courses themselves, once they had become qualified to do so.

As it was now necessary for sisters to commute between their various houses, and also for those in Life Vows to travel the Southern African provincial chapters in Leribe, it became necessary to buy a car, and for sisters to learn to drive it. After several enquiries had been made, a second hand Datsun 1200, with low mileage, but with bodywork which was rather the worse for wear, was purchased. The priest from the neighbouring mission came across each day to give Sisters Audrey and Olpha driving lessons, and, after a few initial difficulties, they both passed their tests.

A fledgling Children's Home came into being at Isandlwana, when a small house in the convent grounds was occupied by an extended family, comprising three schoolgirls and two small boys, with Sister Olpha acting as their housemother. The girls had been sent to the Community for help and training, and attended the local school. The two boys, aged five and seven, had been sent for fostering by the Charles Johnson Hospital at Nqutu, where they had been in-patients for many months. When they no longer required hospital treatment, it was not suitable that they should return to their own homes, and they joined the girls at Isandlwana. Amos suffered with epilepsy and also had learning difficulties, and Mahuwa had had a bad bout of kwashiorkor.[190] The hospital was able to keep an eye on the arrangements, and there was a government clinic just down the road, in case either of them became in need of treatment.

During the 1970s, CHN Zululand continued to expand, six new recruits arriving in 1976 alone, and the convent, originally built for twelve occupants then housed twenty permanent residents, with four more sisters, away studying during term-time, who returned home each holiday – not to mention the sisters at Maphophoma, who returned for Community retreats. The Maphophoma house itself, was full to capacity with five sisters inside, and two girls living in the outside.

By 1978 the novitiate numbered eleven: two who were spending a year in Lesotho, and three others living at Maphophoma. However, despite the overcrowding, it was not feasible to extend the convent, as the water supply was inadequate, and the approach road became impassable in bad weather.

The following year, the Community responded to a request to open a second branch house at Etalaneni, about thirty miles away from Isandlwana. The house, suitably restored by parish council, was opened early in the year, and while two Sisters worked in the parish, another taught handcrafts in the Bambisanani Community Centre nearby.

In response to another request for help, two sisters were sent, for periods of three to four weeks, several times a year, to engage in pastoral work among staff and patients at St Mary`s Hospital, Kwamagwaza.

By 1979, it had become impossible to house the growing Community at Isandlwana and, after exploring various other possibilities, an ideal site was found on mission ground between Kwanzimela Retreat and

Waiting Outside a Mobile Clinic

Conference Centre and Kwamagwaza Mission Hospital, about six miles from the town of Melmoth and on a direct route to several other towns.

Due to the importance placed on gaining educational qualifications and training for professional employment, the new convent initially housed only a small number of sisters during in term-time, but soon filled up during the holidays. In addition, the sisters training at the nearby hospital could pop in and out when they were off-duty. During 1981; six were away in full-time education, two were training in St Mary's Hospital, Kwamagwaza, to be Enrolled Nurses and two were taking a one-year course in Evangelism at the Union Bible Institute. Two other sisters were spending time with the Community in England.

The sisters at Kwamagwaza found scope for work in the hospital, in the parish and in local schools. In addition, the church sewing department was developed and sisters learned how to make their own habits, having previously been supplied by the sisters in Leribe. A small group of sisters remained at Isandlwana, making it a 'House of Prayer and Healing' and looking after the small Children`s Home.

By 1979, the children`s home had been adopted by TEAR Fund of South Africa. Their director had visited the children a couple of times, and had taken photos to be incorporated into a promotional leaflet. This had aroused a lot of interest, and had produced sponsors for the children. The home, despite its obvious value, had previously been a considerable drain on the Community's finances and the receipt of a regular monthly maintenance grant made life much easier. TEAR Fund also gave a capital grant to re-roof the house and to extend the rondavel to make a sheltered play area.

The process of independence for CHN in Zululand followed a similar pattern to that of Lesotho. The first step was taken in 1975 when, in addition to a provincial council for the whole of the Southern African province, regional councils were set up in both Lesotho and Zululand, so that the sisters' knowledge of their local situations could inform the decisions of the joint provincial council. It also served to allow more sisters the opportunity to experience the governance processes of the Community.

Mother Veronica Mary (left) with Sister Gertrude Jabulisiwe

Four years later, in December 1979, a deputy superior was appointed, to work alongside Sister Christian. Two years later, Sister Veronica Mary was elected as the first provincial superior of the new Zululand province of CHN. Sister Veronica Mary was duly blessed and installed as superior on 1st November 1980. A throng of priests and people from all over Zululand, and beyond, converged on St Vincent`s Church where the first part of the service took place within the parish mass of All Saints. Afterwards, everyone formed up outside to process to the convent chapel about a quarter of a mile up the hill, the sisters in front, flanked by the Mothers` Union with their banners, and the Youth Club behind them in scarlet and white. Only members of Religious communities, several of which had sent representatives, were able to squeeze into the chapel to witness the Bishop leading Sister Veronica Mary to her stall and then blessing Sister Gertrude Jabulisiwe as her assistant, but everyone, both inside and out, joined in the singing of the Te Deum. It may be said that it made a fitting contrast to the battle cry of the Zulu warriors, which had sounded, on that same site, during the battle of Isandlwana, just over a hundred years ago.

On 9th May 1981, the new chapel at the Kwamagwaza was dedicated with all due ceremonial; Bishop Alphaeus celebrated, and Canon Philip Mbatha preached the sermon. Chief Buthelezi was able to join the congregation – one of the rare occasions on which he was not expected to make a speech.[191]

After the service and customary feast, Sister Christian said her goodbyes, and departed for the airport to make her return flight to England.

An exchange of sisters between the three CHN provinces has been maintained, and the provincial superiors continue to meet together on a regular basis. Fortunately, the development of better phone links, fax and e-mail makes keeping up-to-date so much easier than it was been in the 1960s. General letters from the three superiors to the sisters of the three provinces have enabled the whole Community to keep up with each other's news and prayer needs.

In 1984 the first aspirant from Swaziland entered the Community and, for much of the time since 1989, there has been a branch house there, at the Usuthu Mission. It is made up of a large bungalow, with a stoep, and three or four rondavels. It has a good garden, and is situated between the church and the school.

Mission work has continued to become move into new areas, facilitated by mobile units of sisters, who work intensively for a few months in a particular parish, before moving on to another.

Since the early 1980s, sisters from Zululand have spent time helping the sisters of St John the Divine in Wentworth, Durban, as they have become more elderly; and, over the years, the sisters have been able to respond to several requests to

help with, or advise on, the foundation of new communities in other countries including Zambia, Mozambique, Malawi and Namibia.

In 2004 a project was begun, to set up an orphanage for children whose parents had died from HIV/AIDS. It was named Isisa House and aimed to provide for their basic needs: food, clothing, schooling, health care and emotional support. A support

Children Receiving Clothing

system for foster parents/guardians was also organised.

In 2014, the Zululand province comprises thirty-nine sisters, some of whom are working professionally: one of the sisters was a nurse-consultant, working to prevent the HIV virus from passing to babies during the birth process, until she was elected Provincial Superior earlier in the year), two more sisters are employed as nurses, and three are teaching.

A household of five sisters has continued to work in Rosettenville, a suburb of Johannesburg, and their work at St Benedict's Retreat House has recently seen the establishment of a food bank, to help those living on the streets.

All sisters continue to be involved in the work of mission and evangelism.

ENDNOTES - CHAPTER 15

[187] The Third Order of the Society of St Francis (TSSF) consists of men and women, single or in committed relationships, who, though following ordinary professions, are called to a dedicated life of service to God through prayer, study, and work, as prescribed in their Rule of Life.

[188] The Beginning, *CHN Community in Zululand* (Sister Christian's Memoirs) p.25.

[189] A kraal is an enclosure for cattle or other livestock.

[190] Kwashiorkor is an acute form of childhood protein-energy malnutrition.

[191] Mangosuthu Gatsha Buthelezi (born 27 August 1928) was descended from an important line of Zulu chiefs. He became a South African politician and then leader of the Inkatha Freedom Party. In 1976 he became the chief minister of the KwaZulu Bantustan, a collection of eleven scattered Zulu exclaves located within the Natal province and worked to help bring an end to the government's policy of apartheid.

CHAPTER 16

The Move from Malvern

Main Convent Building with 1966 Extension

During the 1970s the number of sisters in the Community in Britain continued to decrease, partly due to the death of elderly sisters, but also due to a drop in new vocations. Fewer novices had gone on to profession, and some sisters, who had been professed for several years, had realised that their vocation was not to the Religious Life in CHN, and had asked to be granted release. It had therefore become increasingly clear that the convent buildings were now far too extensive for the Community's needs, and that they were unsustainable in financial terms.

After an initial survey of the property owned by the Community, in January 1982 Mother Penelope was able to report that it would be saleable, if at some future time the Community felt that this was the right course of action.[192]

Over the next few months, the local planning authority prepared a full valuation of the whole property. Having advised the Community to find a new property before starting to sell, Cluttons Estate Agents and Surveyors were asked to look into the possibilities of other buildings which might be appropriate to the needs of the Community. As the sisters began to learn what types of properties were on the market, the terms of the search were clarified; what they were seeking was a place with about thirty bedrooms, possibly a former small school or nursing home.

In January 1984 Sister Mary Patricia was elected to office as the new provincial superior, and proposed that a small group of sisters, with the help of an outside chair, should form a working party, which would assess the use of its buildings and land and discuss the pros and cons of staying put, or of moving. (At that time there were fifty-two Sisters based at the convent and approximately another eighteen living in branch houses.)

The working party looked at other ways of using the convent buildings - Malvern Adult Education Service and other bodies were approached, but none felt that the buildings were suitable for them. The group concluded that the arguments for moving to a more manageable and economic set of buildings were largely self-evident, and drew attention to the fact that any viable possibility would need to provide the appropriate care for a large number of sisters who were elderly or infirm. Consequently, the Community voted to move as soon as a suitable property became available.[193]

Sister Judith was asked to be the representative for building matters, and in the early stages, things moved quite quickly. In May 1985, together with the Community's solicitor, she visited the Charity Commissioners in London, in order to seek permission to sell some of the Community's property in separate lots, and this was granted.

In 1986, an application was submitted asking for planning permission for a simple change of the use of the convent building, and by August the sale of the first three lots had been completed and that of further two agreed, subject to the Charity Commissioners' approval. In addition, permission had been granted for the sale of the Community's orchard to developers.

In June 1987, it was sold for the purpose of building Sheltered Housing, and the whole Community was sent out to pick the gooseberries in case the building started immediately. It didn't – so there was also time to pick raspberries, redcurrants, blackcurrants and even holly before work finally got underway!

In order to make the necessary funds available, so that the Community could put down a deposit on a new property, when the time came, it was agreed that a list be made of past bequests which could be disposed of. In this matter the Victoria and Albert Museum, Sotheby's Auction House and the Bodleian library were very helpful. The list included a 15th century Psalter and some antique silver, which had been found in the Community's cutlery drawer!

One of their buyers came to the convent to view a large picture (part of a triptych) of 'the Death of the Virgin', which hung in the sanctuary. During his visit, he spotted a door-stop at the end of the cloister and this was of much greater interest to him than 'the death of the Virgin'! It was a bronze model of a 'Mother and Child' and had been in that position in the cloister for as long as anyone could remember. It had been fashioned by a very famous French artist, and would have been of great value, had the orange patina not been spoiled by constantly picking it up by the head!

Meanwhile, a letter was sent to any contacts, including all the Anglican diocesan bishops, who might know of a property which was suitable for conversion into a new convent for CHN. There was a lot of response to the letter, and the estate agents provided the Community with the particulars of a selection of large properties. Having considered them carefully, a car full of sisters was dispatched to visit to those properties thought to be worth a closer look. In almost every case it soon became perfectly obvious that the buildings were just not practicable.

In 1981, the option of a complete purpose-build had been ruled out due to the cost, but in August 1985 the option was re-visited, and it was concluded that it would be possible if the new building were on a smaller scale than that envisaged previously.

CHN's various contacts were then asked to look out for sites on which parts of an existing property could be used in combination with a newly, constructed purpose-built block. Numerous properties in various locations were visited, but again none proved suitable and, latterly, the search continued in a climate where house prices were rising rapidly, and, consequently, the interest received on the properties already sold in Malvern was not keeping pace.

The process of sifting through particulars, visiting possible sites over a wide area, waiting and hoping all take a great deal of physical and emotional energy, and there must have been times of sheer exhaustion and of despair over ever finding a suitable place. However, at last, out of the blue, a viable option emerged!

Attending the Church's General Synod in 1987, Sister Carol was approached by the Rural Dean of Derby North who suggested that CHN contact the RC Sisters of the Presentation on the outskirts of Derby, who were looking to sell their provincialate house. It was not even on the market at that point, but Mother Mary Patricia rang them immediately and when asked, 'When would you like to come?' replied, 'tomorrow?'

Although only part of the new Oakwood estate, on the edge of which the convent was situated, had yet been built, the plans showed just how extensive this private housing estate would eventually become. This could have been a major drawback in terms of noise. However, in addition to the convent buildings, plenty of land around it was on offer, so it would not be an issue. There was also a small cottage in the grounds, where an advance party of sisters could live while construction was taking place, and which could later be used to accommodate residential guests. The fact that a suitable chapel already existed was a bonus and the site also had the advantage of good transport links.

As a result of a secret ballot at the chapter held in August 1987, the Community was unanimous in its decision to proceed with the purchase of the house at Derby. It is one of those strange coincidences that in 1887 - exactly one hundred years before - CHN had moved from the parish of Vauxhall, where it had begun its life, to its new convent in Malvern Link!

The architect, Mr O'Neill, who had produced feasibility studies on three previous properties, which were initially thought to be strong possibilities, was asked to prepare an initial study of the Derby property, the brief being to develop the Derby site to accommodate approximately thirty Sisters (several of whom might be disabled or in need of nursing care), and to provide for a range of functions appropriate to the administrative and training centre of the Community. He recommended that the chapel and the cottage be retained, and that the main portion of the original house be refurbished as offices, teaching rooms and common rooms. The various outbuildings/extensions would be demolished in order to provide the space for a new building, which would house the other functions, kitchen, refectory, library etc. In July a local Derby builder began the work needed to renovate the cottage, as permission had been granted for three or four sisters to move into it as soon as contracts had been exchanged. It was planned that the building of the new convent, by Fryers Ltd of Derby who had won the tender, would take place from October 1988 to October 1989.

While the sisters were in chapter, a message was relayed to them to say that contracts had finally been exchanged. Consequently on 12th August the advance party comprising Sisters Diana, Theresa Margaret and Elizabeth Rachel moved to Derby. Their brief was to be on site while construction was under way, and to begin to make contacts in the area. They attended different local churches to see where sisters could helpfully get involved and discovered that St Phillip's, Chaddesden, had recently lost its vicar and would be delighted if a sister could start immediately.

The sisters visited local residents, as the estate continued to expand around them, and it soon became possible to meet people at the newly-opened supermarket, one of the first buildings at the future Oakwood Shopping Centre. A newsagent, dentist's surgery, post office and other amenities soon joined it; and a large primary school, a leisure centre and a small community centre were also to be part of the development.

Sisters from Malvern visited: for holidays, or to break their journey en route to other places, a few visitors called in - to maintain contact with one of the sisters they had seen regularly at another branch house, and a new link was made with students at St John's Theological College, Nottingham.

In the spring of 1989, the convent in Malvern was put on the market, and vacant possession was set for October. This meant that a temporary dispersal of the Community would be necessary to cover the few months until the building in Derby was completed.

The Diocese of Worcester had arranged for a Farewell service to be held, in the context of Vespers,[194] in Worcester Cathedral on 29th July 1989 and CHN's last Eucharist in the Malvern chapel took place on 9th August.

Early September saw fifteen sisters move across the road from the convent to live in St Saviour`s, the former Guest House. Eight sisters departed for Truro, to stay with the Community of the Epiphany and another three sisters moved to a house in a parish in St Helen`s Auckland, where there had been a request for sisters to open a new branch house. All other branch houses were filled to capacity, and three sisters moved into residential homes.

Between September and December, few sisters being left in Malvern, the furniture selected from the eighty-two bedrooms and the offices, as being the most suitable for the new convent, which had been stored temporarily in the laundry was transported to Derby. The rest was sold off, or given a new home, as appropriate, eg., an Italian Church near Northfield, whose members had lost everything, when their church was gutted by fire, received the Lady Chapel altar, and a group of parishes in a team ministry in Leicester, who had bought a pub in a very deprived area and turned it into a Church Centre, took statues of St Joseph and Our Lady from the sacristy.

For nine months, a small caretaking group remained in Malvern, to keep an eye on the old convent until it was sold. After several months, it was sold to an organisation called Evercalm – a company who provided supported living, and the sale was eventually completed on 24th September. However, the organisation was not able to realise its plans for the site, and the property was put back on the market. During this intervening period, the buildings remained unoccupied and unguarded, and it was heart-breaking for both CHN and for the local community to realise the extent of the damage, which those buildings had sustained as a result of vandalism and theft.

Meanwhile, at a meeting in Derby, attended by Mother Mary Patricia, Sisters Edith Margaret and Judith, Mr Dixon, Mr O'Neill and Mr Booth, Foreman of Works for Fryers Ltd., the keys to the new convent were formally handed over.

The chapter meeting in January 1990 took place at the Conference Centre in Swanwick, just outside Derby, as the Community was between convents!

Handing over the Keys

Thereafter, sisters moved into the new convent at a rate of about five a week, until all were assembled.

The benefits of a modern building were soon appreciated: its efficient heating system, the draught-proof windows, the carpeted floors and the small kitchens - in which to make hot drinks - on the bedroom floors. The washbasins in the bedrooms soon dimmed the memory of carting upstairs large jugs of water for washing, and the plentiful supply of hot water for baths and showers put paid to the old twice-weekly bath rota.

Most sisters were accommodated, either in the convent or in one of CHN's branch house, but a local a Nursing Home, within easy reach of the convent, was able to provide a room for the sister who needed more care than could be provided at the convent itself.

Sisters began to meet their neighbours on the rapidly-expanding estate and the convent began to become integrated with the members of the local church congregation, when, soon after their arrival, the Rev'd Mavis Bexon dropped in to welcome them to the area, and to invite them to a barbeque at her house. As the deacon from St Mary's Church, Chaddesden, she was responsible for the congregation on Oakwood, who would start building their own church on the designated site at the Oakwood Shopping Centre, once the funds were available. At that time they were meeting for worship at her house on Appledore Drive, just around the corner from the convent. As the fledgling congregation had soon outgrown her sitting room, she asked if it would be possible to use the convent chapel for their Sunday morning worship, until such time as they could move into their own church.[195]

Welcome to the Diocese

The Community and the congregation both welcomed the new arrangements and, for the younger children, the long sloping ramp, leading from the hall to the chapel, soon found its true identity as a racetrack!

The Provost of Derby, the Very Rev'd Ben Lewers had arranged for a special Eucharist to take place at the cathedral on 3rd March 1990, so that the Diocese of Derby would have the opportunity to welcome the Community. He himself celebrated, and he had invited Bishop Timothy Bavin, Bishop Visitor to CHN, to preach and the Bishop of Derby, the Rt Rev'd Peter Dawes, to give the blessing. The cathedral choir provided the music and invited guests included: the Lord Lieutenant of the county, the Mayor of Derby and the chair of the County Council, as well as other local clergy and members of their congregations.

The occasion also gave the sisters an opportunity to see where the statue of Our Lady from the Malvern chapel had been placed. At the base of the stone plinth on which it stands, a brass plaque bears the following inscription: 'This statue, which formerly stood in the Convent Chapel of the Community of the Holy Name at Malvern Link, was given into the care of this Cathedral Church in the year of our Lord 1990, when the Community moved to Oakwood, in the County and Diocese of Derby.'

After the service, refreshments were provided, giving sisters and guests the opportunity to get to know one another.

On returning to the convent after the service, a formal presentation was made to Messers Eamonn O'Neill, Bill Dixon and George Booth, who had all worked so hard to bring the project to fruition.

Derby Convent

To complete the formalities, on 28th July, the Bishop of Derby came to bless the chapel; this being the first formal occasion to which Companions, Associates, and other friends and contacts of the Community were invited. Tours of the new building were conducted and, when it came to the time for the blessing, the chapel was so full that additional seating had to be put outside.

By May, the grounds around the house were being made good and attention could then be turned towards the landscaping of the grounds, turning them into an attractive area, with newly-planted shrubs and flower-beds, trees and lawns. Specific areas were left to grow wild, in order to encourage bees and butterflies. A network of paths was laid, and suitable seating installed, thus enabling the gardens to become a place of quiet and rest - for the sisters themselves, but also for the many guests who would visit the convent as the sisters' ministry of hospitality continued in this new setting.

During the first few months of the year visitors had dropped in, some of whom had known the Community in Malvern and were coming to see the new house, others who came from Derby and its environs and were visiting a convent for the first time. On 17th December, the Guest Cottage, with its seven bedrooms, a big reduction on the number available in the Community's former guest house, was ready to open its doors to residential guests.

The December of that first year in Derby burst in with high winds and driving snow, bringing down power lines and leaving the convent without electricity and gas for forty-eight hours.

On the Sunday morning a phone call was made to the Oakwood congregation, to make them aware of the situation and to warn them not to come for their service in the chapel. But come they did – bearing flasks to make hot drinks and offers to cook and bring things for lunch. Several elderly sisters even received an invitation to their homes for lunch!

Chapel and Liturgy

The ordering and furnishing of the Derby chapel was a task which could not be rushed, as opinions of what constituted 'simple' and 'conducive to worship' varied enormously. In January 2002, a working party was set up; with the Rev'd Leonard Childs, a local priest with specialist knowledge of such matters, acting as consultant.

Derby Chapel

After investigating various alternative possibilities, it was decided to maintain the simplicity of the apse at first. Several years later, it was agreed to commission a large resurrection cross for the apse, whose shape would be mirrored in a cross to hang over the entrance to the chapel. Upon this latter cross would be mounted the antique corpus which had been brought from Malvern. The designer, Mr Colin Riches, brought examples of the cross using various different colour schemes. After much deliberation, the Community agreed which one should be the final choice. A simple tabernacle was also made, to be fixed beneath the cross.

The rest of chapel remains very simple and uncluttered, but has been enhanced by a set of 'The Stations of the Cross', produced by Sister Theresa Margaret, one of the solitaries who specialises in the painting of icons.

When Anglican Religious communities began to emerge in the late 19th century, some used the form of the Daily Office provided in the *Book of Common Prayer*.[196] Others, including CHN, used the Office in the *Monastic Diurnal*,[197] translated into English. In the 1960s, no further copies being available and in line with several other communities, CHN decided to adopt the Office of *The Day Hours of the Church*,[198] until a longer term solution could be found.

In 1965, a group of Anglican communities' liturgists, led by the superiors of the Society of St John the Evangelist and the Community of the Resurrection, had formed an Anglican Office Book Committee, which began work together to produce a body of texts to be used as each community desired. The committee facilitated the collation and distribution of material for consideration from a wide range of sources, including their own textual and musical compositions.

In 1966, CHN had set up its own `in-house' committee. Changes to its use of *The Day Hours* were introduced gradually, one of the major decisions being to use almost the whole Psalter in the Office, rather than the earlier more limited selection of psalms. This process of experimentation continued over many years. In terms of the music, the Community had already been chanting the psalms to simple ancient modes[199] and in February 1979 began to use simple new chants, based on the original modes, when they adopted *The New American Revised Psalter.*

In 1981, following the publication of the Church of England's new *Alternative Services Book*[200] CHN was able to use modern language in the whole of its liturgy.

In 1985, the committee debated whether to adopt *The Daily Office SSF*, the new Franciscan book,[201] but concluded that it was preferable to produce one of its own. The ASB had introduced new collects and themes for each Sunday and the *Revised Standard Version* (of the bible) was in print. Loose-leaf folders were used to contain a selection of the material collected by the Anglican Office Book Committee and various resources were used for a trial period and then judged for their suitability.

Hymns were selected from a wide range of sources, including several in-house compositions. The antiphon (a sentence sung before and after each psalm and canticle) formulae in the eight modes, with their respective psalm tones, were written by Dom Laurence Bevenot.[202] Music for the other parts of the Office was composed by CHN sisters, who sought to simplify the older plainchant, maintaining its tonal colour and retaining any sequences of notes from the original chant, which were particularly resonant of the saint's day or the liturgical season.

This lengthy process reached its conclusion in 1991, when the new book was printed and the many different folders on sisters' chapel stalls could finally be replaced by a single volume.

[192] Chapter Minutes January 1982.

[193] CM August 1984.

[194] Vespers – the word means evening - is an office said at about 5-6 pm.

[195] Oakwood was to be a Local Ecumenical Partnership, with Anglicans and Methodists sharing their Sunday morning worship, and the small Roman Catholic congregation holding their Mass in the evening.

[196] The *Book of Common Prayer* (published 1549, revised 1662) was the first prayer book to include the complete forms of service for daily and Sunday worship in English. The seven distinct daily offices were consolidated into two: Mattins and Evensong. It was hoped that these would become the form of daily prayer to be used by the Laity, as well as being incumbent on the clergy.

[197] The *Monastic Diurnal* contains only the day hours: Lauds, Prime, Terce, Sext, None, Vespers, and Compline. The full Roman Breviary also includes Matins, the night office.

[198] *The Day Hours of the Church* was an Office Book, adapted from the Sarum Use**,** a variant of the *Roman Rite*. It was first written for use in Salisbury Cathedral, but became popular throughout England, Scotland and Wales; it was widely used until the reign of Queen Mary.

[199] A mode is to a type of scale, coupled with a set of characteristic melodic behaviours; a Gregorian mode (or church mode) is one of the eight systems of pitch organization used to describe Gregorian chant.

[200] *The Alternative Service Book* (ASB), published in 1980, was the first complete prayer book produced by the Church of England since 1662. It was proposed, not as a replacement for the BCP, but merely as an alternative to it. However it soon became the main liturgical text in most churches.

[201] *The Daily Office SSF*, a prayer book for the use of SSF, was first published in 1970.

[202] Dom Laurence Bevenot was a monk at Ampleforth Abbey.

CHAPTER 17

The Ordering of Community Life

The Religious Life of CHN is set out in three complementary documents. The Rule gives its interpretation of the Vows, the constitutions the legal framework for this and the Customary the detail of daily living.

For almost the first hundred years of CHN's life, there had been no major revision of the constitutions (statutes) of 1899; they had merely been updated piecemeal, as the need arose. It is impossible, therefore, to give some of the amendments an exact date; however, it *is* possible to record that, in 1954, Temporary Vows were introduced; ie., rather than proceeding from the novitiate to immediate Life profession, novices would be professed under Temporary Vows first. It had become was apparent that, in the post-war world of restlessness and rapid change, new entrants needed a longer period to adjust to living the Religious Life, than that provided in a two-year novitiate. The profession to Temporary Vows would, nonetheless, be made with lifelong intention.[203]

In that same year there began a thorough revision of the constitutions - one which would take several years to complete, in order to bring them into line with the recommendations of the Advisory Council for Religious Communities.[204] In preparation for their submission, the Constitutions were scrutinised by CHN's legal advisors and the necessary amendments passed by the chapter. Many of them served to clarify the role and term of office of several authorities involved in the governance of the Community including: the mother superior, chaplain general, external confessor, council, finance committee, bursar and trustees.

In effect, the more exact formularies and new additions served to put in place a series of legally-binding checks and balances. For instance, it had previously been the custom for the Reverend Mother, currently in office, to function also as the Community's treasurer. Under the new Constitutions, this could no longer be the case.

It was the role of the mother superior 'to govern according to the Statutes and Rule, with the advice of the chaplain general and the council'.[205]

Consequently, the chaplain general had a major role in the governance and oversight of the Community. Although he usually presided at chapter, *it was his duty to do so*, 'if the agenda included changes to the statutes or rule.'; the reason being that, 'a man was usually much better than a woman in dealing with such matters.'[206] This latter opinion, expressed by Mother Audrey Mary, was a reflection of the general situation with regard to women's communities, and indeed in society as a whole, at that time! In September 1958, Father Alban Russell was appointed as chaplain general and remained in office for the next fifteen years. He was highly involved in the majority of decisions made regarding the Community's life. The extent of that involvement can be perceived when we read that, with regard to the Week of Prayer for Christian Unity,[207] the chaplain general said that he and

Mother Penelope

Reverend Mother had agreed that it would be right for any sister, who wished to do so, to take part in the evening prayer meetings, arranged to take place at churches of different denominations during the week.[208] Father Russell retired in 1973, and Canon Gordon Ireson, when he was appointed the following year, made it known that he wished to break with the old regime by being known as the warden. He and his assistant chaplain began to celebrate the Eucharist on alternate days and, he worked with Mother Penelope, the new Reverend Mother, in a much more advisory capacity. For example, in 1981, when a new constitutions committee was formed, it was stated that the warden 'may be called in, in an advisory capacity',[209] whereas until the 1960s the chaplain general would had a more directive role. Canon Ireson retired in 1982 and, as the role of assistant chaplain had become more firmly established, and other local clergy now came in to celebrate the Eucharist, in 1983, it was decided not to appoint a new chaplain general or warden, but simply a senior chaplain. The wording of the new constitutions, issued in the mid-1980s, makes explicit his more limited role, 'The reverend mother, with the approval of the Council, shall nominate a chaplain for the mother whose duties shall be: to celebrate the Eucharist, to receive confessions as required, to be available ... for consultation, and to take occasional offices, such as Clothings'.[210]

As organisations in general evolved away from a strictly hierarchical model of authority, so too in CHN a move towards a greater devolution of responsibility and a more consultative process of decision-making can be seen. It had previously been the case that a *short* list, selected by the Reverend Mother, with the approval of the chaplain general, had contained the names of those who were to be considered for election to council. This process was made more democratic when the Community began to receive a *complete* list of all those in Life Vows, who were eligible for election. This principle was also applied to the process of election to Life Vows. Formerly carried out by a committee, chaired by the chaplain general, and latterly by the council, it then became the responsibility of the whole Chapter, informed by reports written by those sisters who had had most contact with the sister seeking election.

After the new edition of the constitutions had been passed in 1957, with immediate effect, further amendments would soon become necessary, in order to accommodate the establishment of the new branch house in Lesotho in 1962.

The process of amending the constitutions then became a lengthy one; for - in addition to the fact that they had to be confirmed at a second August chapter in England, a year after they had first been passed - they now had to pass between the two provinces. As every slight amendment to an amendment had to go through this process, it was very time-consuming. But finally, in 1974, a draft revision of the constitutions, containing all the recent amendments, was accepted by the English chapter. However, as the legal framework for an organic community, whose interpretation of its vows was a response, both to the leading of the Holy Spirit and also to the needs of those whom it served in a rapidly changing society, further updates were often necessary.

One series of minor amendments updated the terminology, by which the various officers of the Community were known; and it was settled that 'provincial superior' (a term in common usage among other Communities) should replace that of 'reverend mother'. Another change in forms of address came about when, at a conference for novice Guardians, it became clear that CHN was the only community still to address their novices as novice X, rather than sister X. However, when making the alteration, it was pointed out that this was merely a change in the form of address, rather than a change in status! [211]

1981 saw the establishment of the independent provinces of Lesotho and Zululand, and as they grew in confidence, it became possible, by 1986, to begin work to produce a set of basic constitutions, covering that which was common to the running of all three provinces and separate English, Lesotho and Zululand constitutions which covered those areas where it was more appropriate for each province to have separate arrangements. The basic constitutions were passed in 1996; those for the English province two years later. By 2000, community life in each province had adapted to its own culture and matters of governance had become settled enough to cancel the original basic constitutions, incorporating any necessary clauses from it into each province's own document. A much-simplified document of basic practice stated the joint CHN ethos.

As a charity, CHN's constitutions must comply with the requirements of the Charity Commissioners, and, as a result of changes to Charity Law made during the 1990s, a thorough revision of the constitutions took place. As a result the chapter became the trustee body of the charity; in addition to the superior, her assistant and the bursar, four sisters from among those in Life Vows are elected, and these seven form the trustee committee. In what proved to be a lengthy process, the object of the Community also had to be revised, in order to use wording acceptable in law. However, the purpose and spirit of CHN remained unchanged.[212]

The Community Rule also went through a similar process of change, adaptation and revision. The 1965, sisters were asked to study the Rule during the coming year and identify where minor alterations were needed. In the revised version, the language assumed a gentler tone, having fewer clauses beginning with the injunctions shall (not), will (not) or must (not) and sisters were no longer required to 'examine themselves' but rather to 'renew their specific dedication to God and in light of his love to see their faults.'[213]

The large number of clauses on demeanour and seemly behaviour were no longer deemed necessary and were subsumed into the more general advice that if the soul of the sister be habitually resting in God, it would not be difficult for her to preserve the exterior demeanour of the Religious Life. Also, in a nod towards the changing patterns of deference to authority, novices no longer had to stand when talking to sisters, or to curtsy to the novice mistress.

Eight years later, when Mother Penelope had been in office for four years, she made a request that the Community share their thinking on the meaning of the Religious vocation, in order to agree on a definition of the Religious Life, and in August 1975, in consultation with the Council, she appointed a Rule committee to produce a draft Rule, to enable the Community's discussion.

Their brief was, 'to produce a Rule which was inspirational with basic directives, a Rule which can be lived when, perhaps in the future, we may be scattered abroad or living under more difficulties than at present'.[214] (The 'in-thinking' at that time was that the future for Religious communities was to live in small houses rather than large institutions.)

Gospel-based, it sought to be a positive affirmation of life, to be a guideline for the joyful surrender of the self to God: to allow freedom to explore all avenues of prayer and to foster a sense of personal responsibility, by combining the discipline and support of directives, which set out a minimum, with the inspirational, which pointed to the ideal. It was intended, not to iron out personhood, but to be a guide for a community of human beings of great differences and potential.

The decision of the Rule committee was to leave aside the old Rule, not to go through it section by section, but rather to look at the principles underlying the thoughts submitted it by many members of community and eventually to shape the new Rule on its two main principles: 'the Life of the Counsels' and 'the Life of the Commandments'.

The former section sought to draw attention to the specifics of the Religious Vocation and to search out its biblical roots. The second section sought to apply the general vocation of all Christians to the daily response of the vowed Religious. In doing this it was intended to move explicitly away from any sense that the Religious Life was a superior/more perfect response to the Christian call.

The Rule committee spent an initial week together, and then many hours of work and prayer during the following year, to produce a first draft in time for the pre-chapter days in August 1976. At that stage, sisters had the opportunity to respond to it both in small discussion groups and individually, and it was agreed to live by it, and to discover the need for any alterations over the course of the following year. (After this, small discussion groups were used more often, as several sisters found it less intimidating to speak their mind in a small group, rather than in the full chapter meeting – such groups are now loved by some, but loathed by others!) In August 1979, the final draft was formally accepted by chapter. A summary of the Rule was made available for those who found that a less poetic form was more helpful.

Some alterations were made to bring the language up to date, eg. 'cells' became 'sisters' rooms'; others clarified the Community's common expectations - it was agreed that sisters should say at least two offices a day and maintain their life of prayer when 'on rest'. But other decisions made a more complete break, not with the principle, but with some of the practices which had served the Community well in the past, eg. the daily 'Breach of Rule' in Chapel after Terce,[215] made publicly by all sisters, in which they would be expected to confess to faults such as lateness, noisiness, failure in courtesy, mistakes made in chapel etc., was replaced by the practice of individual confession, either privately, or to a confessor.

By the late 1980s, when the revised Rule, enabling a more holistic approach to the offering of one's whole self to God's service, had been in use for almost a decade, and the decision to move from Malvern had been made, it was possible to focus attention on other important issues concerning the ordering Community's life together. In 1983, a Roman Catholic sister was invited to talk to the sisters about her own community's experience of changing the way in which they lived out their vocation, following the recommendations of Vatican II,[216] in order to help CHN in its forthcoming review. During the review, deep, heart-searching discussions were held on a range of subjects, all relating to the ways in which the Community saw its vocation and future. One of these areas concerned the balance of 'active' and 'contemplative', both in the life of individual sisters and also in the life of the Community as a whole.

Some sisters found that the tightly-structured timetable and the demands of labour-intensive housework and mission work left little time in which to develop a more contemplative prayer life.

During the 1970s, two sisters became increasingly convinced that they had to consider the possibility of living out their Religious Life as Solitaries. This would be for CHN a completely new direction and required that this 'vocation within a vocation' be explored carefully by degrees.

In August 1970, Mother Mary Clare of the Sisters of the Love of God, an enclosed community at Fairacres, near Oxford, came to give a series of talks on 'Prayer and Spirituality' and, in tandem with the revision of the Rule, and a thorough exploration of the roots of monasticism - from the Desert Tradition to the late 20th century, an examination of the history of CHN's vocation also took place. The Community had already been accustomed

Ty Pren

to sisters spending an extended time in retreat, but Solitude, as a way of living out the Religious Life, was not within its experience. In January 1979, Sister Verena was given permission to test a leading into Solitude. SLG allowed her to use the hermitage in their grounds at Fairacres for a trial period, during which time she had no contact with anyone other than Mother Mary Clare. On the Feast of the Baptism 1980, she was blessed into Solitude at the Eucharist in the Malvern Chapel and began to explore the possibilities for a more isolated hermitage. She spent six months living in a caravan in the drive of a farm on the Lleyn Peninsula in north-west Wales, in order to see whether it were possible to cope with the harsh winter there, and, whilst walking in the area, stumbled upon a small wooden cabin in the corner of a field (Ty Pren in Welsh), 100 metres from the cliff top above the Sound, and directly opposite Bardsey Island. This cabin, in an isolated spot and with very primitive facilities, became home until 2007, when she moved into a bungalow in Aberdaron.

Gradually a rhythm of life emerged: prayer, especially in the very early hours - when, for much of the year it was still dark, reading and study, creative crafts - including the production of photocards for sale, manual work in the house and garden, and long spells of contemplation - perched on the rocks in the stillness, being open to God and the intercessory needs of the world.

Life was not without incident, however: an earthquake which registered 5.4 on the Richter Scale, an adder in the compost heap, a hurricane which took off the corner of the roof, and a spectacular electric storm. On that occasion, lightning swept up the field immediately outside Ty Pren's window, a foot or so above the grass, until it hit the fencing and sparked along the barbed wire until it had burnt itself out. On a gentler note, there was also the opportunity to eavesdrop on a group of twenty to thirty seals singing in chorus off the rocks on Bardsey.

Having lived the solitary life for thirty years, Sister Verena was inspired her to write a book, reflecting on her experiences as a Solitary.[217]

Once Sister Verena was established, Sister Michael was given permission to explore her call to the Solitary Life. For two years from August 1980, she occupied two rooms at the top of the convent, living apart from the Community, followed by a time living at the Old Gatehouse on Mull, where she had an interview once a week with Father Keith Joseph, an established solitary living on the island. Consequently, the Community bought a second-hand caravan and were granted permission for it to be stationed on Mull, where Sister Michael stayed for the next six years, returning to the convent and to visit her family once a year.

In 1989, the Fairbairns, who owned the land on which the caravan was situated, decided to sell and Sister Michael moved into the convent gatehouse at Malvern until, when the Community moved to Derby, a two bed, end-terrace house was found for her in the village of Westhouses, which was about a thirty-minute drive away from the convent. There she continued her solitary life: shopping locally, producing lavender bags and using calligraphy skills, honed in the Malvern scriptorium, on the little cards which accompanied them. She spent many hours a day in prayer in her tiny chapel at the top of the house. A priest visited regularly to celebrate communion with her, and to renew the reserved sacrament, and she found a wise Spiritual Director in Father Gregory of the Community of the Servants of the Will of God, with whom she had regular contact. She lived an extremely frugal life and continued to be independent, with occasional visits from sisters at the convent. Finally, aged ninety, she suffered a nasty fall, which precipitated her return to the convent, where she continued to live a slightly adapted form of the Solitary Life until she died.

During the review of the Community's vocation and future, one of the other issues to be discussed was that of the provision of leisure time, in which sisters' individual talents could be cultivated. For some sisters the concept of leisure time was a complete anomaly to that of being totally given, which would involve an element of sacrifice. Others longed for the time to develop their artistic skills and practise a musical instrument in order that such an important part of themselves *might* be used in God's service.

Its introduction was therefore a gradual process. Until the early 1980s, an early night, where a sister could retire after completing any duties at the evening meal, had been the only concession made; but, in 1984, it was decided that each sister should have a half-day per week, free from programmed duties, if she wished. In 1982, it had been decided that sisters would have the option of wearing suitable secular clothes on their 'rests' (holidays), and, on the introduction of a weekly half-day - and then full day, this option was extended to those occasions too.

Whilst the Community was in Malvern, with only a short walk to town and the Malvern Hills on the doorstep, there was little call for sisters to have any personal money. For instance, on an occasion when a sister had to go to the hospital, either for an appointment or to visit a patient, the money needed to make an emergency phone call or to buy a drink was supplied by the bursar as the need arose; however, once the sisters had moved to Derby, it was usually necessary to catch a bus to town. Consequently, in August 1992, in order to reduce the amount of time the Bursar would need to spend providing bus money and other incidentals, and in the spirit of the vow of poverty and good stewardship, it was agreed that each sister *may* ask for an appropriate amount of pocket-money each month, with a limit of £5.

By 2000, free-time had gradually been raised to become a day each week, and, in order to enable sisters to take full advantage of this, it was agreed that the amount of pocket money available, would be increased to a maximum of £15 a month.

Over the years, the way in which sisters relate to one another in community has gradually shifted from a pattern of formal, highly-regulated relationships to one which, whilst retaining the spirit of the Religious Life, is more relaxed and informal. During the Malvern years, there had been very little contact between sisters and novices and, although it had been the practice that at the weekends a walk was organised for each novice, the choice of companion sister was made by the

Novice Mistress. A period of 'Formal Recreation' had been timetabled, for which sisters and novices met separately. Sewing or knitting was to be brought along and all conversation was to be general and non-personal.

During the late 1980s, when Mother Mary Patricia was superior, it was suggested that 'Recreation' be renamed 'Community Time'[218] and that, for sisters living at the convent, this would take place for half an hour once a week in the Common Room. After a period of experimentation, it was generally felt that a longer period was needed in order to build up the common life together and consequently, once settled in Derby, sisters and novices started meeting together for half an hour, morning and afternoon, for coffee and tea breaks. Another innovation, introduced at that time, was to invite a range of speakers, from outside the convent, to come and share their varied experiences with a gathering of sisters, on a regular basis. For some their experience involved living in a different culture, being a member of a different faith, or working amongst groups who were disadvantaged, eg. young offenders. Others had various interests and specialisms including: bee-keeping, wood-carving, wildlife painting and music. The local MP was also invited to address the sisters and to answer any questions they may have. Questions they had in abundance and these were supported by a great wealth of facts, held ready held at their fingertips!

Settling into a new convent demanded a great deal of flexibility as many of the new arrangements had to be tried out and adapted, before they could form part of the continuity with what had gone before. Prior to the move to Derby, in order to help develop an understanding of how different personality types function, a number of sisters had responded to the opportunity to participate in a course offering the Myers-Briggs Typology Assessment.[219]

In contrast with the formality of the convent at Malvern, the Derby building by its very nature required a much more informal style, and while this was a difficult adjustment for some, others found it to be a liberating experience. The work on reviewing the Community's vocation and future continued once the sisters had settled in the new convent, and the Rev'd Gerald Reddington - a priest who was also an experienced group consultant, agreed to work with the sisters, to enable them to look at some of the issues surrounding bereavement and change. In August 1990, he gave a talk entitled 'Ambivalence on Arrival' and then asked the sisters to complete a questionnaire, the answers to which would enable them to give shape and structure to their vision. They were also asked to read The Different Drum by Scott Peck - a book on the workings of communities, prior to his second visit, in January 1991, when he gave feedback from the questionnaires. As a result, in November 1992, two groups of eight sisters, chosen from across the board spectrum of opinion within the Community, held a two-day meeting at Turvey Abbey, working with two Group Analysts. No sudden clarity was achieved, but certain knots were loosened, and the Rev'd Reddington continued to make regular visits to the convent, in order to be available to see individual sisters, whilst the new pattern of Community life continued to evolve and settle.

The question of whether or not to appoint a chaplain to the Community was one of the first to be decided. The chapter in August 1990 decided that an honorary chaplain would be appointed on temporary basis, from among those who already acted as chaplains and the Rev'd Philip Need, the priest at St Philip's Chaddesden, at whose church a sister from the original advance party had continued to work, agreed to take on this role. When he left to take up a new post in Chelmsford, it proved difficult to appoint a replacement, but the rota of local clergy, who were willing to come and celebrate the Eucharist, had proved to be a most satisfactory arrangement on both sides.

The novitiate had been closed for the period immediately before and after the move; and further discussion had taken place regarding the nature of the commitment made at profession to First Vows (Temporary Vows) and that at profession to Life Vows. Prior to the beginning of the 1970s, if a novice or sister in First Vows had left, having discerned that her vocation was not to the Religious Life, this had been seen as shameful. After that time, it was no longer the case; however, there was still a high degree of disquiet surrounding any sister who left after taking Vows. Consequently, in August 1989, it was agreed that for an experimental period, following her time as a novice, a sister would spend at least three years in 'Dedication under Promise' ie. they would make promises to live in the spirit of the Rule, and not be professed under Vows. This experiment lasted until January 1995, at which point the sisters agreed that 'Profession under First Vows' more adequately expressed the character of the post-novitiate commitment within CHN.

This reflection on the process of deepening one's commitment to God in community went hand-in-hand with an exploration of the form the novitiate should take, at a time when fewer aspirants asked to be admitted, and those who did come were often older than those who had come in former years.

In Malvern, the novice guardian (formerly novice mistress) had had sole responsibility for the novices. New arrangements were now put in place for the time when the novitiate would re-open in Derby. These provided that one sister would be appointed to be the novices' main point of reference, but that, in organising their experience of the Religious Life and the testing of their vocation, she would draw upon contributions from various other sisters.

In February 1992, the first two postulants were received, but left after a couple of months. It was decided that the Community needed more time to settle into its new convent, with all its attendant changes, and the next two postulants were admitted in February 1993.

In 1996 the Rule was translated into inclusive language, and was updated to take into account the changes which had taken place over the previous twenty years. The first sister to take Life Vows in Derby did so on 1 March 2001.

Changes to the Community's distinctive clothing was one of the areas in which changes to its previous custom was most obvious. From the early 1970s, postulants had been allowed to wear their own clothes, instead of the dress and veil previously prescribed by the Community and in August 1971, work began on the modernisation of the habit. The last sisters to be clothed in a wimple became novices in 1972, and it was decided that the traditional black habit should be replaced with one in blue. Materials in various weights and shades were tried out, but, unfortunately, the one which suited best was taken off the market. However, after an extensive search, another material was found and blue habits were introduced in 1974.

CHN Superiors from 1970 – 2013 (from left to right)
Sister Mary Patricia, Sister Monica Jane,
Sister Penelope, Sister Jean Mary

It was not until 1981 that novices were allowed to wear a scapular, and were allowed to wear their crucifix outside – the previous custom had been to hide it within the habit.

In 1995, after a period where sisters were allowed to experiment with wearing the veil, or not, it was agreed that veils should be worn on formal occasions in chapel, but may be discarded on other occasions at the sister's discretion.' Further reflections, over a decade later, on the value of the habit and the symbolism of the veil led, in 2012, to the offices for Clothing and Profession being re-written to allow sisters to receive a veil or not, as they felt appropriate.

Holy Name Associate Orders
During the Community's history there have been a number of associate groups, whose early years have been documented in Part One. By the mid-20th century, those who felt called to live a form of dedicated life, but who did not have a vocation to enter CHN as a sister, could commit themselves either as a Companion or as an Associate.

Companions were governed by a sister, appointed by the Reverend Mother. They had a time of probation, followed by a period of five years between making their First and their Final Dedication, when they took vows of Celibacy and of Obedience to a Rule of Life. This Rule consisted of: attendance at the Eucharist, half an hour's personal prayer, spiritual reading and the saying of two offices daily. They were also required to make a four-day retreat at the convent, and to live in the spirit of poverty and simplicity. Founded in 1919, it reached its peak in the 1930s with a membership of around thirty-five. The last new entry in the Roll Book was recorded in 1968, and the final surviving Companion died in the early 2000s.

Associates Badge

Associates were those who wished to be 'associated' with the Community and would support it by prayer and the payment of an annual subscription. They were expected to keep the Associates Rule and to be in regular contact with the Associate Sister. Their Rule consisted of: attendance at the Eucharist on Sundays and one weekday; a quarter of an hour's personal prayer or spiritual reading, intercession and the saying of the Holy Name collect daily. They also made an annual retreat of between one to three days. In 1954 there were 155 members, men and women, named in the Roll Book and, of this number, twenty-nine were Priest-Associates. In addition to keeping the standard Rule, they committed to make the Community their intention at a Eucharist, celebrated on either 7th August - Holy Name Day, or 1st January - the Feast of the Naming of Jesus. They also committed themselves to further the 'Object of the Community' and to advance its interests.

In 1988, after a major review, Associates and the few remaining Companions amalgamated under the new title of 'the Fellowship of the Holy Name' (FHN) and in 1997, it became an ecumenical group.

Prospective members, with the help of a sister, create an individual Rule of Life, designed to accommodate their current circumstances and responsibilities. It is based on daily prayer, worship with others and service to others. In addition to making time for their relationship with God to deepen and grow, members are encouraged when they make their Rule to consider the needs of family and friends, and also to include time and space for their personal creativity and well-being.

Each member can, if they wish, have a particular sister, with whom they think they can share their faith journey and review their Rule, to be their 'contact sister', and they keep in touch in person or by letter, phone or e-mail. An Admittance Office takes place, usually within the context of a Eucharist at the convent, and the member's Rule is placed on the altar until the end of the service, as a symbol of the link between their offering and that of the Community. Members are encouraged, where possible, to make an annual retreat.

In 1988, regional groups, with a co-ordinator from among their members, have met twice a year, for a time of meditation and fellowship, and to pray for the needs of Community and of other members of FHN. Quarterly letters are sent from the Fellowship Sister to all members, bringing recent news and prayer needs; and, since 2008 members have received the Community's annual magazine - *CHN News*, comprising articles, reports, poems etc. from both sisters and FHN members.

FHN Badge

Each year, a small Fellowship Retreat is held prior to the annual Fellowship Day. Fellowship Day is held at the convent, for all who are able to attend. On these occasions there is a celebration of the Eucharist, an outside speaker, and a session where Community and Fellowship news is shared. Coffee, lunch and afternoon tea punctuate the day, giving plenty of opportunity for informal conversation between the members and with individual sisters.

Since the turn of the century, those members whose circumstances permit them to do so, have been invited to spend a couple of weeks living alongside the Community, especially during the months when sisters take their holidays. They join in the daily round of worship, work and community times, whilst having plenty of space for themselves in between. In addition a few local members opt to help out for a day each week.

As various CHN branch houses have closed, some regional groups have ceased to meet and consequently, in 2010 it was decided that a small group of Fellowship members, with a couple of sisters, should form a Steering Committee to address issues regarding the future development of FHN. In 2013, a new regional group was formed in Stafford.

[203] CM August 1953

[204] The Advisory Council for Anglican Religious Communities comprises bishops and Religious, who meet to discuss issues relating to religious communities, and it produces a Directory, which gives advice on how to proceed in a number of situations which can occur in several communities.

[205] CHN Statutes c.1957.

[206] CM August 1954.

[207] The Week of Prayer for -Christian Unity is traditionally celebrated between 18-25 January. There is an exchange of pulpits between local churches of different denominations, and special ecumenical celebrations and prayer services are arranged, based on a common biblical theme.

[208]CM August 1966.

[209] CM January 1981.

[210] Constitutions Part 1, XI. CM January 1983.

[211] CM August 1993.

[212] The Object of the Community in its dedicated life of poverty, celibacy and obedience is to spread the gospel of Jesus Christ in accordance with the Anglican tradition and the vision of the Founders of the Community by: its constant witness in life, work, words and worship to the Holy Name of Jesus, and its mission to support and engage in charitable work, both spiritual and social, responding to world-wide need in the love of Jesus'. CM August 1999.

[213] CHN Rule c.1966.

[214] Working Party Document

[215] Terce (the third hour of the day after dawn) is the main morning office, usually said about 9 a.m. .

[216] The Second Vatican Council, (Vatican II), held between 1962 – 1965, made many sweeping changes, several of them affecting those in Religious orders.

[217] *A Simplified Life* was published by Canterbury Press in July 2010. (ISBN: 9781848250253)

[218] CM January 1985

[219] The Myers-Briggs Typology Assessment looks into the ways people of differing temperaments prefer to operate, and how these ways of behaviour complement or conflict with each other.

CHAPTER 18

Outreach and Mission: Recent Years

The call of three more sisters to the Solitary Life in the early 1990s, represents one pole of the way in which the Religious Life in CHN has developed.

In 1991, Sister Lisbeth began to test a vocation to the Solitary Life, living in a small caravan in a field which was part of the estate of the Society of the Sacred Cross at Ty Mawr, in Wales. In 1993, when CHN agreed that she should continue on an open-ended basis, a larger caravan was purchased, and she moved to a more isolated spot on the estate. Later, she moved to a small terraced house in a small village near Caernarfon.

Presenting an Icon

In 1995, Sister Theresa Margaret, began her solitary life in Keswick before moving to Anglesey, a small island off the north west coast of Wales. Later she moved to a cottage on the Lleyn Peninsula, to the south west of Anglesey. A painter of icons, she has continued to undertake commissions, both for parish churches and for individuals, including one as a gift for the Dalai Lama, on his visit to the former Archbishop of Canterbury, the Most Rev'd Dr Rowan Williams.

In 1996, Sister Carol began to test a life as a 'solitary with minimal engagements', being careful to limit the number of retreats, addresses and conferences she agreed to lead. She began a time of testing the vocation in a property on the Lee Abbey Estate, where she had just completed her time as a lay chaplain and then spent many years in a house in Wells Cathedral Close, before moving to Clevedon in 2013.

All the solitaries are used as 'companions along the way' by people who visit, or correspond by post or telephone.

Meanwhile, at the other end of the spectrum, the more active forms of CHN's mission and outreach continued at the convent and in the branch houses.

When the Community moved from Malvern to Derby, sisters were working at the following houses: Chester Retreat House, Newcastle, Keswick and Nottingham. During the few years leading up to the move, the Community had considered a number of requests to open new branch houses, but had agreed that it was not the right time to make any long-term decisions.

In September 1989, however, the Community was ready to open a house of prayer in the parish of St Helen's, Bishop Auckland, and, in 1991, another branch house was opened in the parish of St Anne's, linked with that of St John's, both on the outskirts of Derby city centre. St John's had specified that one sister should take on the role of Accredited Lay-worker, but both had agreed that the other sisters would be free to develop whatever ministries seemed appropriate. The house (which had formerly housed the curate) was blessed, and Sister Lilias took her place on a Training Course for Lay Readers. When it became necessary to close the house in December 1994, Sister Lilias was able to continue her ministry at St John's from the convent.

One sister had, for many years felt drawn to live among other elderly people, experiencing the same daily problems as they did in terms of managing the house, shopping, getting about etc.. The opportunity presented itself in 1998, when the Community was offered the use of an almshouse on the outskirts of Nottingham; and two sisters moved in to live among and minister to the people there. CHN remained there until 2004.

In 1994, the Community responded to an invitation from the Archbishop of Canterbury for two sisters to live in a cottage in the grounds of Lambeth Palace: to fulfil the duties of sacristan to the Archbishop, to be a 'praying presence', to provide pastoral support for the staff, and to be a listening ear for anyone in distress - including those who phoned the Archbishop, and others who came to the doors of Lambeth Palace, asking for help.

They also supported the Anglican Communion in its dealings with overseas churches and, as part of the hospitality team, assisted in welcoming visitors from home and abroad. Otherwise they were free to develop such ministry as they saw fit. One sister spent several years involved with those living with AIDS, visiting the Mildmay Hospital;[220] another worked at Westminster Abbey. Other sisters have helped in schools and at a hostel for men. Sisters have also contributed to the pastoral work at a wide variety of local churches, including St Peter's Vauxhall, where CHN started.

In January 2012, Sister Catherine SLG moved to Lambeth to share the work with CHN, initially for one year, but in 2013, due to CHN's need for more sisters to be based at the convent, it became necessary to withdraw from the work.

During the early 1990s, several other requests to open new houses were followed up, but all fell through. However, in 1998, CHN was able to send two sisters to live in a council house in Welland, a high density social housing estate a short distance from the city centre. It forms part of the parish of Christ the Carpenter, Dogsthorpe, but is rather isolated from it, and the sisters were asked to be a praying presence on the estate as part of the church's mission to and care for the locality.

High unemployment, low incomes, dependence on welfare, lack of roots and a constantly changing population all compound to make the people there especially vulnerable. As well as the recent cuts in public services, private service providers have also lost much of their funding and competing charities have failed to attract sponsorship, thus putting more pressure on the local residents. The sisters can do little to compensate for those losses, but their awareness of the problems encountered enable them to do a little networking, to befriend their neighbours, to offer encouragement to neighbourhood and local church initiatives, and to be more actively involved where appropriate eg. in schools, at a local community garden scheme, food bank, hospice and city centre chaplaincy.

A Listening Ear in Welland

Several years later, in 2009, two sisters moved into St John's Rectory, Longsight, in response to an invitation from the parish of St Chrysostom's and the Diocese of Manchester, to be 'a praying presence', living among and engaging with the local community in that vibrant multi-ethnic, multi-faith area, and contributing to the ministry of the local church and diocese. The house provides a home to one of the parish assistants (a young adult having a year's experience at the church, whilst preparing to attend a selection conference for ordination) and offers hospitality for groups and individuals. Sisters assist at the English conversation group for mothers at the local primary school and support the school in other ways. Visiting the same shops, using the buses and walking around the neighbourhood all provide the opportunity to engage in conversation with some of the other local residents to develop, and also with the local Community Police Support Officer. In an area which is just emerging from the hold of a violent gang culture, and is plagued by drug- and alcohol-related issues, sisters have been available to provide a listening ear for some of those affected. In the wider diocese, sisters have contributed to the Bishop's Advisory Group on Prayer and Spirituality and have supported a small group, as they prepared to found a Manchester 'Order of Mission'.

Community has not been exempt from addressing some of the same issues which have challenged the Church, and sisters do not all hold the same point of view. Prior to the vote on whether women should be allowed to enter the priesthood at the November 1992 General Synod, the sisters also voted, in order to clarify where the Community stood on the matter. After lengthy discussions, the following statement was agreed. 'We accept in principle the possibility of a woman celebrant in any of our houses, with adequate provision being made for those who cannot be present for reasons of conscience and with the exception of major feasts and occasions (for the time being), for the sake of unity in the Community.'[221]

Consequently, in 1995 Sister Rosemary was given permission to explore this 'vocation within a vocation', and was ordained priest in 1999. That same year Sister Lindiwe, of the Zululand province, began her training at the College of the Transfiguration, Grahamstown, South Africa and in 2006, Sister Diana became CHN's third priest, when she was ordained in Derby Cathedral. All three have exercised their priestly ministry in local parishes.

Sister Diana at a Baptism

One of the major issues facing most communities at the end of the 20th / beginning of the 21st century, at a time of decreasing numbers of sisters and fewer new vocations, is how to make suitable provision for the elderly and infirm, whilst maintaining the Community's commitment to mission and outreach. In April 1993, a house 'without strings' was bought in Oakham, Rutland, for a small group of the 'ambulant elderly', who soon found themselves involved in the life of the parish church and local community, especially in a ministry of listening to those facing the difficulties of advancing years, like themselves.

In 1990, when the move to Derby took place, sisters were available to maintain their commitment to mission and outreach and also to cover all the work of the convent, with a little help in the kitchen, and two staff to help on Ground Floor (the infirmary wing) in the mornings. By 1998, however, it had become necessary to employ more secular staff in the kitchen, and also to provide 24-hour cover, under the management of a care manager on Ground Floor.

In 2000, the Community considered three options, when exploring ways of improving its future care provision: a) to open a new branch house (possibly ex-nursing home) for those needing nursing care, b) to build a house in the grounds for that purpose or c) to adapt the present building and timetable to their needs.

Several properties were visited, and a feasibility study was carried out, which ruled out the second option on financial grounds. However, it became clear that the mind of the Community was to take up the third option and to adapt the current building and timetable.

An immediate consequence of the decision was to move the celebration of the Eucharist, on two days each week, to take place just before lunch. Another was to engage in a longer-term project, this time to adapt the building by adding a conservatory to Ground Floor. Two of the original rooms were knocked together and the conservatory extended out at the back. In 2006, it was ready for use, as was the new wheelchair-friendly passageway, leading from Ground Floor to chapel. This provided a very welcome alternative to the narrow passageway at the opposite side of the convent, which had previously been the only access route.

Consequently, with all these arrangements in place, it has been possible to sustain the Community's commitment to mission and outreach.

Some of this takes place outside the convent. Sisters have been involved in the following: Reader ministry, membership of the General Synod of the Church of England and of the Advisory Council for the Religious Life. The two ordained sisters were called on to act as chaplains, one for the Community of St Clare at Freeland, near Oxford, the other at St Deiniol's Library.[222]

One sister acted as a school governor, another led a regular service in a couple of nursing/residential homes, and several were engaged in pastoral work at a number of local churches.

BET Bricklaying Skills

Four sisters acted as trustees of other charities, one of these being the Basotho Education Trust. BET is a charity which funds tuition fees for men and women in Lesotho to study practical skills, such as motor mechanics, carpentry, brick-laying, electrics and leatherwork, tailoring, computing and catering. It also supports students undertaking schooling and college courses. The service to mark its thirtieth anniversary, held on 30th June 2012, celebrated the fact that, since its inception, it has been able to support over 800 students.

Not all sisters engage in mission work which takes them outside, however; many have a ministry within the convent and its grounds, as a number of men and women, priests and lay, make regular visits to see an individual sister for spiritual accompaniment and, in addition, several sisters have a 'telephone ministry'.

Accommodation for residential or day guests has remained a major aspect of the Community's work and, in recent years, it has become possible for those who wish to stay for a short period to 'live alongside' the Community and to experience its way of life, to do so.

In 2015, the Community will commemorate the 150th anniversary of its founding – the year in which Sister Gertrude, CHN's first sister made her profession in St Peter's Church, Vauxhall – the year in which the Community began its journey into the Religious Life. A Special Eucharist of Thanksgiving will be held on 7th

August (Holy Name Day) in Derby Cathedral to give thanks for all the blessings the Community has received over those 150 years: for the pioneering spirit of the founding sisters and for those who remained faithful during the years when it struggled to became firmly established , for those sisters who prayed to discern the shape of the Rule by which it would live, for friends made in its parochial work and in the life of its homes, mission and branch houses, for its Companions, Associates and Fellowship members, and for all who have joined in its work of prayer and intercession, and for all the CHN sisters, who have tried to be faithful to their call to live the Religious Life to the glory of His Holy Name.

The service will thank God for his faithfulness and love to CHN in the past, and will ask for the guidance of his Spirit and for his blessing on its future.

To the Holy and Undivided Trinity, Father, Son and Holy Spirit, be praise and glory from every creature. Amen.[223]

ENDNOTES - CHAPTER 18

[220] The Mildmay Mission Hospital, is where the UK's first AIDS victims were cared for, and where Princess Diana famously shook hands with a patient when fear surrounding the illness was at its height.

[221] CM January 1994.

[222](St Deiniol's Library (recently renamed The Gladstone Library) is a residential library, founded by the Right Hon William Gladstone, which continues to attract scholars, clergy and educators from all over the world. Morning Prayer, Evening Prayer and the Eucharist are held in the Chapel daily.

[223] This is the acclamation made at the end of every CHN office.

APPENDIX I

Father G Cosby White

This history has contained few references to the wardens and chaplains general who have guided the inner life of the community. This has been almost inevitable for their work was necessarily a hidden one, and they were men whose uneventful lives have little general interest. However, an exception must be made for Father G Cosby White, the second warden, who was an unusually interesting man. Although he was not one of the great figures in the nineteenth century Church he was one of the foremost of the lesser men of the later Tractarian movement and a study of his life provides a valuable illustration of that movement in its second phase.

George Cosby White was born 23 February 1825, the son of a War Office official. He was educated at Kensington Proprietory Grammar School and then at Trinity College, Cambridge. While he was at the university an older friend (possibly George Williams of King's) brought him into contact with the Tractarian movement, and this must have been a turning point in his life, for he appears as a convinced, almost militant, High Churchman from the beginning of his ministry.

He was made deacon by Bishop Wilberforce in 1848 and served a short curacy under Butler of Wantage, but in 1849 he became warden of the House of Charity in Soho, and the next two years were spent in London. It was in London too that he was ordained priest.

In 1851 he became the first provost of the College of the Holy Spirit on Cumbrae Island (Firth of Clyde), which had recently been built by GF Boyle,[223] one of the most devoted laymen of the Oxford movement. The institution was a remarkably interesting one. The Gothic revival buildings designed by Butterfield were a symbol of the spirit of the new foundation; even the domestic buildings have an ecclesiastical, positively a monastic air about them. [224] For the college was intended to be a monastery in spirit and purpose, though free from the restrictions and rigorisms of ancient monasticism. The aim of the new institution was the offering of Catholic worship in its completeness or, as it was phrased, 'the frequent celebration of divine service by a collegiate body under circumstances favourable to religious learning.'[225] It seems that the canons were expected to recite the day hours of the breviary, as well as Mattins and Evensong, in choir, and a translation called *The Hours of Prayer* was intended to be used in the church. At Christmas 1851 there was a midnight Celebration, then a very rare observance, and a sure sign of the 'advanced' character of the worship. Mr Boyle did not wish his clergy to degenerate into mere Mass priests, however, and he therefore included educational and mission work amongst the aims of the institution. A wing of the college intended for young men training for the English universities was completed in October 1851, and a home was also provided for aged and infirm clergy. It had been hoped that the college would serve as a centre for mission work in the islands and on the mainland of western Scotland, and Father Cosby White threw himself heartily into this work, especially at West Kilbride on the mainland where he built up a considerable congregation. But the climate did not suit his somewhat delicate health. In June 1852 he was ordered abroad and a year later he resigned his post. He was not forgotten, however, and when the church eventually became a cathedral the bishop made him one of the canons.

After a few years as curate at Chislehurst he was ready for more strenuous work. In 1857 he became curate in charge of St Barnabas, Pimlico, and when this was made an independent parish he was appointed its first vicar. In 1857 St Barnabas was the leading church of the Catholic revival, and it had succeeded Oxford as the storm centre of the movement. Modest though its ceremonies and fittings were, they aroused such animosity that in 1851 the church was the scene of mob violence and had to be held as a beleaguered city by armed men. In 1855 suits were made against Liddell, the vicar of the mother church of St Paul's, Knightsbridge, for the removal of certain fittings in both churches.[226] The prosecutors won their suits and the judgment was confirmed on an appeal to the Court of the Arches, though a further appeal by Liddell to the Judicial Committee of the Privy Council in 1857 reversed the judgment on several counts and might be reckoned as a modified victory for the High Church party. It took a man of resolution and courage to accept a post at such a church, and in undertaking the curacy Father Cosby White made himself a marked man. When he accepted the appointment there can have been little prospect of anything except trouble ahead. As it was, Liddell had a great tussle with the bishop, who threatened to withhold Father Cosby White's licence unless he surrendered to him the power to order the details of the Church services. The bishop was wrong and had to give way, but it was not an encouraging start for the new curate.

As things turned out, the worst of the troubles at St Barnabas ended in 1857, and the attack was soon transferred to the churches of St George's in the East and St Alban's, Holborn; thus Father Cosby White's years at Pimlico were unexpectedly peaceful ones, and there is little to record of them except the steady building up of parish life. The church was a centre of Catholic devotion. Its daily seven o'clock Eucharist was the only one for miles around and its morning and evening choral services were well attended, the former by a large and regular body of middle-aged laymen, and the latter by a very large number of the poor. The principal leaders of Catholic teaching, men like Bennett, Mackonochie, Lowder and Carter, delivered their message from its pulpit. On Easter day 1858 the throng of communicants was so great that the church could not hold them and St John's chapel had eventually to be built to relieve the pressure on St Barnabas.

After his resignation of St Barnabas in 1875, Father Cosby White's life takes on a different pattern as he sinks into the relative obscurity of a Worcestershire parish. It seems right, therefore, before turning to his years at Newland, to discuss the other evidences of the pioneering spirit which was so characteristic of his earlier years. For Father Cosby White was always to the fore of the Catholic movement. Thus he was a founder member of the Confraternity of the Blessed Sacrament and one of the earliest members of the Society of the Holy Cross, acting as its master from 1858 to 1862. He was a supporter of the early retreat movement and was present at the second 'proper' retreat (1859) to be held for Anglicans. The midnight Celebration at Cumbrae in 1851 has already been mentioned. His claim to have been the first priest of the English Church to preach the Three Hours seems to be well founded, for though the honour is more usually claimed for Mackonockie or Lowder, the dates given for them are a few years later.[227] He was one of the signatories of Pusey's *Declaration on Confession* (1873). His appointment at St Barnabas led him to be called as a witness before the Ritual Commission (1867), and he was one of the group of priests who met the archbishop at Addington in 1874 to ask him to check the ritual prosecutions. Yet one feels he could never be described as a Ritualist himself, and the fact that he abandoned the use of vestments at Newland for a time at the command of his bishop is good evidence of this. His pioneering spirit was shown also in mission work, and when the Society of the Holy Cross began St George's Mission amongst the poverty, misery and debauchery of Wapping, he was one of the first to take part.[228] He played a prominent part in the Twelve Days Mission of 1869, and the retreat day for missioners was held at his vicarage. His love for souls drew him into penitentiary work, and he was one of the first council members of the Church Penitentiary Association.

The second part of his life was quiet and uneventful, though during his short time as vicar of St Matthias, Malvern Link (1875-77) he improved the vicarage, built a wall to the churchyard and began a mission room at Upper Howsell, which was a sort of precursor of the Church of the Ascension. Perhaps such energy explains his churchwarden's description of him as, 'The best commercial clergyman I ever met.' In 1877 he became warden of the Beauchamp almshouses and vicar of the small parish of St Leonard's, Newland. Here he spent the rest of his working life, absorbed in the care of his parishioners and of the old pensioners. It was a pleasant retreat. Photographs still remain which show him with the old people. The women are neat and demure in gathered cloaks adorned with large badges; dark bonnets cover their white frilled caps. The old men, attired in sleeveless gowns, look burly and sometimes a trifle belligerent. On the ground sit the choir boys in cassocks and mortar boards, for Newland was known for its plainchant and a small choir school was maintained.

There is little to record of these 20 years at Newland, but before passing on to his retirement, something must be said about certain aspects of his work which are especially interesting. It is difficult to estimate the real extent of Father Cosby White's work since much of it was hidden, for he was a priest who was trusted as a guide by many souls. Skinner, his predecessor at Newland, described him as 'one of our best confessors', while Canon Newbolt wrote that he was said to hear more confessions than any other priest in England, though he could not himself vouch for the truth of this statement.[229] During his years at Newland he travelled a good deal, for if his penitents could not come to him he went to them, and his friends were never surprised to find him in any part of England on some pastoral errand.

He was a great supporter of missionary work. His only son, Bernard, had been killed in Basutoland during the Oun War, and this gave him a great interest in that country. He collected money for the erection of a church at Mafeteng, where his son fell, and after Father Cosby White's death his daughter Mary continued his work, so that in 1921 the church at Quacha's Nek was dedicated to St Barnabas in his memory.

His work as a compiler of *Hymns Ancient and Modern* brought his name before a wider public. Although there were many hymn books in use by the mid-nineteenth century, the need for one on true Church lines was widely felt. The first move was made by the rector of Chislehurst, the Reverend FM Murray, who enlisted the help of Sir HW Baker. Together they approached Father Cosby White, whose Hymns and Introits were widely used, and in the autumn of 1857 a committee of five met in his Pimlico parsonage. Two years later a trial book was published, and in 1861 an edition with tunes appeared. The definite Church character of the compilation challenged, and received criticism, but hostility ensured its success and it became the most popular of Anglican hymn books, passing through many editions. From 1889 to 1904 Father Cosby White was chairman of the compilers, but when the edition of 1904 was published he resigned, for he felt that his age and ill health made this essential.

The community owed much to Father Cosby White. He was honorary chaplain to the sisters at Malvern from 1880 to 1895, and his influence became increasingly important after 1887 when the mother house was established there. He had had considerable experience of sisterhoods which made his advice especially valuable, and it was fortunate that his short term of office as warden (1895-98) occurred at a difficult time when important constitutional changes were being made. He built the New Wing of the convent, complete with cells and refectory, and his concern for moral welfare work and his generosity towards this community's homes have already been told.

Finally, something must be said of his amazing generosity. It is, of course, impossible to trace all his benefactions, but some could not be hidden, and the most obvious of these must now be mentioned in order to give some idea of his munificence. Newland benefited especially by his gifts. The frescoes on the walls of the church were completed and a great clock given for the gatehouse tower. He added largely to the Beauchamp charity and the interest on £1,000 was devoted to the choir school. He also founded the St Barnabas Hostel where four aged priests of small means could live in their own little houses free of rent and rates. After he had left Newland, he built the library to the east of the quadrangle and endowed it with many of his books. He built a little school with a master's house attached for the children of Newland parish, and when he retired to Clevedon he was the unknown benefactor of the mission church of the Good Shepherd.

It is difficult to describe his character adequately, since the references to it belong exclusively to his latter years. A photograph of him, as a man in his prime, shows a face of unusual resolution and decision, and suggests a person who could not lightly be trifled with. Canon Butler seems to have sensed this when he wrote of his former curate: 'Who follows next? He whose whole strength has lain in confidence and quiet, with high charge oft trusted, ne'er has swerved to right or left, wining the mood? God gives to upright souls.'[229] His courageous spirit was shown in his latter years, for when the 1914-1918 war broke out he longed to help, and at the age of 90 he inserted the following advertisement in the *Church Times*: 'An aged priest, holding his bishop's licence, desires to assist the chaplain of a hospital for sick and wounded in the war. No stipend required, or any payment for board and lodging.' [230] His offer could not be accepted, for the work was far too strenuous for a man of his years, yet his desire was so strong that he repeated his advertisement two years later. Throughout his life he did everything to the uttermost and when he was in his old age, Bishop Gott noticed that, 'he is happier when he is doing almost too much.' A priest who knew him in his retirement spoke of him as 'a heroic figure, resolute in the face of slowly increasing infirmity ... preaching when, owing to increasing deafness, he could no longer hear confessions; celebrating when he could not preach; and an assiduous attendant at our altar almost to the last.'[231] Three years before his death, he admitted that he felt sad to know that his work was at an end, but his reaction to the situation was typical. 'I must try to spend more time on prayer.' For prayer was one of the great characteristics of his life. A priest who knew him at Clevedon said that he 'never knew any priest who was such a man of prayer. Whatever he did, he prayed over it, and whatever he gave he gave with his prayers as well.' His devotion to the Blessed Sacrament was the key to his whole life, and the priest who ministered to him when he could no longer come to the altar said that it was an unforgettable experience. His modesty and humility, his unworldliness and his great courtesy were amongst his most attractive characteristics. Stuckey Coles noticed that he was a reserved and somewhat lonely man (though he had gifts which drew to him those who needed help and comfort), but when Bishop Frere knew him it was the attractiveness of 'his many enthusiasms and his infectious Christian joy in life' that he noticed. Yet probably the best summary of his character came from Mr H Badwell, who said: 'He was one of those whom one always felt the better for seeing ...'.

His last years were spent at Clevedon with his daughter Mary and her husband, the Reverend EJ Eyre, though for a few months he acted as resident chaplain to Bishop Gott of Truro. At Clevedon he became an honorary assistant at St John's Church where he regularly took the 8 a.m. Eucharist on Sunday mornings. He died on 9 December 1918 at the age of 93, having lived just long enough to see the end of the war which brought so much suffering to his country.

ENDNOTES – APPENDIX I

[223]Later Earl of Glasgow.

[224]For a full description of the College, see W. Perry, The Oxford Movement in Scotland, 1933, pp.56-61. A photograph of the church, now known as the Cathedral of the Isles, Millport, may be found in Marion Lockhead, Episcopal Scotland in the Nineteenth Century, 1966, p.107. There are also several interesting photographs in an article on 'Cathedral of the Isles' by Hubert Fenwick in Anglican World, vol. 7, nos. 3/ 4, 1967, pp.46-48.

[225]Quoted in PF Anson, The Call of the Cloister, 1964, p.47.

[226]These included the high altar and its cross, candlesticks, coloured altar cloths and the credence table.

[227]Father Cosby White first preached the Three Hours at the House of Charity, Soho, in 1851. A copy of the addresses is preserved in the library of the Beauchamp Alms Houses, Newland, Worcestershire.

[228]The mission developed into the famous parish of St Peter's, London Docks.

[229]WCE Newbolt, Years that are Past, n.d., p.128.

[230]Quoted from a pamphlet preserved in the library of the Beauchamp Alms Houses, Newland, Worcs.

[231]5 November, 1915.

APPENDIX 2

Some Notes on the Early Training of Novices

In the Community's earliest years there was no real novitiate, and novices had little formal training. They simply learnt their life and work by practical experience. This is illustrated by the story of Sister Mary (professed 1872) who, when asked in her old age, 'Sister, who was your novice mistress?' replied placidly, 'My dear, I never had one.' Not only was there no novice mistress, frequently there was no postulancy either. It is true that the First Rule asked for a postulancy of three months and also expected the candidate to spend a month as a visitor before her admission, but the records suggest that only one sister was actually received as a postulant before 1876, though several had been associate sisters, and this seems to have been regarded as equivalent experience.

In 1875, when Sister Eliza was appointed as the first novice mistress, the duties of the office were discussed. It was resolved that the mistress, 'Train the novices in the knowledge and obedience of the Rule, and the better understanding of the Religious Life. That for this end she hold two classes a week, and have opportunity of speaking to the novices privately. That she offer advice on the internal life.' A rather amusing touch is the resolution: 'That when novices constantly break rule the mistress appeal to the authority of the mother,' which suggests that novices were not always all that they might be. When Sister Faith Louisa became mistress in 1879, Father Herbert preached a sermon on the qualities necessary in a novice mistress. The first thing he looked for was spiritual experience – in both life and work. She must know the temptations the novices would have to face and she must also have experience of mission work since the novices needed guidance being, as he put it, 'often without knowledge of souls'. Patience and a readiness to impart what she knew in a sympathetic spirit were also important, but he laid the greatest stress on example, for although classes might last one or two hours, an example was there all the week. The mistress was not so much to show the way as to lead the way.

The appointment of the novice mistress at first lay with the priest, although the draft constitutions of the '90s changed this to the mother and warden acting conjointly.

Even when a mistress was appointed, the novices' life cannot have been a highly organised one. They must have shared the life of the sisters very fully and, as far as can be estimated, they had no separate quarters of their own until 1896 when the New Wing was completed. Until this date they were addressed as 'Sister X' but this was replaced by 'Novice X' which remained the custom for the next century. The practice of spending part of the novitiate in a branch or mission house began quite early, however, for it goes back to the time when the mother house was moved to Malvern (1887). As a result it was decided that 'Novices shall pass a part of their probation in the London House according as the superior and priest shall arrange.' This was later expanded to include other mission and branch houses.

The actual length of the novitiate varied, though from the first a minimum of two years was normally required. From 1877 onwards lay novices had a novitiate of at least three years, and in 1887 a complicated system was established whereby a lay novice had a novitiate of three or four years, followed by a period of several years as a 'dedicated novice'. Novices' promises were regarded as binding for the full term of their novitiate and, if they wished to leave, they had to ask the chapter for release from what were called their 'temporary vows'.

An early register remains, which gives a good picture of the novitiate at the turn of the century. A study of the entries concerning admissions for 1892-1903 shows that all but seven of the 60 postulants received were clothed, and 40 of them reached profession. This suggests a stable novitiate without a lot of comings and goings. The big majority were choir novices, for the names of only nine lay novices appear. Almost all were between 20 and 40, but three girls were still in their teens and there were five women over 40. The date of entrance as a visitor (or occasionally as a worker) was often recorded, and was obviously considered important. The register always gives the dates of first confessions, and the use of this sacrament seems to have been a condition of admission. Communion was less frequent than today. Most novices were allowed Sundays, red letter days and one week day, but some had less. The type of work the novice did was always carefully entered. Orphanage, district visiting, penitentiary, Sunday school and mothers' meetings were frequently mentioned and many novices worked in chapel or acted as sub-sacristan. Lay novices almost always did district visiting, and frequently Sunday school, in addition to their housework, and both choir and lay novices worked in the embroidery room. The names of the mission houses to which they were sent were also entered. It is clear that all novices were being definitely trained (by practical experience) in mission work.

Not very much is known about the type of spiritual teaching they received, but fortunately some notes for novices' classes still survive. These belonged to Sister Emma, who was twice appointed novice mistress (1877 and 1887) and who also gave classes when she was not in office. They give some idea of the teaching which was provided in the 1880s. Classes seem to have been of two kinds. Firstly, there was instruction on 'religious vocation' as such. This tended to be rather abstract and legalistic, and though it was occasionally illustrated by 'types' there were no concrete examples and no applications to daily life. Secondly, there were meditations on Biblical themes such as Esther, the Song of Songs, and the stories of Jonah and Abraham. These were always treated mystically, and the text served as a peg on which to hang the teacher's thoughts. This method of instruction was probably popular, but it had serious defects, since subjects were frequently alluded to, but seldom treated exhaustively. It is probable, however, that there were additional classes given by other sisters (dogma is known to have been taken early in the 1900s), and these would have helped to provide balance.

APPENDIX 3 – List of Houses and Officers 1865-2014

Visitors
Father Elwin SSJE	1895 - 1897
Father Page SSJE	1897 - 1908
The Right Reverend Bishop Yeatman-Biggs	1908 - 1922
The Right Reverend Bishop Chandler	1922 - 1933
The Right Reverend Bishop King	1933 - 1941
The Right Reverend Bishop Roxborough Smith	1941 - 1955
The Right Reverend Bishop Askwith	1955 - 1962
The Right Reverend Bishop Gresford Jones	1962 - 1972
The Right Reverend Bishop Guy	1972 - 1975
The Right Reverend Bishop Trillo	1975 - 1985
The Right Reverend Bishop Bavin	1985 - 1995
The Right Reverend Bishop Smith	1995 - 2007
The Right Reverend Bishop Inge	2007 - present

Wardens
The Reverend GW Herbert	1865 -1894
The Reverend G Cosby White	1895 -1898

Chaplains General
The Reverend G Custance	1898 - 1911
The Reverend CJ Jones	1911 - 1938
The Reverend LD Heppenstall	1938 - 1955
The Reverend SG Chance	1955 - 1958
The Reverend AE Russell	1958 - 1973
The Reverend G Ireson (Warden)	1974 - 1982
The Reverend H Sly (Chaplain)	1983 - 1989
The Reverend P Need (Chaplain)	1990 - 1991

(*The term Warden and Chaplain General denote the same office)

Mothers Superior
Sister Charlotte	1867 - 1876
Sister Ellen	1876 - 1879
Mother Frances Mary	1879 - 1888
Sister Emma	1888 - 1897
Sister Agatha	1897 - 1915
Sister Vera	1915 - 1925
Sister Agnes Mary	1925 - 1945
Mother Elfrieda	1945 - 1953
Sister Audrey Mary	1953 - 1970
Sister Penelope	1970 - 1984
Sister Mary Patricia	1984 - 1994
Sister Jean Mary	1994 - 2004
Sister Monica Jane	2004 - 2013
Sister Pauline Margaret	2013 - present

Mission Houses

It should be noted that this is a list of mission houses, not of parishes in which the sisters worked. The number of parishes would, of course, be far more extensive.

1865 – 1950	St Peter's Vauxhall. 21 Brunel Street (1865), Eldon Lodge, 171Upper Kensington Lane (1866 -1874), 141 Upper Kensington Lane (1874 -1950).
1875 - 1877	St Andrew's, Wolverhampton.
1877 - 1911	St James', Wednesbury, Staffordshire.
1883 - 1887	All Saints, Emscote, Warwickshire.
1888 - 1957	St Alban's, Birmingham.
1889 - 1894	St Paul's, Walden, Hertfordshire.
1898 - 1899	St Mary's, Tewkesbury, Gloucestershire.
1898 - 1917	St Patrick's, Birmingham.
1899 - 1905	Christ Church, Lisson Grove, London.
1899 - 1916	St Paul's, Balsall Heath, Birmingham.
1900 - 1926	St Barnabas', Hove, Sussex.
1902 - 1945	St Aidan's, Birmingham.
1906 - 1934	St John Baptist, Coventry.
1907 - 1918	St Mary's, Wimbledon.
1910 - 1916	St Mary's Priory Church, Worksop, Nottinghamshire.
? - 1918	St Leonard's, Newland, Worcestershire.
1926 - 1930	Christ Church, Wolverhampton.
1934 - 1954	St John Baptist, Staveley, Derbyshire.
1940 - 1943	Holy Trinity, Reading.
1948 - 1969	St John Baptist, Coventry.
1950 - 1955	St Saviour's, Pimlico, London.
1950 -	St Mary's, Wellingborough, Northamptonshire.
1954 - 1973	The Annunciation, Brighton, Sussex.
1955 - 1961	St Dunstan's, Stepney, London.
1953 - 1971	St Marychurch, Torquay, Devon.
1961 - 1969	St Matthew's, Elswick, Newcastle upon Tyne.
1969 - 1981	St George's, Jesmond, Newcastle upon Tyne.
1973 - 1989	St Peter's, Basingstoke
1978 - 1984	St Martin's, Basildon
1981 - 1993	Christchurch, Walker, Newcastle upon Tyne.
1985 - 2009	St John's, Keswick.
1985 - 2009	St Peter's, Radford, Nottingham.
1989 - 1994	St Helen's, Bishop Auckland.
1990 - 1994	St Anne's, Derby. St John's, Derby to present.
1994 - 2013	Lambeth Palace, London.
1993 - 2007	All Saints', Oakham.
1998 - 2004	St Peter's in the City, Nottingham – Almshouse.
1998 - present	Christchurch, Dogsthorpe, Peterborough.
2009 - present	St Chrysostom's, Victoria Park, Manchester.

Homes

1879 - 1966	Home of the Good Shepherd, Malvern Link, Worcestershire.
1880 - 1933	Worcester Diocesan Refuge (known as Field House from 1898).
1880 - 1883	St Michael's Home for Penitents, Leamington.
1890 - 1894	Holy Name Home for Incurables, Parkstone, Dorset.
1891 - 1898	Home of the Holy Family, Malvern Link, Worcestershire.
1945 - 1969	St Catherine's House, Malvern Link, (transferred to St Edward's House, West Malvern in 1955).
1947 - 1955	The Howsells, Malvern Link, Worcestershire.

Overseas Houses

1891 -1901	St John Baptist, St John, New Brunswick, Canada.
1931 -1962	Convent of the Holy Name, Bolshun, Liberia.
1962 - present	Convent of the Holy Name, Leribe, Lesotho.
1969 - present	Convent of the Holy Name, Kwamagwaza (formerly at Isandlwana), Zululand.

Guest Houses and Retreat Houses

	St Mary's, Hartfield, Sussex.
	The Wilderness, Mayfield, Sussex.
1924 - 1955	St Catherine's Guest House, Malvern Link, (removed in 1944 to St Edward's House, West Malvern, Worcestershire).
1955 - 2000	St Saviour's, Malvern Link.
1919 - 1925	17 Queensberry Place, London, SW (headquarters of the Daughters of the Holy Name).
1958 - 2000	Chester Retreat House, Chester, Cheshire.
1961 - 1974	Diocesan Retreat House, St Alban's, Hertfordshire.
1969 - 1978	Diocesan Retreat House, St Teilo's.